AN **INTRODUCTION** TO

POPULATION GEOGRAPHY

Second Edition

D1364092

William F. Hornby

Formerly Principal Lecturer in Geography
Sheffield City Polytechnic

Melvyn Jones

Principal Lecturer
Recreation and Countryside Division
School of Leisure and Food Management
Sheffield Hallam University

CAMBRIDGE
UNIVERSITY PRESS

Published by the Press Syndicate of the University of Cambridge
The Pitt Building, Trumpington Street, Cambridge CB2 1RP
40 West 20th Street, New York, NY 10011-4211, USA
10 Stamford Road, Oakleigh, Melbourne 3166, Australia

First published 1980
Second edition 1993

ISBN 0 521 42360 0 paperback
(First edition ISBN 0 521 21395 6)

A catalogue record for this book is available from the British
Library.

Designed and produced by The Pen and Ink Book Company
Ltd, Huntingdon, Cambridgeshire.

Printed in Great Britain at the University Press, Cambridge

Acknowledgements

The publishers would like to thank the following for permission
to reproduce photographs and diagrams:

Fig. 2.3, Oxfam; Fig. 2.7, David & Charles Publishers; Fig. 2.17,
Family Life Education Coordinating Unit, Ministry of Health,
Singapore; Figs 3.4, 3.5 and 6.10, Longman Group UK Ltd; Figs
4.1 and 4.16 Mike Goldwater, 8.4 Martin Cottingham, Christian
Aid Photo Library; Fig. 3.12, Macmillan Education Ltd; Fig. 3.13,
The American Geographical Society; Fig. 4.6, Weidenfeld &
Nicolson; Figs 5.1, 5.2 and 8.3, Camera Press; Fig. 7.1,
Popperfoto; Fig. 7.2, David Park; Fig. 7.4, J. Allan Cash; Fig. 7.5,
Network SouthEast; Fig. 7.8, Old Dronfield Society.

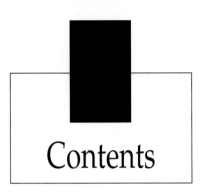

Contents

Case Studies
and Exercises

PART ONE:
POPULATION GROWTH AND DISTRIBUTION

1

Introduction:
Components of population change and problems of measurement

Recent forecasts suggest that during the 1990s the population of the world will increase, on average, by approximately 100 million every year. If such forecasts prove accurate, then before the year 2000 the Earth will be populated by more than 150 people for every 100 who were alive in 1975. Rates of increase of population vary dramatically from place to place, however, with most countries in Africa, Asia and Latin America recording growth rates much higher than those of the more economically developed countries of Europe, North America and Australasia. Of the nations with population increases of over 3% per annum in 1990, more than three-quarters were in Africa. By contrast, many European countries had rates of increase well below 1% with some even showing a decrease. Geographers are concerned with attempting to explain these and other spatial variations in the world's population as well as

with understanding changes in the total world population. They are also concerned with the implications of population growth and change for the quality of life of the world's peoples and the varied environments in which people live.

In this first chapter we shall briefly examine the basic components of population change and some of the problems encountered in measuring change. In subsequent chapters of Part One we shall consider various aspects of world population growth, population distribution and relationships between population growth and resource utilisation. There will inevitably also be some mention of population movements, but an examination in depth of such movements is the primary concern of the second part of the book.

First, it is important to be clear about what we mean by the term 'population' and to appreciate some of the difficulties involved in population measurement. The word 'population' can be used in several different ways. For example, a biologist might refer to a collection of animals or plants as a 'population', whereas a geographer is more likely to use the term in relation to a group of human beings. Thus a geographer might refer to, say, the 'population of Glasgow', but on consideration it can be seen that such an expression has no very precise meaning unless further details are given. Does it refer to the people who are normally resident in Glasgow? If so, what does 'normally' mean in this context? Or does it refer to the people who were resident in Glasgow on a particular day in a particular year? If it does, should not a particular time also be specified, as the number of residents will obviously change in the course of a day as a result of births and deaths and of people moving into and away from the city to live? And does the 'population of Glasgow' include other people who have homes outside the city but who travel daily to work in Glasgow?

Consideration of questions such as these makes it clear that the term 'population' is often used by geographers in ways that are difficult to relate to precise numerical values. Indeed, the term is often applied to collections of people of which the exact numbers and composition are changing all the time. In such circumstances it may be virtually impossible to provide a numerical value for a population that is both up to date and accurate. In short, a study of population is essentially a study of a dynamic and not of a static situation.

Components of population change

There are two basic ways in which population change occurs. First, a population may increase or decrease as a result of natural change – that is, as a result of the number of people being born or dying within the community. Secondly, it may alter as a result of migration, with people moving into or away from the place where the community lives. Thus the total population of any particular community represents the balance between two components: the natural change component and the migration change component. This can be shown diagrammatically as in Fig. 1.1. This diagram emphasises the dynamic nature of population and can be applied at different scales – to a country or to a city, for example.

The relative significance of the two components varies greatly through time and from place to place. The migration change component is likely to be of greater relative importance, for example, in part of a town where new, moderately-priced houses are being built than in the same area when building programmes have been completed. After the initial occupation of such an area, migration would be likely to become less important than natural increase because there is a high probability that the area would be largely populated by young couples, many of whom would remain in the area while they had children. Migration would not cease entirely as some people would move away to be replaced by new migrants, but it would be considerably less significant than earlier. In time, further changes would occur as the population aged, fewer children were born, the death rate increased and new migrants moved in. Similar dynamic patterns can be traced on a larger scale in, for example, some parts of the United States that were settled by European migrants in the nineteenth century. In general, however, the natural change component is far more significant at a national level than the migration change component and, of course, the latter can be ignored when dealing with changes in the total world population (though this might change if other planets suitable for human settlement were discovered and developed).

Population censuses

Most national population censuses attempt to overcome the difficulties arising from the continuing changes in population totals by basing calculations on a rigid series of instructions concerning the date and time to which census data refer and the categories of people that should be included or excluded from the totals. It is easy to see that problems can arise in carrying out a census. Although it is common to base the collection of data on the places where people reside and so exclude problems such as daily travel to work, many other difficulties exist. For example, should people who are working temporarily overseas be included in population totals?

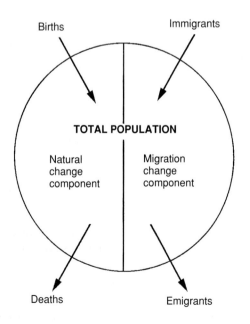

Fig. 1.1 Components of population change.
Source: after Haggett, 1975.

Should sailors be excluded if they are at sea when a census is taken? Should someone who lives and works in London from Monday to Friday but returns to spend the weekend with his or her family in Lincoln be recorded as a resident of London or Lincoln? No doubt you can think of other problems involved in taking a census in a country like Great Britain, but these almost pale into insignificance in comparison with some situations elsewhere. In some areas severe difficulties have been encountered in attempting to record the numbers in nomadic groups (as in Mauritania where up to a third of the population may be nomads), while in many developing countries low levels of literacy and poor communications have made it difficult to record populations accurately. Political factors have also influenced the reliability of census returns in many countries, particularly when individuals or groups have felt threatened by demands for information required as part of the census. Even in Great Britain fears that census information may be used to the detriment of particular groups can cause problems, as is evidenced by the difficulties encountered in framing questions concerning ethnic origins in recent censuses.

The sheer scale of the problem in a country like India is difficult for us to comprehend. In 1991 some 1.7 million people were involved in actually carrying out the national census in over 600,000 settlements, ranging from major cities like Bombay and Calcutta (where densely populated slums and homeless pavement dwellers cause particular problems of enumeration) to the scattered homes of semi-nomadic tribal groups in remote hill areas. Add to this the variety of languages spoken (the census questionnaire was printed in 20 languages), the low literacy levels in some areas, doubts and fears felt by many people about the motives of the enumerators in asking certain census questions, and the administrative difficulties involved in checking the accuracy and co-ordinating the results of a survey carried out by such a multitude of people, and some idea of the problem of making an accurate assessment of India's population size and characteristics begins to emerge.

Census errors may have significant financial implications. It is widely accepted that the United States 1990 census seriously under-enumerated the population – probably by about 5 million – tending to miss mainly poor, homeless, non-English speaking and/or immigrant members of the population. This probably cost the local authorities where such people lived some $17 billion (£10 billion) in federal aid and was strongly resented in New York, for example, where the census is thought to have undercounted the population by about 250,000. When errors of this magnitude can occur in a country with one of the most sophisticated systems for recording population data, it is easy to imagine what errors there may be in less favourable situations.

In Nigeria, early censuses were little more than rather vague estimates. The first attempt at a full enumeration was over a period of about nine months from July 1952 to April 1953. Planned in this way to overcome staff shortages and organisational problems, this census indicated that the total population was approximately 30 million. The next census, in 1962, was considered so unreliable by the government that a new census was taken in the following year. This recorded a population of 55.6 million but many observers still doubted its accuracy. It implied a population growth rate in excess of 6% per annum since the previous census – almost an impossibility unless natural increase had been accompanied by massive immigration, of which there was no evidence on the scale necessary. Most demographers concluded that the 1952/53 total probably represented an under-assessment and the 1963 total an over-assessment of the true population, which several estimates suggested was by then just over 50 million.

Despite government attempts to ensure accurate enumeration at the next Nigerian census in 1973, preliminary results recorded an astonishing total of 79 million people. Even on the basis of the original 1963 total of 55.6 million, this represented an increase of over 3.5% per year in the period between the censuses, very much higher than most estimates had anticipated. Census data for individual states were extremely confusing, with three of the twelve states having almost doubled their populations, two having apparently decreased in numbers and others having increased more or less as expected between the censuses. The controversy surrounding the results eventually led to them being officially repudiated by the government. A decade later, in 1983, sample surveys rather than a full enumeration were used to provide an estimate of Nigeria's total population. This suggested that Nigeria's population was just over 92 million, a figure in reasonable conformity with the United Nations estimate. In 1991, however, the most recent census, carried out with help from the United Nations and several developed countries, surprised everyone by recording a total population of only 88.5 million, at least 20 million fewer than most recent estimates, and a result that suggests earlier censuses had greatly over-estimated Nigeria's population. Although Nigeria's census problems have had more publicity than those of many other countries they are by no means unique and some countries have not even attempted a full enumeration. The collection of population data between censuses in many developing countries is also very limited in both quantity and quality. The registration of births and deaths, for example, may be limited to sample areas or be absent altogether. In this context it is perhaps worth making the point that even in the United States it was not until the mid-1930s that complete territorial coverage for the registration of deaths was achieved.

Clearly, any study of population must take into account the possibility that estimates and even official statistics based on census enumerations and other forms of demographic data may be imprecise and misleading. It is important to remember this in relation to the comments made in the remainder of this book and the statistics on which such comments are based.

2

World population growth

Introduction

Although population data for many countries in the modern world may be of doubtful validity, information concerning earlier periods is generally even less reliable. Despite this, various efforts have been made to chart patterns of population growth and distribution in the distant past based on such evidence as archaeological remains and the population structures and densities of modern communities with economies similar to those of earlier groups. For more recent periods, a variety of written evidence and estimates based on surveys of different kinds have also been used.

The origins of humanity are still the subject of considerable dispute, speculation concerning this being based on a limited number of fragments of skeletons discovered in locations as diverse as China, East Africa and Indonesia. Archaeologists have suggested that *Homo sapiens* probably first became distinct from its hominid (man-like) predecessors about 100,000 years ago and some recent discoveries point to an even earlier date. During most of the period since *Homo sapiens* first appeared on the scene, however, the number of people on Earth has been very small in comparison with the present population. Early rates of population growth were extremely slow, with the economic basis of existence being hunting and food-gathering. Primitive human communities with this kind of economy gradually spread, possibly from early bases in Africa and Asia, to occupy much of the world. As recently as 10,000 years ago, at about the time when people first began to cultivate crops and domesticate animals, estimates suggest that the entire world population probably totalled only about 5 million, a figure not much different from the present populations of small countries such as Finland or Denmark.

This period of economic change when people first became farmers rather than hunters or food-gatherers (often described as the Neolithic Revolution) drastically altered the relationships between people and their environment. Further changes followed. These included the development of permanent rather than the earlier shifting cultivation, the introduction of new technological aids such as the plough, increases in production and exchange of agricultural and other commodities (which in turn helped to make possible the growth of cities) and the discovery of how to smelt and make use of metals. During the long period between the Neolithic Revolution and the beginning of early modern times (about 1650) population is thought to have increased at a considerably faster average rate than in the pre-Neolithic era, though still very slowly by modern standards, with an average growth rate of below 0.1% per annum. The rate must have fluctuated through time and between different groups, however.

The total world population probably reached 500 million by about 1650 and thereafter grew at an increasing rate (see Fig. 2.1). Between 1650 and 1830, a period of 180 years, the total population approximately doubled to reach a billion (1,000 million). In the following 100 years it doubled again and in the 45 years between 1930 and 1975 it doubled yet again to reach 4 billion. Forecasts at that time suggested that the next doubling might take only 35 years to give a population of 8 billion by the year 2010. Subsequent estimates based on some slowing of growth rates in the 1970s and 1980s have suggested that the 8 billion mark may not be reached until about the year 2020, but it has proved extremely difficult to forecast changing birth rates with accuracy, and this leads to some doubts about future rates of growth. The period for which population will continue to grow is also unclear

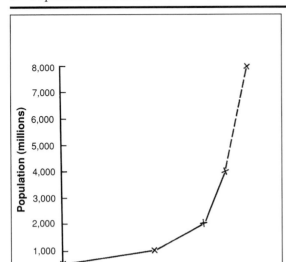

Fig. 2.1 World population growth (generalised) 1650–1975, and forecast growth 1975–2020. See text for comment.

the world as a whole. The diagram makes it clear that the relationship between births and deaths is fundamental to this. Measurements of births and deaths can be expressed in several different ways, but they are most commonly indicated in the form of crude birth rates and crude death rates. These can be simply calculated, as shown below, on the basis of data that are fairly easily available.

Crude birth rate (expressed as the number of live births per 1,000 persons)

$$= \frac{\text{Total number of live births in 1 year} \times 1,000}{\text{Total mid-year population}}$$

Crude death rate (expressed as the number of deaths per 1,000 persons)

$$= \frac{\text{Total number of deaths in 1 year} \times 1,000}{\text{Total mid-year population}}$$

though most estimates in recent years have anticipated that population will eventually stabilise at perhaps 11 or 12 billion by about the year 2150. Even that represents a population roughly twice that of 1990 and with an average annual increase of approximately 100 million in the 1990s, as already mentioned, many people see population growth as a major threat to human survival. The use by some commentators of terms like 'population explosion' tends to encourage such concern and it is easy to view the future of the world with considerable gloom. If the situation is to be better appreciated, however, it is important to examine what has happened in the recent past in rather more detail so that likely future developments may be set in a more meaningful context.

Crude birth and death rates

Look again at Fig. 1.1. From what has already been said, it is clear that only the natural growth component of total population need be considered when dealing with population growth for

The difference between the two rates is known as the rate of natural increase, though this is usually expressed as a percentage. Thus in 1990 Tanzania had a crude birth rate of 51 per thousand, a crude death rate of 14 per thousand and a rate of natural increase of 3.7% per annum. Although the rate of natural increase is related solely to birth and death rates, the rate of population growth is also concerned with changes brought about by migration. Jamaica's situation in the mid-1970s clearly indicated the significance of this. In 1976, Jamaica had a crude birth rate of 31 per thousand, a crude death rate of 7 per thousand and therefore a rate of natural increase of 2.4%. The island's population growth rate, however, was only 1.9% because of the considerable emigration occurring at that time.

The terms 'crude' birth rate and 'crude' death rate are used because it is possible to use more precise, less 'crude' ways of measuring fertility and mortality. For example, fertility might be calculated by relating the number of births to the number of women of child-bearing age in the community rather than to the whole population. We shall consider some of these alternative measurements later. In the meantime, it is

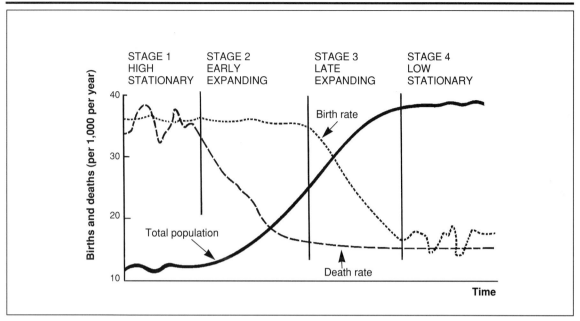

Fig. 2.2 The demographic transition model.
Source: after Haggett, 1975.

important to remember that crude rates may conceal quite marked variations within a population – between different age groups or ethnic communities for example – as well as suffering from inaccuracy, in some cases, because of a shortage of sound basic data. Where the terms 'birth rate' and 'death rate' are used elsewhere in this book they should be taken to mean crude birth and crude death rate.

Demographic transition

An examination of the information available concerning birth and death rates, and of population changes resulting from the difference between these, led to the suggestion that many European countries appeared to have passed through four main stages of population change in modern times – seen as being associated with contemporaneous socio-economic changes. This pattern of population change has been described as the *demographic transition*, and Fig. 2.2 is an attempt to represent this in the form of a model. Further research has shown that particular countries rarely, if ever, conform in detail to all aspects of the pattern suggested by the

model, and this has led to much criticism of the model and to some re-assessment of its value. If it is remembered that, like any model, it is primarily a *generalisation* of reality and cannot therefore be expected to reflect detailed changes in every country, it can still serve quite a useful purpose in providing an indication of past patterns of change and a yardstick against which the experience of different countries can be measured.

Until at least the middle of the eighteenth century, the limited evidence available suggests that both birth and death rates had fluctuated between 30 and 40 per thousand in many European countries for several centuries. It seems likely that fluctuations were greater in death rates as populations were affected by periodic wars, famines and diseases, but the long-term effect of these was, with a few major exceptions, usually slight. One such exception was the fourteenth-century plague, later known as the Black Death, variously estimated to have resulted in the deaths of between 10% and 50% of the population of England. The general situation, however, was one in which the population remained at a low, though fluctuating, level with high birth and death rates maintaining a rough balance so that changes in population totals were slow and slight in comparison with those of later periods. This situation is represented by stage 1 in Fig. 2.2 and is usually called the 'high stationary' stage. This term can be slightly misleading but refers to the levels of fertility and mortality rather than the total population.

During the eighteenth or early nineteenth century the death rate began to decline in many European countries, initiating the 'early expanding' stage of demographic transition. It seems likely that this declining death rate was initially associated with improvements in nutrition as agricultural production increased and with greater political stability but, by the late nineteenth century, better sanitation, improved personal hygiene, better housing and increased medical knowledge had become important contributory factors (although the decline in certain infectious diseases is not fully understood) and the death rate fell more rapidly. There was usually no immediate corresponding fall in birth rate (see stage 2 in Fig. 2.2) and the difference between birth and death rates resulted in rapid population growth. Indeed in some areas fertility actually increased, perhaps partly as a result of people marrying earlier because of changing socio-economic conditions in this period. The United Kingdom is an example of one such area and here, as death rates fell and fertility increased, population growth reached a maximum of 1.6% per annum in the 1820s. It is worth noting that this figure, though high for the period in which it occurred, is considerably lower than the rates of growth experienced in many Asian, African and Latin American countries since 1950. In some cases these have exceeded 3% per annum. In most European countries, however, the nineteenth century was a period of population growth on a scale not previously experienced, though there were variations in the pattern of growth between different countries both in degree and in the dates at which changes occurred.

As many of the major diseases of temperate areas were brought under control and improved

standards of health and sanitation had their effect, the death rate in most European countries gradually levelled off at a much lower level than that of stage 1. By the 1920s and 1930s countries such as the Netherlands, Sweden and the United Kingdom had death rates well below 20 per thousand and although these continued to decline, largely as a result of the greater control over infant mortality, the rate of this decline was much slower than previously. In this same period (represented by stage 3, the 'late expanding' stage, in Fig. 2.2) birth rates began to decline dramatically in many countries. This is less easily explained than the earlier fall in death rates but in most European countries seems to have been associated with the establishment of a predominantly urban-industrial society in which the desire for, and possibly the economic value of, large families decreased. In addition, better methods of birth control and a gradually widening awareness of these made it possible for parents to restrict the size of their families if they so wished.

More recently both birth and death rates in such countries have reached a stage where they are relatively stable and where population change is in the form of a slow natural rate of increase with the birth rate slightly higher than the death rate on average (represented by stage 4, the 'low stationary' stage in Fig. 2.2). It is interesting to note that, in contrast with the situation in stage 1, the model indicates a tendency for the birth rate to fluctuate more than the death rate in stage 4. This is discussed in more detail in Case Study 2A. By the middle of the twentieth century many European countries appeared to have entered a phase similar to that suggested by stage 4 of the demographic transition model, and natural increase rates for much of Europe have now fallen below 0.5%. A departure from the detailed pattern suggested by the model is apparent in many European countries where death rates have declined to levels well below those indicated in the model for stage 4 – falling below 10 per thousand in the Netherlands, France, Ireland, Switzerland and much of southern Europe by 1990, for example. Indeed, by that date, estimates suggested that death rates did not exceed 13 per thousand in any European country.

In some cases, too, birth rates have declined to a level below that of death rates, giving rise to some suggestions that the model should include a fifth stage in which birth rates are below death rates and population eventually declines. The fear that such a situation might develop has been a factor influencing the population policies of several states in Eastern Europe in recent times (see Case Study 2B) but to date it seems to have been a short-term phenomenon only, so it is perhaps premature to add a fifth stage to the model on the evidence so far available.

A pattern of demographic change similar to that outlined in the model has also occurred, or appears to be occurring, in several countries outside Europe. Many of these, for example Canada, the USA and Australia, have populations strongly linked to Europe in terms of their origins, but a demographic transition bearing some similarity to the 'European' type has also occurred in some areas that have no clear ethnic links with Europe. Japan provides an interesting illustration of this which, as it developed into an industrial state similar to some European countries, also appeared to develop along rather similar demographic lines (see Exercise 2.1). The rapid fall in death rates in Japan after the Second World War is generally attributed to the widespread adoption of improved medical techniques initiated during the American occupation of Japan. This pattern of change is interesting in relation to similar patterns observed in many developing countries at a slightly later date which appear to be related more to medical improvements than changing socio-economic conditions. Singapore is another Asian state that appears to be following a somewhat similar pattern to that of the 'European' demographic transition though at a later date than Japan and again with some individual variations (see Case Study 2C).

Demographic transition in developing countries

Much interest and attention is now focused on the demographic situation in a large number of countries, mainly in Africa, Asia and Latin America, that are at lower levels of economic development than those mentioned so far and are sometimes grouped together as 'developing' countries. In many such countries a situation similar to that of stage 1 in Fig. 2.2 was succeeded in the mid-twentieth century by a period in which the death rate declined dramatically but no substantial decline occurred in the birth rate until some time later, if at all. In some countries birth rates have actually increased during part of the period in which death rates have been falling. This appears to have been the case in several Latin American and Asian countries in the 1940s and 1950s, and often more recently in African countries. Birth rates in Algeria, for example, appear to have peaked in 1970 to 1974 in a period of very high natural increase extending from the 1950s onwards. At present, natural increase rates in excess of 2.5% are quite common in developing countries and average rates over 3%, though less common than in the 1970s and 1980s, were still being recorded in 1990 in some countries, including Kenya, Zambia, Ghana, Saudi Arabia, Jordan and Nicaragua. This situation is comparable in some ways with stage 2 and early stage 3 of the demographic transition model. In nineteenth-century Europe, however, fertility was generally lower than has been the case in many developing countries since 1950 and natural growth rates have also generally been higher in developing countries since 1950 than they were in nineteenth-century Europe. One factor influencing this has been the early age at which many women in developing countries are married but in most cases it seems likely that a series of factors relating to changing lifestyles and cultural attitudes may be involved. Some of these will be considered later in the discussion of family planning issues in developing countries.

Attempts to show the pattern of demographic change in developing countries in the form of a diagrammatic model have often been misleading, especially where a time scale has been included. For example, such diagrams have often implied that declines in death rates began

Exercise 2.1

Changing birth and death rates in Japan, 1921– 87

a) Construct a graph to show the following
information concerning Japan.

Year	Total population (millions)	Crude birth rate (per 1,000)	Crude death rate (per 1,000)	Year	Total population (millions)	Crude birth rate (per 1,000)	Crude death rate (per 1,000)
1921	56.7	35.1	22.7	1955	89.3	19.4	7.8
1922	57.4	34.3	22.4	1956	90.2	18.4	8.0
1923	58.1	35.2	22.9	1957	90.9	17.2	8.3
1924	58.9	33.9	21.3	1958	91.8	18.0	7.4
1925	59.7	34.9	20.3	1959	92.6	17.5	7.4
1926	60.7	34.6	19.1	1960	93.4	17.2	7.6
1927	61.7	33.4	19.7	1961	94.2	16.9	7.4
1928	62.6	34.1	19.8	1962	95.2	17.0	7.5
1929	63.5	32.7	19.9	1963	96.2	17.3	7.0
1930	64.5	32.4	18.2	1964	97.2	17.7	6.9
1931	65.5	32.1	19.0	1965	98.3	18.6	7.1
1932	66.4	32.9	17.7	1966	99.1	13.7	6.8
1933	67.4	31.5	17.7	1967	100.2	19.4	6.8
1934	68.3	29.9	18.1	1968	101.3	18.6	6.8
1935	69.3	31.6	16.8	1969	102.5	18.5	6.8
1936	70.1	30.0	17.5	1970	103.7	18.8	6.9
1937	70.6	30.9	17.1	1971	105.0	19.2	6.6
1938	71.0	27.2	17.7	1972	107.5	19.3	6.5
1939	71.9	26.6	17.8	1973	109.1	19.4	6.6
1940	72.2	29.4	16.5	1974	110.6	18.6	6.5
1941	72.9	31.8	16.0	1975	111.9	17.1	6.3
1942	73.9	30.9	16.1	1976	113.1	16.3	6.3
1943	74.4	30.9	16.7	1977	114.2	15.5	6.1
1944	73.8	n.a.	n.a.	1978	115.2	14.9	6.1
1945	72.1	n.a.	n.a.	1979	116.2	14.2	6.0
1946	75.8	n.a.	n.a.	1980	117.1	13.6	6.2
1947	78.1	34.3	14.6	1981	117.9	13.0	6.1
1948	80.0	33.5	11.9	1982	118.7	12.8	6.0
1949	81.8	33.0	11.6	1983	119.5	12.7	6.2
1950	83.2	28.1	10.9	1984	120.3	12.5	6.2
1951	84.5	25.3	9.9	1985	121.0	11.9	6.3
1952	85.8	23.4	8.9	1986	121.7	11.4	6.2
1953	87.0	21.5	8.9	1987	122.3	11.1	6.2
1954	88.2	20.0	8.2				

Source: Japan Statistical Yearbook, 1989.

b) Comment on the features indicated on
your graph in relation to the demographic
transition model (Fig. 2.2).

c) On the basis of more general reading,
suggest reasons for changes in birth and
death rates in Japan since 1920.

only in 1950 yet there is considerable evidence that many developing countries had already undergone a decline in death rates to a level of 20 per thousand or thereabouts by the late 1930s or early 1940s. Additionally it is still very obvious that the time sequence for a substantial reduction in birth rates varies very considerably between different developing countries. These issues are examined in rather more detail in Exercise 2.2.

Suggestions that developing countries will, in time, follow a pattern similar to that suggested by stages 3 and 4 of the demographic transition model, may or may not be correct. Even if it did happen, however, the time scales involved are critical since massive annual increases in population are already occurring in Asia, Africa and Latin America – in some cases in countries that face considerable problems in feeding their existing populations. (During the 1980s the populations of both China and India increased by more than twice the total population of the United Kingdom, for example.) The basic problem is that whereas death rates have fallen markedly in response to such developments as the provision of better medical facilities, improved hygiene and successful disease eradication programmes, in many countries, as already suggested, birth rates have remained high – even where family planning programmes have been strongly promoted.

Exercise 2.2

Demographic transition in developing countries

a) Using the data in the table below, construct a series of line graphs to show birth and death rates for the countries named in the table between 1940 and 1990. (It is suggested that you produce three graphs, each representing three or four of the countries named, with the line graphs for the different countries superimposed.)

b) Comment on similarities and differences revealed by your graphs concerning the process of demographic transition between 1940 and 1990 in the countries for which data are provided.

c) Suggest to what extent it is possible to produce a generalised model of demographic transition for developing countries based on the data provided. (You may find it helpful to attempt to produce such a model.)

Crude birth rates and crude death rates in selected developing countries, 1940–90.

	Crude birth rates (per thousand)						Crude death rates (per thousand)					
	1940	1950	1960	1970	1980	1990	1940	1950	1960	1970	1980	1990
Singapore	45	45	38	22	17	20	21	12	6	5	5	5
Malaya/Malaysia	41	44	38	37	31	30	20	16	10	8	8	5
Ceylon/Sri Lanka	36	40	37	32	29	21	21	12	9	8	7	6
Egypt	41	45	44	42	41	38	26	19	17	15	11	9
Mauritius	30	50	39	27	28	19	26	14	11	8	7	7
Venezuela	36	43	48	41	36	28	17	11	8	8	6	5
Chile	33	34	35	27	25	22	22	15	12	11	7	6
Costa Rica	45	49	45	45	32	29	17	12	9	8	4	4
Mexico	44	46	45	42	33	30	23	16	11	9	8	6
Jamaica	31	33	43	33	27	20	15	12	9	8	6	5

Sources: various.

Thus, in addition to continuing high birth rates in many developing countries, death rates in many countries have reached very low levels. In most of Latin America, East and South-east Asia and the Middle East and in several developing countries elsewhere, death rates had fallen below 10 per thousand by 1990. A few countries even had death rates of 5 per thousand or below including Malaysia, Qatar, Costa Rica, Hong Kong, Jamaica and Venezuela. Although the reduction in death rates can be related to some extent to general socio-economic development, it is principally the greatly improved health facilities and medical knowledge that have made possible the control of major tropical diseases and a great reduction in infant mortality. The infant mortality rate (i.e. the number of deaths of infants under one year of age per thousand live births in a given year) had been reduced to below a third of its 1950 level in many countries by 1990. Scope for much further improvement is still apparent, however, when the average rate for European countries (12 per thousand) is compared with those for Latin America (54), South-east Asia (70), South Asia (101) and Africa (109). The low death rates already present in many developing countries clearly mean that the detailed features of demographic transition in such countries will be different from those experienced by most European countries. As already suggested, however, much attention is now focused on the attempts by developing countries to bring about reductions in fertility levels before further massive population growth has occurred, and this leads us to a consideration of family planning issues in such countries.

Family planning issues in developing countries

The attitudes towards family planning of both governments and individuals in developing countries vary considerably. During the 1950s and 1960s many governments accepted the need for family planning programmes and have since endeavoured to introduce them – with varying degrees of success. In India, for example, despite a strong government commitment to family planning, birth rates have declined only slowly since 1950. Early plans to reduce the birth rate to 25 per thousand by 1980 were soon revised to 30 per thousand as a result of the slow progress being made but even this higher figure had still not been achieved by 1990. Kenya, with a birth rate of approximately 50 per thousand in 1970, saw this actually increase to 54 per thousand by the early 1980s – despite government encouragement for family planning – though a decline seems to have commenced later in the decade. Elsewhere some family planning schemes have met with more obvious success. In Jamaica, the birth rate fell from 43 per thousand in 1960 to 22 per thousand in 1990. In a similar period it dropped from 35 to 13 per thousand in Hong Kong and between 1970 and 1990 in Indonesia it declined from 47 to 27 per thousand.

Not all governments have sought to encourage family planning, however. Some have argued that population increase is an essential element in the economic development of their countries. Some Brazilian government officials, for example, have suggested that the resources of the Amazon Basin can only be developed effectively if Brazil has a larger population than at present, and several of the oil-rich Middle Eastern states have adopted pro-natalist policies largely on the grounds that they need an increased labour force to develop their resources effectively. Arguments of this kind clearly raise the issue of what is the optimum population for an area, a theme examined in more detail in Chapter 4. There is also a feeling in some developing countries that the efforts of people in areas like North America and Western Europe to encourage family planning programmes in less affluent areas than their own are not without self-interest. It is argued that people in more economically developed areas are concerned to preserve present world economic patterns and so ensure that rapid population growth in the Third World does not result in a shortage of products at present consumed by people in North America, Western Europe and similar areas. In short, programmes of family planning are seen as a means of preserving high standards of living in some areas at the expense of others that may already have much lower living standards.

Attitudes of this kind may have been fostered by the way in which some family planning programmes have emphasised the necessity of birth control with little reference to the circumstances or needs of individuals affected by such programmes. There has in the past been an unfortunate tendency to group together all developing countries and imply that they have identical problems – notably that of having too many people and not enough food. It has also been implied that the provision of contraceptive devices and advice on an extensive scale, especially if accompanied by massive propaganda, will resolve most of these problems. It is now widely recognised that in many cases such approaches are doomed to failure or, at best, to only limited success. Birth control is unlikely to

be very attractive to a peasant farmer who relies on his children to help him to farm his land and to act as an insurance for his old age in a situation where, as in most developing countries, there is no such thing as an old age pension. In these circumstances, family planning might rightly be viewed as having more rather than fewer children. This kind of individual attitude provides one reason why birth control programmes have been of limited success, despite strong government backing, in countries like India. There are many other factors that also militate against birth control methods being widely adopted. For example, in much of Latin America and in some other areas, the influence of the Roman Catholic church has restricted the spread and effectiveness of family planning. The widespread attitude that a man's social standing is to some extent determined by the

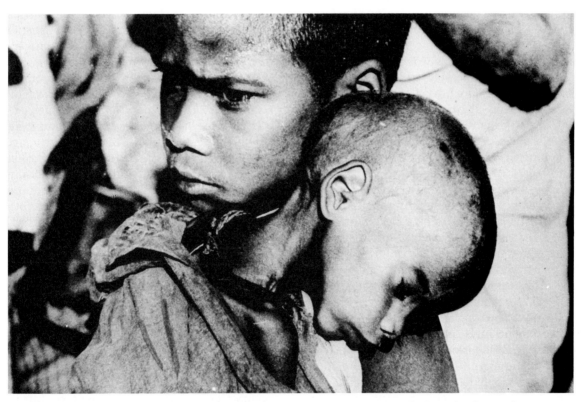

Fig. 2.3 Two brothers in Bihar, India, during one of the droughts that have frequently affected this area. Child mortality rates are still quite high in much of rural India where children are usually seen as economic assets and a large family may be perceived as a kind of insurance against the possible loss of some children at an early age.

number of children he has sired is another powerful cultural force against birth control in countries like Kenya and some Muslim countries where a desirable size for a family is still often seen to be six or seven children.

Clarke (1985) pointed out that, on the evidence of data available at that time, nine of the ten countries in the world with total fertility rates of over 7.0 were countries with a Muslim majority, Kenya being the exception. The total fertility rate (TFR) indicates the average number of children that would be born to each woman if she were to live through her childbearing lifetime (usually considered to be ages 15–49) bearing children at the same rate as women of those ages actually did in a given year. A TFR of 2.1 to 2.5, depending on mortality conditions, represents 'replacement level' fertility, i.e. the level at which a country's population would eventually level off (assuming no net migration). Clarke suggested that a major reason for the high fertility levels in many Muslim countries was the status of women in such countries – though acknowledging that this was difficult to quantify and that many of the indices frequently used to do this, such as literacy, educational enrolment, and labour force participation, were perhaps 'Western-orientated'. Other writers have suggested that high fertility levels might be influenced by a reduction in the extent of early widowhood as male mortality rates rapidly decrease so that more married women continue to produce children throughout all or most of their fertile years. A decline in traditional means of birth control such as breastfeeding and the previously widespread practice of sexual abstinence for a lengthy period after the birth of a child may also have significant effects in some communities.

It would be wrong to assume from these comments about high fertility levels in Muslim countries that the Islamic religion is opposed to family planning. In fact, several Muslim countries have adopted strong family planning policies in recent years. As already mentioned, some of the most pro-natalist countries have tended to be oil-rich Arab states such as Saudi Arabia, Iraq, Libya and Oman but, not surprisingly,

some of those most concerned about high levels of fertility have been those where population pressure is perceived to be a problem such as Egypt, Bangladesh, Indonesia and Tunisia. Of the first group of states, the only one with a TFR below 7 by 1990 was Libya (5.5) whereas all four in the second group had TFRs below 5.0. Indonesia, with the largest population of any country with a Muslim majority, has had particular success with its family planning policies in recent years and by 1990 had a TFR of only 3.3 and a birth rate of 27 per thousand, the latter having shown a decline of over 10 per thousand since 1975. The success of family planning policies in Indonesia has been attributed to several different factors including rising standards of living, improved health services, better education, more widespread availability of contraceptives and family planning advice, and a wider acceptance of sterilisation. The general experience of the Muslim states, however, emphasises amongst other things that it is simplistic to assume that economic growth alone will necessarily result in falling birth rates.

Obviously a wide range of factors may influence the success or failure of family planning programmes. The influence of individual factors may also be quite complex. For example, in many countries education seems to have a significant influence on the size of families. Better-educated parents tend to have fewer children for a variety of reasons. Such people are more likely to be aware of effective methods of contraception and may live in circumstances which make it easier to utilise such methods. They are also likely to be more aware of the wider range of economic opportunities available to better-educated people in most societies. Indeed, it is interesting to note that the most successful family planning programmes have generally been conducted in areas where economic changes have also been occurring, as in Hong Kong and Singapore (see Case Study 2C).

The relatively recent widespread provision of primary schooling for the majority of children in many developing countries may also have a considerable effect on birth rates in the future. It changes the situation of many families, especially in rural areas, from one in which children could be used to carry out a wide range of domestic and economic activities at little cost to the family, to one in which children often become a financial burden because of the expense of school fees, books and uniforms. (All these items frequently have to be provided by parents in developing countries.) Education may also result in children having increased expectations of what is a 'normal' lifestyle – again putting a stress on the family budget. Although the value of education is generally highly regarded in developing countries because of the new opportunities it is perceived to offer, parents may find it difficult to educate a large family and may therefore be encouraged to limit their family size. How they respond is likely to depend largely on cultural attitudes in their society which may themselves be changing as a result of education and many other social or economic factors. Caldwell (1980) and others have argued that one of the main reasons why fertility in Europe, North America and Australia did not decline substantially until the late nineteenth century despite major social and economic changes having begun much earlier, was that universal compulsory education only became established in such areas from about 1870 onwards. This, it is suggested, resulted in a crucial change from children being a net financial asset to being a net financial cost for a family, and was a major cause of changed attitudes towards family size. It seems probable that similar changes in attitude may now be occurring in many developing countries.

Despite some individual exceptions, it seems apparent from the evidence currently available that in most cases people in developing countries are more likely to adopt birth control measures if radical changes occur in their traditional way of life to provide them with improved economic standards, better educational opportunities, greater social security in their old age, and a higher degree of female emancipation. In short, people must usually be in a situation where they perceive some real advantage in restricting the size of their families before they are likely to practise birth control. Thus so-called family

planning programmes that are dominated by attempts to encourage birth control without paying attention to other aspects of social and economic change are unlikely to be very successful.

The potential for further increases in the population of developing countries would seem to be very considerable. Death rates are likely to continue to decrease – relatively slowly in most cases – as infant mortality rates decline. Birth rates may also decline in most developing countries but this decline is unlikely to be very rapid. Some reasons for this have already been suggested but at least one other factor may be of considerable significance. In many developing countries, rapid increases in population in the relatively recent past mean that a large proportion of the population still has to pass through the fertile age range. In many African countries, for example, approximately half the population is under the age of 20 and, however successful family planning programmes may prove to be, it seems likely that major increases in total population will occur during the period in which these young people pass through the fertile age range. This leads us to an investigation of the age structures of particular populations and the effect these have on population growth.

Age structure and population growth

The age structure of a particular population is likely to have a major influence on the rate of population increase. Figure 2.4 shows the percentage of the population aged less than 15 years for selected countries in 1970 and 1990. The differing patterns of change between countries for this period are worth further consideration (see Exercise 2.3). The data provided in Fig. 2.4 also help to emphasise the point made earlier that as those at present in the under-15 age groups pass through the fertile age range it will be difficult to bring about significant reductions in population growth rates in many developing countries simply because of the large numbers of people within the fertile age range. If, however, the number of children born to each woman can be substantially reduced then the

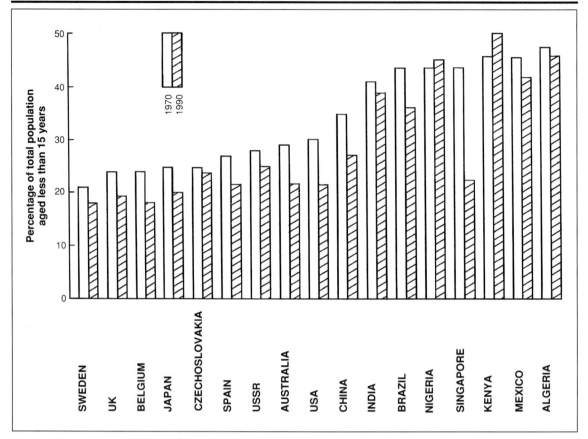

Fig. 2.4 Percentage of total population aged less than 15 years in selected countries in 1970 and 1990.
Sources: World Population Data Sheets of the Population Reference Bureau, Inc. and UN estimates.

prospect of continuing high growth rates in the longer-term future will be reduced. This kind of situation lies behind some of the more extreme population control policies carried out in countries fearful of the pressure on resources that may result from continuing high rates of growth. China's attempts in the 1980s to restrict the number of children to only one per family (see Case Study 4A) provide a good example of this.

Exercise 2.3

Youthful populations

Examine the information provided in Fig. 2.4 concerning the proportion of the total population aged less than 15 years in selected countries in 1970 and 1990.

a) Summarise the main changes between 1970 and 1990 that are evident from the figure, suggesting reasons for any important features you identify.

b) Suggest what future difficulties may result for a country that currently has a large proportion of its population aged under 15 years. By reference to particular examples, indicate what approaches have been adopted by countries in the past in an attempt to overcome such difficulties, and comment on the extent to which they have been successful.

Exercise 2.4

Age-sex pyramids

a) Construct age-sex pyramids for countries A, B and C using the data provided in the table below. (All values given are percentages of the total population.)

Age group	Country A		Country B		Country C	
	Males	Females	Males	Females	Males	Females
0–4	10.1	10.1	5.8	5.6	3.1	2.9
5–9	7.6	7.7	5.0	4.9	3.1	3.0
10–14	6.1	6.2	5.0	4.9	3.5	3.4
15–19	5.0	5.1	5.1	5.0	4.3	4.1
20–24	4.1	4.3	5.1	5.0	4.5	4.3
25–29	3.2	3.6	4.5	4.5	4.3	4.1
30–34	2.6	3.1	3.8	3.8	4.1	3.9
35–39	2.2	2.6	3.1	3.2	4.2	4.0
40–44	1.9	2.1	2.6	2.7	3.4	3.2
45–49	1.6	1.7	2.1	2.2	2.9	2.7
50–54	1.3	1.4	1.8	2.0	2.6	2.6
55–59	1.0	1.1	1.6	1.8	2.4	2.5
60–64	0.7	0.9	1.2	1.5	2.2	2.5
65–69	0.5	0.6	0.9	1.2	1.7	2.1
70–74	0.3	0.4	0.7	0.9	1.4	1.9
75–79	0.2	0.2	0.4	0.7	0.9	1.5
80+	0.1	0.1	0.4	0.6	0.9	1.8

b) The three age-sex pyramids you have constructed relate to Chile (1986), Malawi (1987) and the Netherlands (1986), though not necessarily in that order. Describe the main features of each of the pyramids and suggest, with reasons, which relates to each country named.

When a high proportion of the population is under the age of 15 years this is also likely to impose pressure on government resources, especially with regard to expenditure on education. In Africa this has been a particularly severe problem in recent years with, in 1990, approximately 45% of the African population under the age of 15 years. In many African countries major advances in educational provision were made in the 1960s but these have rarely been maintained through the 1970s and 1980s, with falling levels in expenditure per child becoming the norm. This is not surprising in economically poor countries where the absolute number of children under 15 years old has increased dramatically during this period – in some cases, as in Kenya and Zambia, doubling in only 20 years or so through to 1990.

In addition to having an effect on future fertility patterns, as mentioned earlier, the presence of a disproportionate number of young people in a country is also likely to give rise to relatively low death rates. This is a feature of many developing countries today but future changes in the age structure of populations in such countries may have a negative effect on death rates. Whether this will be sufficient to counter-balance other factors such as improved hygiene and public health services is difficult to predict.

A helpful indication of the age structure of a

particular population can be made through the use of population pyramids (also known as age-sex pyramids). These are diagrams that consist of a series of horizontal bars representing successive age ranges (normally in five-year groups) with the total males in each group recorded to the left and females to the right of a vertical axis, each five-year total of males or females normally being expressed as a percentage of the total population. Figure 2.5 shows a series of such pyramids selected to illustrate some contrasts in population structures.

The pyramid for Kenya, with its broad base and narrow tip, is fairly typical of many African countries, representing a situation in which there is a large percentage of young people and relatively few old people. Kenya had, however, a slightly higher proportion of its people in the lower age groups than any other country in the mid-1980s. The pyramid for Peninsular Malaysia is not dramatically different but has a considerably smaller percentage of the total in the lowest age groups (37.5% under 15 years old compared with 51.4% in Kenya) and also a smaller difference between the totals in successive age groups in the lower part of the age range. These differences reflect the effect of family planning schemes and the greater control over mortality, especially of children, in Malaysia where it is significant that living standards have risen noticeably since the 1950s. With regard to older people the difference between the two pyramids is perhaps less obvious although in Peninsular Malaysia almost twice as large a proportion of the population is aged over 65 as in Kenya (3.9% compared with 2.0%).

It is important to remember that a population pyramid for a country reflects not only births and deaths but also migration. This is apparent from the pyramid for Jamaica (Fig. 2.5). Considerable employment problems in Jamaica from the 1950s onwards coupled with employment opportunities elsewhere, especially in the UK and North America, led to large-scale emigration until immigration controls in the receiving countries had a limiting effect. Most of those who migrated were in the younger working age groups and the effect of this on the age structure of Jamaica by the early 1980s is apparent in the narrowing of the middle section of the population pyramid. The lower section of the pyramid mainly indicates the increased effectiveness of family planning in the more recent past but also reflects to some extent the lower numbers in the fertile age range resulting from earlier emigration.

The population pyramids for more economically developed countries contrast strongly with those for developing countries, tending to show less variation between different age groups and thus being more rectangular than triangular in shape. The pyramids for Sweden, France and Japan all show the effects of much lower birth rates and generally lower death rates over a considerable period of time. In marked contrast to Kenya, Malaysia and Jamaica, both France and Japan have just over 20% of their population under the age of 15, mainly as a result of their much lower birth rates, while Sweden has only 17.8% of its population in this category. All three developed countries have more than 10% of their population aged over 65 with Sweden having 17.8% in this category, as many as those aged under 15. At a more detailed level the pyramids indicate certain specific features. For example, the low numbers in the age range 40–49 evident in the French population pyramid reflect the high death rates and low birth rates occurring during the Second World War, with the largest age group (35–39) representing the period of the post-war 'baby boom' in France. A similar 'baby boom' was experienced in Japan (clearly evidenced in the population pyramid) and in most other countries affected by that war. An earlier pyramid showing France's age structure in, say, the 1960s would indicate just as clearly the effects of the First World War on population numbers. These are less obvious in the 1987 pyramid because anyone born during that war would by 1987 have been at least 69 years old and so general death rates have had a considerable effect on the numbers surviving from the age groups born in and soon after that war.

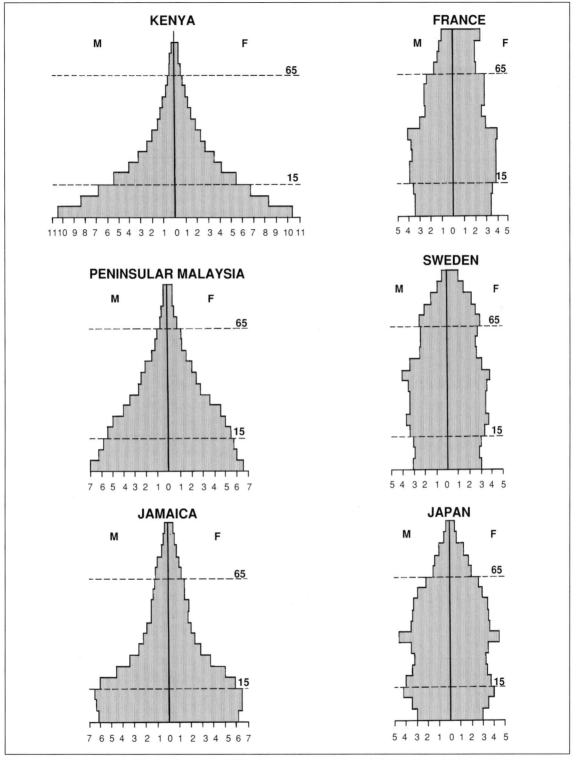

Fig. 2.5 Population pyramids for Kenya (1985), France (1987), Peninsular Malaysia (1984), Sweden (1988), Jamaica (1982) and Japan (1986). In these and all subsequent population pyramids the data are arranged in five-year age groups represented as a percentage of the total population (with the exception of the oldest age group which includes all those over the age of 80 in the case of Kenya, 85 in the case of France, etc.).

Fig. 2.6 Mineworkers in Malaysia. The clothing and vehicles of these mineworkers reflect a standard of living that is higher than that of many people who live in developing countries. In Malaysia, although variations in living standards inevitably still exist between different sectors of the population, the general improvement in social and economic conditions in recent decades is considered to have had a significant effect on attitudes towards family planning.

Fluctuations in birth rates, mentioned earlier as a typical feature of the fourth stage of the 'European' demographic transition, are clearly reflected in the lower (more recent) parts of the pyramids for Sweden and Japan. In most cases these fluctuations can be related to changes in social attitudes, economic conditions or aspects of the provision and use of contraceptives – perhaps most notably in developed countries the introduction of the contraceptive pill and subsequent fears about possible side-effects of this means of contraception. Birth rate fluctuations may also relate to much more traditional attitudes, however, as in China and Japan where certain years in the calendar are considered either lucky or unlucky times in which to have children. The birth rate in Japan fell from 18.6

per thousand in 1965 to only 13.7 in 1966, rising again in the following year to 19.4, a dramatic change usually attributed to the fact that it was considered unlucky to have a female child in 1966.

A general feature of the population structure, apparent from careful examination of the pyramids in Fig. 2.5, is that in the early years there is usually a slight preponderance of males but in later years females normally form the larger group. This reflects the tendency for there to be an excess of males over females at birth, believed to be a natural adaptation to the higher pre-natal and infant mortality rates amongst males. The generally lower mortality rate of females eventually leads to a situation in which they form the majority. Thus, whereas there are more males than females in the lowest three age groups for all the countries represented in Fig. 2.5 (e.g. 19.2% males compared with 18.3% females in Peninsular Malaysia and 10.75% males compared with 10.1% females in France) women form the majority of those aged over 65 in each country. The excess of females over males in the older age groups tends to be slightly more marked in the developed countries, perhaps because of the more physically demanding lifestyles of many women in developing countries.

As crude birth and death rates are calculated in relation to the whole of a population, the age structure of the population can clearly limit the value of these rates in showing fertility and mortality levels. For example, other things being equal, a population with a large proportion of its people within the fertile age range is likely to have a higher birth rate than a country of similar total population that has fewer people within the fertile age range. Alternative measures have thus been devised to overcome this limitation. These include the following:

a) *General fertility rate*   This relates the number of births in any year to the number of women in the fertile age range (usually taken to be 15–49 years). It is normally expressed as so many births per thousand women in the fertile age group per year.

b) *Age-specific fertility rate*   This relates the number of births in any year to the number of women in a specific age group (e.g. 20–24 years) and is again usually expressed as so many births per thousand women in the specific age group per year.

c) *Age-specific mortality rate*   This is similar to (b), being calculated on the basis of the number of deaths per thousand persons in a specific age group in a selected year.

d) *Total fertility rate (TFR)*   This indicates the average number of children that would be born to each woman if she were to live through her child-bearing lifetime (15–49 years) bearing children at the same rate as women of those ages did in a given year (see earlier comment on page 14). This rate is sometimes expressed per thousand women.

e) *Gross reproduction rate*   This is calculated in a similar way to the TFR but only female children are considered – thus it represents the average number of female children that would be born to each woman if she were to live through her child-bearing lifetime with current fertility rates prevailing.

f) *Net reproduction rate*   This is calculated in the same way as (e) but is amended to take account of women who die before passing through the fertile age range. A net reproduction rate of 1.0 implies that a population is exactly replacing itself, of less than 1.0 that it is failing to do so and of more than 1.0 that the population is likely to increase because the number of potential mothers in the next generation is being increased.

Whatever means are used to measure rates of population change, it is difficult to forecast the future pattern of growth with any certainty. Future developments will inevitably be affected by influences that change through time, such as social attitudes to family planning. However, the case studies in this chapter and elsewhere in the book illustrate some of the developments that have already taken place and may suggest some likely future patterns of change.

Disease and population change

The fact that disease may be an important influence on population change has already been briefly mentioned. Disease is likely either to have severe socio-economic effects (e.g. an above-average number of days' absence from work through sickness, which may lead to worsening housing conditions and nutritional standards, which in turn may lead to susceptibility to other diseases, etc.) or to lead to death. Widespread disease-induced deaths obviously unbalance age structures and may have crippling demographic consequences, sometimes for generations. For instance, early deaths on a large scale as a result of disease will obviously affect fertility rates in the immediate future if they occur among adults in the fertile age range and in the longer term if they occur among infants. It is important to distinguish between the two major groups of diseases – infectious (communicable) and degenerative – for they are of varying significance in different parts of the world.

Infectious diseases are caused by pathogenic (disease-carrying) bacteria and viruses. Bacteria are amongst the smallest of living organisms and they penetrate or are engulfed by body cells. Viruses are even smaller. They are parasitic and cannot survive outside living cells. The rate of reproduction of bacteria and viruses is extremely high. Howe (1972) cites the example of a cut infected by a thousand of the streptococcal bacteria that will, within 12 hours, produce approximately 10–100 million streptococci if left to grow unchecked. This number is sufficient to kill a human being.

Bacteria or viruses may be introduced into the body directly, by swallowing (as with cholera, dysentery or typhoid), by breathing in (diphtheria or scarlet fever) or through wounds (tetanus). Alternatively they may be introduced indirectly by a carrier or vector as in the case of malaria via the *Anopheles* mosquito, the plague via the rat flea (*Xenopsylla cheopsis*) and typhus via the body louse (*Pediculus humanis corporis*).

One of the most important characteristics of infectious diseases is their ability to spread rapidly as epidemics. This is well illustrated by selected British examples, perhaps the best known of which is the bubonic plague (Black Death) that reached Britain in 1348. This is an infectious disease of certain rodents and is passed on to humans through the bite of infected fleas that live on the rodents. The host in medieval times was the black or house rat (*Rattus rattus*) and the vector was the rat flea. The house rat infested the dwellings of the poor and was particularly widespread in towns. The disease is thought to have originated in the Indian subcontinent between 1340 and 1342. It expanded into Europe via the Crimea in 1346, having been brought there by an invading Tartar army which probably contracted it in Asia Minor. The plague entered Britain at what is now Weymouth in Dorset early in August 1348 from Calais or the Channel Islands. The disease spread through Dorset, Devon and Somerset and reached Bristol by 15 August (Fig. 2.7). It had affected Gloucester, Oxford and London by the autumn, and East Anglia and Lincolnshire by the spring of 1349. By May of that year it had reached York and by midsummer was in North Wales. Most of Scotland was affected by spring 1350. Some scholars claim that the population of Britain was halved between 1348 and 1350, and

others that it was reduced by 30%; one has suggested that no more than 10% died. What is clear is that the effects of the plague were uneven, with pastoral and hill districts suffering least and sea and river ports most.

Since the Black Death a large number of other rapidly spreading but fortunately less potent diseases have been recorded in these islands. In the sixteenth century, for instance, a disease of uncertain origin called sweating sickness or English sweat diffused over the country with varying degrees of severity on a number of occasions. In the seventeenth century there were several outbreaks of plague, from which the inhabitants of London were the worst sufferers: in the epidemic of 1603 over 33,000 died in the capital; in 1625 the London death toll was over 41,000 and in the Great Plague of 1665 there were more than 65,000 deaths in the city. In the

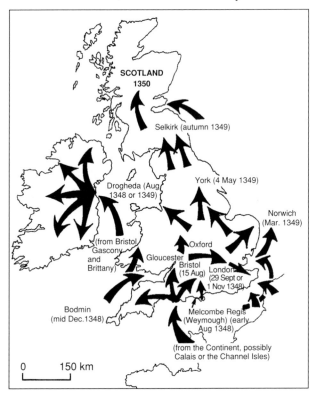

Fig. 2.7 The progress of the Black Death in the British Isles in the fourteenth century.
Source: after Howe, 1972.

nineteenth century cholera epidemics occurred in 1817–23 and 1827–33. The second of these began in the Ganga Valley and quickly spread through the Punjab and Afghanistan into south-east Europe. The disease reached Berlin by August 1831 and first occurred in Britain in Sunderland on 19 October 1831. By early 1834 almost 22,000 had died in England and Wales, over 25,000 in Ireland and 9,500 in Scotland.

A relatively small cholera epidemic that occurred in the Soho district of London in 1854 is renowned because of the map showing deaths from the epidemic that appeared in the second edition of John Snow's essay 'On the Mode of Communication of Cholera' (Fig. 2.8). The 'cholera field', as Snow called it, was centred on a pump in Broad Street and extended for about 200 metres around it. Within this area more than 500 people died from cholera between 1 and 10 September 1854. Snow pointed out that most of the dead had been users of the Broad Street pump whereas those living in the area but obtaining water elsewhere were unaffected. This was the first time that a relationship between cholera and contaminated water had been proven.

By the early twentieth century the significance of infectious diseases in Britain had been

Fig. 2.8 The 'cholera field' around Broad Street pump, Soho, London 1854.

greatly reduced and continued improvements in public water supplies, sewerage systems and public and private hygiene had virtually eliminated them as major killers by the 1970s. However, occasional outbreaks have occurred, some of which have been severe. Between 1947 and 1958, for instance, over 50,000 people contracted poliomyelitis, but vaccination programmes that began in 1956 have since made the disease extremely rare. More recently, much concern has been expressed in Britain and elsewhere at the spread of AIDS, a viral disease first recognised in New York in 1979. This has resulted in people dying from infections that the human body can normally resist without much difficulty. As this condition results from a breakdown of the normal immune system, it is called 'Acquired Immune Deficiency System' or AIDS. The virus causing AIDS is the Human Immunodeficiency Virus (HIV) and while at the time of writing considerable numbers of people are known or suspected to be infected with the virus, the number who have developed full-blown AIDS or died from the disease is statistically small. There are, however, major fears that numbers dying from AIDS may increase dramatically in the future with significant effects on population structures in some countries. For example, in 1990 the World Health Organisation (WHO) estimated that one in 40 women in sub-Saharan Africa carried the HIV virus, that one in three of the children of these women would receive the virus from their mothers and that more than 10 million African children would be orphaned in the 1990s as their parents died from AIDS.

National and international programmes to eradicate infectious diseases have been significant features of the development of health systems since the Second World War. Perhaps the most successful of these has resulted in what appears to be the final eradication of smallpox. Although an effective vaccine against the disease had been developed by Edward Jenner as early as 1796 it was not until the mid-1960s that widespread use of the vaccine and control over the movements of infected individuals ultimately led to the disease being eliminated in the developed countries of the world. In 1967 WHO turned its attention to an 'Intensified Smallpox Eradication Programme' involving systematic vaccination on a global scale and repeated field investigations to find and isolate remaining cases. The last recorded case was in Somalia in 1977 (except for an accidental case in an English laboratory) and in 1979, after a two-year smallpox-free period, WHO announced the official eradication of the disease.

The fight to eradicate malaria has proved more difficult though rapid progress was made in many developing countries in the 1940s and 1950s. In Sri Lanka, for instance, the estimated expectation of life at birth rose from 43 years in 1946 to 52 in 1947, the sort of change that had taken 50 years or so to achieve in West European countries. This was attributed at the time to the spraying of malarial areas with DDT, an insecticide developed during the Second World War. Scholars now disagree about whether there was a single cause-effect relationship between spraying with DDT and population change in Sri Lanka. Because of the ambiguous way in which deaths were recorded in Sri Lanka in the 1940s it is not possible to make a statistical comparison of deaths from malaria before and after 1947. It has been argued that the use of insecticides not only reduced the number of deaths from malaria but also indirectly affected population growth by reducing the number of malaria-induced miscarriages and by increasing the amount of sexual intercourse among adults no longer weakened by the disease. Other observers have pointed out that during the critical period of initial post-war population growth, wartime food shortages ended, milk and milk products became more widely available and maternity services were substantially increased.

The optimism generated by the apparent success in many developing countries of programmes of malaria eradication similar to that in Sri Lanka was short-lived and the disease has recently undergone a resurgence in many countries, especially in Africa. The WHO estimated in the early 1990s that worldwide there were 110 million clinical cases of malaria annually – four-fifths of them in Africa – and that a million African children still died from the disease every year. There are several reasons for this. These include the fact that many eradication schemes were initially funded from external sources and local governments have often been unable to maintain the necessary expenditure to continue such programmes or have chosen to spend their money in other ways. This problem has been heightened by the debt crisis that has affected many developing countries since the early 1980s. Also, some of the main malarial vectors have become genetically resistant to insecticides and the chief malarial parasite (*Plasmodium falciparum*) transmitted by the vectors into the human body has developed a resistance to some common anti-malarial drugs, especially the widely used chloroquin. Attempts to eradicate the disease continue but while these have been successful in some – usually more affluent – countries such as Singapore and Taiwan, there is still much to do before malaria is eradicated throughout the world. The same is true of many other infectious diseases that are still potent disablers and killers in many developing countries.

By contrast, in developed countries such diseases have largely been brought under control or eliminated by a combination of environmental improvements, health education, legislation and the widespread use of vaccines and antibiotics. (It is still, of course, possible for new infectious diseases to develop in such areas, as the recent spread of AIDS indicates.) In general, however, deaths from infectious diseases in such countries have been 'replaced' by deaths from degenerative diseases in middle and later life. Although called 'degenerative' their aetiology (cause) is still imperfectly understood and for some at least there is evidence that environmental factors contribute to their development. The most important degenerative diseases are circulatory diseases such as coronary heart disease and cerebro-vascular disease (stroke), various kinds of cancer and respiratory diseases such as bronchitis and asthma. Howe (1986a, 1986b) has emphasised the importance of investigating the locational incidence of such diseases through his mapping of mortality patterns in

the UK based on Standard Mortality Ratios (SMRs) for more than 490 administrative districts. The calculation of these has been restricted to the 15–64 age group to emphasise the incidence of premature deaths. The SMR is calculated so that a district with an SMR of 100 has the mortality incidence equal to the national expectation of mortality. Districts with SMRs under 100 have fewer mortalities than the national average and those with SMRs over 100 exceed the average.

Figures 2.9a and 2.9b show the distribution of deaths of males from coronary heart disease and lung cancer in the UK using SMRs in 1980–82. Coronary heart disease was, on average, responsible annually for the deaths of 24,434 men and 6,521 women under the age of 65 in that period. As Fig. 2.9a indicates, the southern parts of Britain tended to have lower SMRs for this disease in men than the north, though there are considerable variations within the pattern. Even within London there are marked differences between, say, Sutton (SMR 51) and Croydon (56) in comparison with Newham (117) or Barking and Dagenham (122). Figure 2.10a shows some of the areas with a particularly high or low risk from coronary heart disease in men. In the UK the general pattern of distribution of mortality from this disease for women is similar to that for men. It is difficult to relate these patterns of distribution to acknowledged causal factors for this disease such as heavy cigarette smoking, high blood pressure, obesity or high stress levels. This obviously raises the issue of what other factors may be involved.

Although the pattern of distribution of mortality from lung cancer is perhaps less clearcut, there once more appears to be a tendency for the higher risk areas to be in the more northern parts of Britain. Figure 2.10b indicates some areas with particularly high or low levels of mortality. Cigarette smoking has again been strongly implicated in the occurrence of lung cancer but distributions of the kind shown suggest that other factors may also be involved. Breast cancer was responsible for the deaths of over 6,000 women annually in the early 1980s. Spatial variations in SMRs for this disease in the

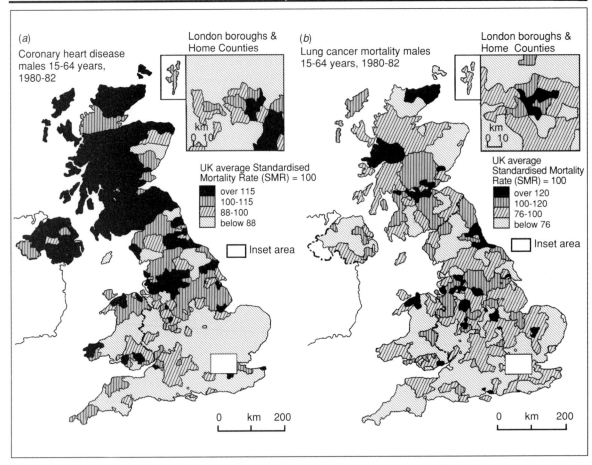

Fig. 2.9 Mortality in males 15–64 years, 1980–82: (*a*) from coronary heart disease, (*b*) from lung cancer. *Source:* Howe, 1986a.

UK show no clearcut pattern, however, with adjacent districts frequently showing strong contrasts in the levels of mortality. Even from these few examples it is obvious that the study of spatial variations in mortality raises various questions about patterns of health that have an effect on the age structure of different parts of the UK. Pollution by certain chemicals is now a widely accepted but imperfectly understood factor. Other environmental factors may also be of significance. So may the genetic characteristics of people living in different parts of the country. Howe has, for example, raised the issue of whether there is a relationship between premature death from several diseases and the Celtic fringe with its high frequencies of people

with blood group O in comparison with the largely Anglo-Saxon population of the South East dominated by blood group A. It is likely to be some years before such issues are resolved but it may be that investigations of the kind carried out by Howe result in more attention being paid to a wider range of factors that may influence health than has customarily been the case.

(a)

District	SMR relative to UK average 100
Low risk	
South Norfolk	35
Suffolk Coastal	42
Isle of Man	44
Mid Suffolk	45
Huntingdon (Cambs)	46
Dinefwr (Dyfed)	50
Aylesbury Vale (Bucks)	50
Coventry (West Midlands)	50
Wychavon (Hereford & Worcs)	51
Chichester (West Sussex)	51
Sutton (London)	51
High risk	
Afan (West Glamorgan)	169
Hamilton (Strathclyde)	170
Omagh (N. Ireland)	171
Motherwell (Strathclyde)	174
Western Isles	178
Inverclyde (Strathclyde)	179
Monklands (Strathclyde)	186
Dungannon (N. Ireland)	194
Lochaber (Highland)	195
Tweeddale (Borders)	197
Caithness (Highland)	209

(b)

District	SMR relative to UK average 100
Low risk	
Stroud (Glos)	45
Elmbridge (Surrey)	50
Chiltern (Bucks)	50
Waverley (Surrey)	52
Reigate & Bansted (Surrey)	53
Woodspring (Avon)	54
Harrow (Greater London)	56
High risk	
Stoke-on-Trent (Staffs)	161
Hartlepool (Cleveland)	164
Southwark (Greater London)	165
Middlesbrough (Cleveland)	167
Knowsley (Merseyside)	179
Glasgow City (Strathclyde)	182

Fig. 2.10 Ranking by standardised mortality ratios (SMRs) 1980–82, of selected districts in the UK with low or high risk of premature death (i.e. before 65 years) in males: (a) from coronary heart disease, (b) from lung cancer.
Source: Howe, 1986b.

England and Wales: stages in demographic evolution

England and Wales: stages in demographic evolution

When the first decennial census was taken in England and Wales in 1801 the population was about 9.2 million. One hundred years later it stood at over 32 million and in 1991 it was 50.9 million. This growth reflects a number of far-reaching demographic changes which were taking place and which in turn influenced and were influenced by economic, technological, cultural and social changes. At first sight the main features of the demographic evolution of England and Wales appear to offer a straightforward example of progress through the demographic transition. The application of this model to England and Wales is, however, fraught with the problems of sparse and unreliable data before 1837 (when the civil registration of births, deaths and marriages began) and awkward facts before and after that date. As a result this model has come in for much re-evaluation and criticism by English demographers in the last 40 years.

Figure 2.11 shows, in generalised form, population growth in England and Wales since the begin-

ning of the eighteenth century. Three periods with different rates of change are recognisable: (i) a slow rate of growth throughout the eighteenth century, followed by (ii) much more vigorous growth throughout the nineteenth century and the first decade of the twentieth century, leading to (iii) a phase in which growth has gradually slowed down.

If changing rates of births and deaths are plotted on the same graph, we can see the relationship between these two demographic variables and total population growth, and the apparently close parallel between the population cycle of England and Wales and the demographic transition model. Figure 2.12 reveals four stages:

A) *Stage 1, ending in the 1740s* This period appears to have been characterised in England and Wales by high and fluctuating birth and death rates, though the long-term trend was for population to increase slowly.

B) *Stage 2, 1740s –1880* This long period of development, whose onset coincided broadly with the early years of the Industrial Revolution, witnessed a rise in population from about 5.6 million to 25 million. The acceleration in the rate of population growth was a remarkable one and there has been much research in recent years on the causes of this demo-

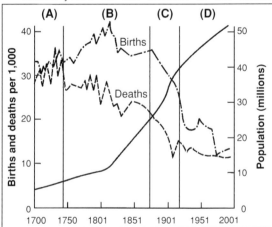

For the period 1700–1839 the birth and death rates are those calculated by Wrigley and Schofield (1981) using back-projection (see text for explanation) plotted at 5-year intervals. After 1839 the birth and death rates shown are based on official registration data.

Fig. 2.12 England and Wales: stages in demographic evolution.

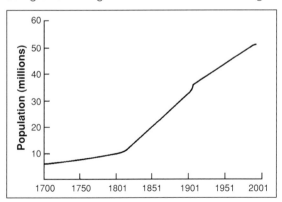

Fig. 2.11 England and Wales: population growth, 1700–1991.

graphic change. The three variables of fertility, mortality and net immigration are all possible determinants of this change. As immigration is generally thought to have been of only minor importance, attention has been focused on birth and death rates. If reliable national statistics were available for the period 1740 –1837 (official registration of births, deaths and marriages only began in July 1837), much of the problem would be resolved, but this is not the case and researchers have been forced to concentrate on detailed studies at the local and regional levels using parish records of varying accuracy and completeness.

Foremost among the questions that researchers have been addressing are:

i) Was the rise in the rate of population growth the result of a fall in the death rate or was it due to a rise in the birth rate because of the lowering of the average age at which people married?

ii) Were the supposed advances in surgery, midwifery, medicines, hospitals and dispensaries, major factors in reducing mortality or were they of negligible importance? There is conflicting evidence here. Indeed some scholars believe that in the short term the supposed advances probably increased mortality.

iii) What was the contribution of improved public health, through improved nutrition, to the changing rate of growth?

More light has been shed on the first question by a major piece of research published in 1981 by the Cambridge Group for the History of Population and Social Structure (Wrigley and Schofield, 1981). The technique of *back-projection* was employed to calculate birth, death and marriage rates and total populations for England for the period 1541–1871. This involved using data from a sample of 404 parishes and developing a computer program to run the data backwards in time to produce estimates of population size and the other key indices at five-year intervals. The authors concluded that in the three centuries before 1841, the population growth rate was determined more by changes in fertility than in mortality

and that the fertility changes were almost entirely caused by variations in the timing and incidence of marriage, which in turn were responses to changing economic conditions. Thus, in times of economic growth when wages tended to rise (e.g. during the century beginning in 1740), more marriages took place, the age at which people married was lower, and the number of births in each family was likely to be greater than in periods when fewer marriages took place and brides and bridegrooms were older.

C) *Stage 3, 1880 –1920*   Death rates fell steeply for much of this period and, in contrast to the previous period, were accompanied by a sharp decline in birth rates. By the early years of the twentieth century the falling birth rate was reflected in the slowing rate of population increase. Living standards rose during this period, and together with the spread of birth control propaganda came a desire to limit family size. The effect of the First World War at the close of this period is clearly shown on the graph.

D) *Stage 4, since the 1920s*   During this period birth rates and death rates have stayed at a relatively low level and population growth has slowed down. Birth rates have shown most fluctuation, rising and falling again as the depression years of the 1930s and the war years gave way to the post-war 'bulge', followed in the 1960s by the widespread use of 'the pill' and the legalisation of abortion. Figure 2.13, which appeared in *The Times* in 1974, shows changing birth rates in the UK in a critical period of medical advance, medical controversy and changing social attitudes.

The 1970s were a period of particularly low birth rates. The birth rate fell from 17.7 in 1966 to 15.9 in 1971, and to an all-time low of 11.8 in 1976 before recovering to 12.8 in 1981 and 13.8 in 1990. Throughout the period from the mid-1960s death rates have been fairly constant, varying between a high of 12.1 in 1976 and a low of 11.3 in 1987 and 1988. During the last two decades (1970–90) the total population has grown more slowly than in any 20-year period since the early eighteenth century – at a rate of only 0.1% in the early 1980s, and at a slightly higher rate of 0.3% between 1984 and 1989. Between mid-1988 and mid-1989 population growth in England and Wales resulting from an excess of births over deaths was 125,000. This was the largest increase in population arising from natural change (i.e. excluding migration) since 1971–72.

As England and Wales passed from one stage in their demographic evolution to another, so the population structure changed. The population pyramids (Fig. 2.14) for 1881, 1931 and 1986 reveal three markedly different populations and show clearly the pyramid shapes associated with different stages of a country's demographic evolution. The 1881 pyramid shows a young population with 70% of the population under 35 years of age. By 1931 there had been a significant change. The broadest part of the pyramid is no longer at the base, but among the adults. In addition there is a broadening in the upper ranges reflecting greater lifespans. The 1986 pyramid shows a further narrowing at the base reflecting the generally low birth rates in the previous 15 years, and the upper age ranges show more broadening as more people, particularly women, survive beyond 65. The noticeable broadening of the pyramid in the 35–40 age range reflects the baby boom of the late 1940s and early 1950s. The bulge in the 15–25 age range is the result of the increase in births that occurred when the baby boom cohort entered the reproductive age range some 20 years later.

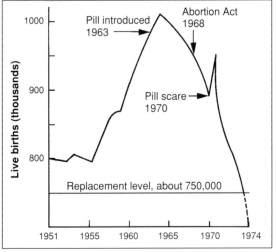

Fig. 2.13 UK: live births, 1951–74.

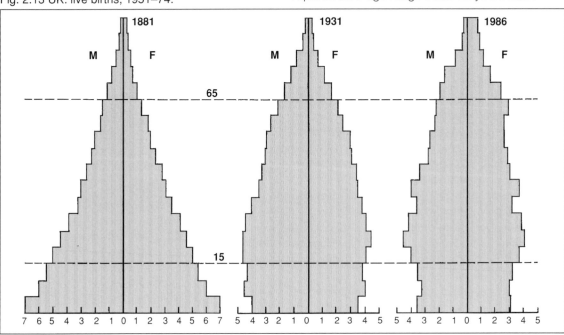

Fig. 2.14 England and Wales: population pyramids for 1881, 1931 and 1986.

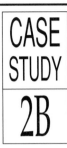

Family planning issues in Eastern Europe

As already indicated, fluctuations in birth rates may result from a variety of influences. A brief examination of recent experience in the countries that formed the communist bloc of Eastern Europe until the political upheavals at the end of the 1980s is interesting in this context. In this region, population totals stagnated or declined in the 1980s and often even earlier (see Fig. 2.15). Largely because of this, the already complex interaction of factors that ultimately determine personal attitudes to family size – such factors as changing social conditions, economic pressures and opportunities, education, and religious beliefs – have been further complicated by state policies motivated largely by a concern about low birth rates and influenced by currency problems that have made it difficult to import contraceptive devices even when this was thought desirable. Despite Marxist philosophies that suggested women should play a full part in society and employment, leading to an acceptance in priniciple of family planning by most states, there has often been little attempt to encourage the use of modern contraceptive methods. Thus, in most of the region, with the notable exceptions of Hungary and the German Democratic Republic (GDR), contraceptive methods were generally of a traditional and not very reliable kind and, largely because of this, abortion became a widely used means of birth limitation.

In *Romania*, the decline of the crude birth rate from 24 per thousand in 1946 to below 15 per thousand in the mid-1960s led to concern about low levels of population growth and to anti-abortion legislation in 1966, whereupon the crude birth rate rose to 27.4 per thousand in 1967. This legislation and the banning from sale of modern contraceptives had only limited long-term effects, however, with the crude birth rate fluctuating around 15 per thousand during most of the 1980s. A major problem has been the large number of illegal abortions, often carried out in unhygienic, and thus dangerous, conditions. A similar pattern of birth rate decline in *Yugoslavia* from 30 to 15 per thousand between 1950 and 1990, again involved birth limitation being based largely on abortion though, in contrast to Romania, this was legally available free of charge up to the 10th week of gestation. Only an estimated 12% of married women used modern contraceptive methods in the late 1980s but even this was a higher proportion than in Romania or Bulgaria (see Fig. 2.15).

	Total population (millions)		CBR (per 1,000)		CDR		Married women using modern contraceptives (%)
	1970	1990	1970	1990	1970	1990	
Albania	2.2	3.3	36	26	8	6	not known
Bulgaria	8.6	8.9	17	13	10	12	8
Czechoslovakia	14.8	15.7	16	14	11	11	25
GDR	16.2	16.3	14	13	14	13	not known
Hungary	10.3	10.6	15	12	11	13	62
Poland	33.3	37.8	16	16	8	10	26
Romania	20.6	23.3	23	16	10	11	6

Fig. 2.15 Population data for selected countries in Eastern Europe.

In *Bulgaria*, birth rates fell to just over 20 per thousand before the Second World War and, after a brief post-war 'baby boom', began a further slow decline to 13 per thousand by 1990. Official surveys in the 1980s suggested that low birth rates were related to inadequate housing provision and the reluctance of women (over 80% of whom were in paid employment) to give up their jobs because of the difficulty of surviving on a single income – an even greater problem in much of Eastern Europe than in other parts of the continent. These factors seemed to outweigh the many benefits offered by the government to encourage larger families: grants of increasing value on the birth of children of successively higher birth order, child allowances up to the age of 16, housing bonuses for parents of two or more children, maternity leave and a guarantee against job loss because of such leave, free health care during pregnancy and extensive child care facilities. Legal abortion was again easily available and widely practised, as it was also in Yugoslavia, with little use of modern contraceptive practices.

By the 1980s most families in *Hungary*, too, felt it necessary for both parents to be in paid employment and it was also common for men to have a second job. This situation was important in the failure of many marriages with over half ending in divorce in recent years. Until 1956 modern contraceptives were largely unavailable and abortion was prohibited, but an estimated 150,000 illegal abortions occurred annually. Abortion increased after legalisation, to 207,000 in 1969 (134 per 100 live births) then declined to below 80,000 by 1980 as family planning clinics were established and modern contraceptives became widely available. Abortions increased by some 10% again in the 1980s although over 60% of married couples were estimated to be using modern contraceptives by 1989 – a very high figure for Eastern Europe. By then, the most widely used methods were the contraceptive pill (manufactured locally) and IUD but the use of condoms was still not being promoted despite the dangers of the spread of AIDS. Hungary's negative growth rate by the end of the decade (-0.2%) seemed to be related mainly to the difficult economic circumstances of many couples. This situation was evident in most of the region including *Czechoslovakia* where, despite the low birth rate (see Fig. 2.15) and economic problems, legal changes in 1987 encouraged the use of modern contraceptives by making these (with the exception of condoms) available free of charge. Abortion regulations were also changed to discourage abortion after eight weeks of pregnancy and in a situation where some 80% of women seeking legal abortions had never used reliable modern methods of contraception, these changes seemed likely to encourage a move away from abortion to more socially acceptable methods of birth restriction rather than markedly altering birth rates.

The situation in the *German Democratic Republic* had much in common with that in Hungary with very high levels of female employment and free family planning services despite serious government concern about a decline in population from 18.4 million in 1950 to 16.3 million by 1990. Encouragement to have children was provided through generous social welfare provisions including a year's paid maternity leave for mothers, child allowances and interest-free loans for parents up to the age of 30, through a lack of discrimination against unmarried parents and through price subsidies on baby equipment, children's clothing, etc. The contraceptive pill (again locally manufactured) was provided through family advice centres set up in the 1960s and was being used by over 40% of all women of child-bearing age in the 1980s – one of the highest levels of use in the world. Abortion laws passed in 1972 made abortion available on demand during the first 12 weeks of pregnancy and thereafter for certain medical and other reasons but a ratio of about 40 abortions to 100 live births in the late 1980s was the lowest in the region.

Poland is often portrayed as an exception to the general situation in Eastern Europe because of its largely Roman Catholic population. Despite official church opposition to the use of modern contraceptives, however, the birth rate in Poland is little different from that in the rest of the region. Government financial involvement in providing family planning services has, however, been relatively limited and recent, with the main family planning organisation being dependent chiefly on foreign financing until 1982. In the early 1990s, only about a quarter of married couples were estimated to be using modern contraceptive methods, there was strong opposition to abortion on moral grounds, and the reluctance of many pharmacists to sell contraceptives to young people was cited as a significant factor in the increasing problem of teenage pregnancies. The influence of the Church remains strong both amongst individuals and at government level, so changes in policies relating to family planning may be slower to occur in Poland than elsewhere in the region.

The dramatically changed political situation in the region from the late 1980s may in time bring about changes in attitudes to family planning, though the underlying economic difficulties that influenced the attitudes of both individuals and governments were initially exacerbated in some cases by the political changes. At the time of writing the lack of widely available means of modern contraception and consequent high levels of abortion seem likely to continue for a considerable period in several countries.

CASE STUDY 2C

Singapore: demographic change and population planning

The Republic of Singapore had, in 1990, a population of approximately 2.7 million living at a density of about 4,300 per square kilometre. The vast majority live in urban areas and this, together with the high levels of literacy and education in Singapore, has greatly helped in the spread of ideas and attitudes concerning population control. In particular, government attempts to reduce birth rates in Singapore have been dramatically successful – so much so that in recent years policies have begun to change because of fears that current low birth rates may restrict economic growth in the future.

The National Family Planning Programme was launched in 1966, soon after Singapore achieved full independence, as a central feature of the state's overall development strategy, with the Singapore Family Planning and Population Board (SFPPB) being responsible for 'initiating, implementing and co-ordinating all family planning and population activities in the Republic'. in 1966, Singapore had a population of 1.9 million and the rate of natural increase had already declined to 2.3% from 3.3% in 1950 (see Fig. 2.16). This rate was still considered too high by a government facing the possibility of mounting unemployment and perceiving a need for heavy investment in housing, social services and the economic sector. Population control was thus seen as essential for the new state if economic and social advances were not to be negated by population increases, and it has since remained a central aspect of development planning.

Prior to the formation of the SFPPB in 1965, family planning services had been mainly provided by the Singapore Family Planning Association, a voluntary agency that received some financial aid from the government. Between 1950 and 1965 the crude birth rate fell from 45.4 to 29.5 per thousand but a major aim of the first five-year national family planning programme (1966–70) was to reduce this to 20 per thousand. This marked the beginning of a period through to the early 1980s, in which the SFPPB consistently sought to reduce birth rates and so restrict population growth as part of a range of national policies aimed at raising living standards in Singapore. It was hoped that this would be achieved by providing easy access to professional advice and contraceptive supplies

Year	Population (millions)	CBR (per 1000)	CDR (per 1000)	Rate of natural increase (%)
1950	1.02	45.4	12.0	3.3
1960	1.65	37.5	6.2	3.1
1965	1.89	29.5	5.4	2.4
1966	1.93	28.3	5.4	2.3
1967	1.98	25.6	5.3	2.0
1968	2.01	23.5	5.5	1.8
1969	2.04	21.8	5.0	1.7
1970	2.07	22.1	5.2	1.7
1971	2.11	22.3	5.4	1.7
1972	2.15	23.1	5.4	1.8
1973	2.19	22.0	5.4	1.7
1974	2.23	19.4	5.2	1.4
1975	2.26	17.7	5.1	1.3
1976	2.29	18.7	5.1	1.4
1977	2.33	16.5	5.1	1.1
1978	2.35	16.8	5.1	1.2
1979	2.38	17.1	5.2	1.2
1980*	2.28	17.6	4.9	1.3
1981*	2.32	17.6	4.9	1.3
1982*	2.37	17.5	4.9	1.3
1983*	2.41	16.3	5.0	1.1
1984*	2.44	16.5	4.8	1.2
1985*	2.48	16.6	4.9	1.2
1986*	2.52	14.8	4.6	1.0
1987*	2.55	16.6	4.7	1.2
1988*	2.60	19.8	4.9	1.5
1989*	2.65	17.5	4.9	1.3

Refers to resident population

Fig. 2.16 Singapore: total population, crude birth rate, crude death rate and rate of natural increase, 1950–89.
Source: Ministry of Health, Singapore.

for all those wishing to practise family planning and by motivating people to seek such help through publicity. The crude birth rate fell to 21.8 per thousand in 1969 but thereafter began to increase slightly and by 1972 had risen to 23.1 per thousand (see Fig. 2.16). This was associated with the growing numbers of women in the fertile age groups, reflecting the high birth rates of the period following the Second World War. The response to this situation was an intensification of most aspects of the existing family planning programme and the introduction of some new features.

The family planning programme through the period into the mid-1980s was based on the following elements:

a *The establishment of easily accessible advisory and clinical services for family planning.*

At a maximum, more than 50 maternal and child health clinics and the National Family Planning Centre provided free advisory services, while a full range of contraceptives was available at nominal charges.

b *A massive publicity programme aimed at educating and motivating people with regard to family planning.* Information was disseminated via radio, television, newspapers, magazines, posters (Fig. 2.17), pamphlets, car stickers, etc. with considerable stress laid on the two-child family norm and the social and economic benefits likely to accrue from having such a small family. This publicity was reinforced through a motivational programme based on interviews with newly married couples and women attending ante-natal, postnatal and infant welfare sessions. From 1974

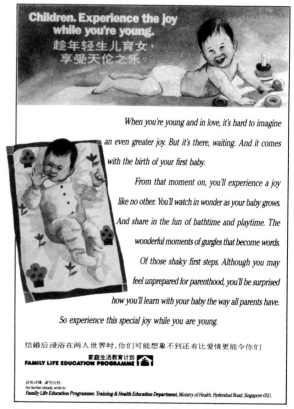

Fig. 2.17 Two family planning posters that indicate some of the changes in the family planning programmes of Singapore. The first emphasises clearly but humorously the desirable family size in the early stages of the family planning programme.

The second relates to the situation in the early 1990s and encourages parents to begin their family early – perhaps in the hope that such parents might eventually have a larger family than had become the norm by that date.

onwards a confidential telephone information service on family planning was also provided.

c *Legislation concerning abortion and sterilisation.* Acts legalising abortion and sterilisation were passed in 1969 and modified at later stages. The 1974 Abortion Act specified that operations must be carried out in government hospitals or other approved institutions, and made abortion available on socio-economic as well as medical grounds. Abortion has been widely practised since then, and in the late 1980s Dwyer (1987) suggested that over one-third of pregnancies were aborted. Sterilisation also became an important means of population control with the number of female sterilisations increasing from 2,071 in 1970 to 9,045 in 1975 but declining thereafter to about half that number by the mid-1980s. Male sterilisations have been much less common, never exceeding 500 per year in the same period. The nominal fees for abortion and sterilisation ensured there was no economic bar to such operations.

d *The introduction of social and economic disincentives to the practice of having large families.* These have included increased hospital delivery fees for children of higher birth order, paid maternity leave for mothers for their first two but not subsequent children, the absence of any income tax relief measure for the fourth and subsequent children and priority in the choice of primary school for the children of a parent who had undergone sterilisation when there were two or fewer children in the family and the parent was under 40 years old.

Figure 2.18, showing changes in age-specific fertility rates, indicates more effectively than can mere changes in birth rates the scale of the fertility decline in the period between 1966 and 1982. Between 1966 and 1976, for example, the number of women aged between 15 and 44 increased by more than 50% whereas the population of Singapore as a whole increased by less than 20%, thus providing the potential for a considerable increase in the crude birth rate if the number of children born to each woman had remained constant. That this did not happen is evident from Fig. 2.18. For the whole period for which data are provided, it is evident that age-specific fertility rates fell markedly though not uniformly. The most dramatic changes were in the older age groups with the age-specific fertility rate declining by 1982 to below one-quarter of what it had been in 1966 for those in the 35–39 age group and to below one-tenth for those in the 40–44 age group. This suggests effective birth control once a 'suitable' size of family had been achieved. With regard to what was considered a suitable size of family in this period, it is interesting to note that the total fertility rate between 1966 and 1982 declined from 4.5 to 1.7, suggesting that the government's 'Stop at Two' policy had been very successful.

It is difficult to assess to what extent the changes that took place in the pattern of births between 1966 and the early 1980s were a function of family planning policies rather than other factors. Certainly rapid economic growth and improvements in education in Singapore also played a part in encouraging changes in attitude to the practice of family planning. Perhaps, more than anything, the experience of Singapore emphasises that family planning policies are most likely to prove successful in a situation where a

Age group (yrs)	1966	1968	1970	1972	1974	1976	1978	1980*	1982*
15–19	33.0	30.9	25.9	25.3	20.8	16.2	11.8	12.4	11.2
20–24	218.5	165.8	139.0	137.4	118.9	107.2	86.8	82.9	78.6
25–29	261.2	236.6	208.8	218.0	172.2	160.2	140.9	141.1	133.6
30–34	202.0	152.0	138.0	139.2	102.9	95.9	86.8	85.7	82.8
35–39	124.8	85.2	74.5	66.1	42.6	33.8	26.7	27.4	30.4
40–44	51.7	35.3	26.7	20.9	12.7	8.1	5.3	5.7	4.8

* Refers to resident population

Fig. 2.18 Age-specific fertility rates, Singapore, 1966–82. All figures are expressed per thousand of the female population within the particular age group concerned.
Source: Singapore FPPB reports and Ministry of Health, Singapore.

range of socio-economic improvements are taking place at the same time. In 1983, however, government thinking began to take a new direction. The 1980 census indicated that better-educated women were having far fewer children than those who were less well educated. In 1980, Singaporean married women with no educational qualifications had, on average, given birth to 4.34 children each whereas the mean number of children born to married women with a degree or postgraduate diploma, was only 1.56. Additionally, 28% of women with a university education remained unmarried at the age of 30 compared with only 10% of women with no educational qualifications.

Government concern that the most highly educated section of the population was producing so few children led to various measures to encourage graduates and other educated women to have more children. These included enhanced child relief that could be claimed against income tax and preferential education arrangements for the third and subsequent children of graduate mothers. These measures were strongly opposed by other sections of the community and led to alternative policies such as computer dating and trying to persuade more women graduates to marry and have larger families without using financial or similar incentives likely to offend the rest of the population.

By about 1986, however, these concerns had begun to be superseded by a wider anxiety about the effect of falling birth rates throughout the whole population. Continued economic expansion is considered difficult without some increase in the labour force, currently totalling about 1.6 million. A rise of some 50% in two years in the number of foreign workers (to about 150,000 by late 1989) emphasised the problem, and efforts continue to attract skilled labour from abroad to help meet economic needs. A related concern is that if current fertility rates are maintained, the changing age structure and particularly the growing proportion of older people will increase the burden to be borne by a workforce of decreasing size. With the average size of completed families down to about 2 children and a net reproduction rate of below 0.9, some population projections suggested that Singapore's population would reach a maximum of about 3.3 million by the year 2030 unless birth rates began to increase again.

Government planners have suggested that Singapore could accommodate a population of about 4 millions, and have set a 'target' of 50,000 live births per annum 'but in spite of an active campaign to encourage a higher fertility rate, birth rates are failing to match the population replacement rate' (*Financial Times*, 30 April 1991). In 1989 there were 47,735 live births. Tax incentives to encourage couples to have more than two children have been introduced; those contemplating restricting the size of their family by abortion or other means are being encouraged to consider whether this is necessary; encouragement is being given to couples to marry and start a family earlier than was customary (see Fig. 2.17); and the family planning slogan is no longer 'Stop at Two' but 'Have three, or more if you can afford it'. The Population Planning Unit that has replaced the former SFPPB faces a very different challenge. Singapore's demographic transition has happened much more rapidly than that of most other countries, largely because of its successful family planning programmes in the first 20 years of independence. The challenge now is to change to a programme of controlled growth rather than drifting into decline.

3

Some aspects of population distribution

World patterns

The present uneven spatial distribution of population throughout the world represents just one stage of a continually changing pattern of adjustment by millions of individuals to the variety of physical and socio-economic factors that influence their lives. Although modern technology makes it possible for people to live on almost any part of the Earth's surface if they choose to do so, certain areas have tended to discourage settlement, partly because of the physical discomfort and difficulty of living there but also because they offer few opportunities for providing a livelihood. Such areas include zones of extreme aridity, the highest mountain areas, and zones with very low temperatures. However, although these zones are usually very sparsely populated, some limited areas of more dense settlement may occur within them as, for example, in the oil-producing regions of the Sahara and the urban centres of northern Russia. Other parts of the world, such as the agriculturally productive alluvial lowlands of southern Asia, offer particular physical attractions for human settlement and therefore may be more densely populated than adjacent areas. It would be misleading, however, to suggest that patterns of population distribution are determined by physical factors alone, for within the broad framework of physical attractions and constraints the detailed pattern of population distribution is strongly influenced by socio-economic factors.

These socio-economic factors are of many different kinds. Levels of economic development and technology, for example, affect the number of people that can be supported in a particular area. The industrialised and commercialised society of the United Kingdom can support far more people than could a society based on shifting cultivation for subsistence purposes in the same area, and the irrigation farming of the Nile Valley supports more people than was possible in that area before irrigation was introduced. Perhaps less obviously, such factors as political organisation, religious beliefs, levels of education and social attitudes can influence, directly or indirectly, birth and death rates, population mobility, and types and patterns of settlement, which all contribute to the pattern of population distribution in a particular area.

Population distribution at a continental scale is marked by some striking contrasts, as is evident from Fig. 3.1. Almost three-fifths of the world's people live in Asia (excluding the former USSR) on just over one-fifth of the world's land area, with more than four times as many people living in Asia as in any other continent. Africa now ranks second in terms of total population, having 'overtaken' Europe (excluding the former USSR) in the early 1980s. Since it also has the highest rate of natural increase for any major continental unit, Africa seems likely to increase its proportion of the total world population substantially in the period through to the year 2020, but on current estimates Asia will still have more than three times as many people as Africa by that date. Asia and Europe have much higher densities of population than any other continent at present and seem likely to remain by far the most densely populated continents for many years to come, although Europe will gradually fall further behind Asia in this respect because of its lower rate of natural increase. Such variations in rates of increase clearly emphasise the dynamic nature of patterns of population distribution and it is important to remember that migration as well as natural increase has played an important part in distrib-

	Population estimate mid-1990 (millions)	Total population as % of world total 1990	Area as % of world area	Population density/ km² 1990	Annual rate of natural increase	Population projection to 2020	Total population as % of world total 2020	Est. population density/km² 2020
World	5,321	–	–	39.2	1.8	8,228	–	60.6
Africa	661	12.4	22.4	21.7	2.9	1,481	17.9	48.7
North America	278	5.2	15.8	12.9	0.7	328	4.0	15.2
Latin America	447	8.4	15.1	21.7	2.1	705	8.6	34.3
Asia (excl. former USSR)	3,116	58.5	20.3	113.0	1.9	4,805	58.4	174.2
Europe (excl. former USSR)	501	9.4	3.6	101.4	0.3	516	6.3	104.5
Oceania	27	0.5	6.3	3.1	1.2	38	0.5	4.5
Former USSR	291	5.5	16.5	13.0	0.9	355	4.3	15.8

Fig. 3.1 World population data (by region).
Sources: 1990 World Population Data Sheet,
Population Reference Bureau, Inc., and *UN Demographic Yearbook, 1988.*

utional changes in the past. Despite a recent tendency for there to be greater restrictions on large-scale movements across international boundaries, it may still prove a significant factor in the future, for such restrictions are usually dictated to a large extent by the social attitudes and economic needs of recipient nations and these can change through time. This has been clearly evidenced by the changing attitudes of several European nations to receiving migrants from such areas as North Africa, the Middle East and the West Indies as well as from other parts of Europe in the period since the Second World War.

There are, of course, also very significant variations in distribution within particular continents. Fielding (1974) has suggested that three major generalisations can be made.

1 The highest densities are in areas of favourable physical environment, irrigation being an important 'cultural' improvement of some areas that have seasonal or unreliable rainfall but are otherwise physically attractive.
2 People are attracted to live in areas of low elevation, with more than half the world's population occupying areas below 200 metres above sea level.

3 Population clusters along the borders of continents and countries, leaving interiors empty by comparison. Approximately two-thirds of the world's people live within about 500 kilometres of the coast.

These generalisations are clearly exemplified in Asia, where there is a particular concentration in the marginal lowland areas of India, Southeast Asia, China and Japan, in marked contrast to the sparsely populated upland interior of the continent. The other major concentrations of dense population on a world scale are associated with the industrialised societies of Europe and North America, which have developed high levels of urbanisation during recent centuries.

There is also a striking concentration of the world's people into a relatively small number of countries. Figure 3.2 shows the 'top 20' countries in terms of their total populations in 1990. Very dominant even in this group are China and India which contained between them well over a third of the 1990 world population total. Perhaps almost as striking is the fact that although there were over 170 recognised nation-states in 1990, only about a quarter of the world's people lived outside the 20 states named in Fig. 3.2.

Variations in rates of population growth between different countries inevitably lead to changes in the rank order of countries in any such table as time passes. If the population

	Population estimate mid-1990 (millions)	Rank order total population 1990	Total population as % of world total 1990	Rate of natural increase 1990	Population projection to 2020 (millions)	Rank order projected population 2020	Total population as % world total 2020
China	1,119.9	1	21.0	1.4	1496.3	1	18.2
India	853.4	2	16.0	2.1	1374.5	2	16.7
Former USSR	291.0	3	5.5	0.9	355.0	3	4.3
USA	251.4	4	4.7	0.8	294.4	4	3.6
Indonesia	189.4	5	3.6	1.8	287.3	5	3.5
Brazil	150.4	6	2.8	1.9	233.8	8	2.8
Japan	123.6	7	2.3	0.4	124.2	12	1.5
Nigeria*	118.8	8	2.2	2.9	273.2	6	3.3
Bangladesh	114.8	9	2.2	2.5	201.4	9	2.4
Pakistan	114.6	10	2.2	3.0	251.3	7	3.1
Mexico	88.6	11	1.7	2.4	142.1	10	1.7
Germany**	79.5	12	1.5	0.0	77.3	17	0.9
Vietnam	70.2	13	1.3	2.5	119.5	13	1.5
Philippines	66.1	14	1.2	2.6	117.5	14	1.4
Italy	57.7	15	1.1	0.1	56.1	20	0.7
UK	57.4	16	1.1	0.2	60.8	18	0.7
Turkey	56.7	17	1.1	2.1	93.8	15	1.1
France	56.4	18	1.1	0.4	58.7	19	0.7
Thailand	55.7	19	1.0	1.5	78.1	16	0.9
Iran	55.6	20	1.0	3.6	130.2	11	1.6

Data for Nigeria as given in this table seems likely to be inaccurate on the basis of the 1991 census data (see chapter 1).
Data for Germany based on combining that for the former Federal Republic of Germany and German Democratic Republic.
Note comments in text about ranking of most populous countries by the year 2020.

Fig. 3.2 Population data for selected countries.
Source: 1990 World Population Data Sheet,
Population Reference Bureau, Inc.

projections for the year 2020 listed in Fig. 3.2 are reasonably accurate, the five countries with the highest population totals in 1990 seem likely to retain their relative positions in 2020, though the political break-up of the USSR into several states in the period since the table was compiled obviously complicates the picture. Indonesia's population total seems likely to exceed that of the USA soon after 2020. Several countries in the list seem likely to show a considerable fall in rank, notably Japan, Germany and Italy as their populations stabilise or even begin to decline. Others, such as Pakistan, Thailand and, easily the most striking, Iran are likely to show a marked rise in rank. You are asked to consider these and other changes in Exercise 3.1. What is not apparent from Fig. 3.2 is that if all the world's countries are considered and not just the 20 most populous countries of 1990, the same series of projections suggests that three of the four European countries in the table will have been 'relegated' from the 'top 20' altogether by 2020. By that date Zaire (with a projected population increase from 36.6 million in 1990 to 90.0 million in 2020), South Africa (39.6 to 83.5 million) and Tanzania (26.0 to 68.8 million) are projected to replace the UK, France and Italy in the list of the 20 most populous countries. Clearly, several of the points highlighted in this section of the chapter reflect assumptions that relatively high population growth rates will continue in many devel-

Exercise 3.1

World population distribution

a) Discuss the main features of the changing pattern of world population distribution indicated in Figs. 3.1 and 3.2, suggesting reasons for the features you describe.

b) Explain why care must be exercised in drawing conclusions from data provided in tables of this kind.

c) Discuss briefly some of the major economic and political implications of the changes in world population distribution indicated in Figs. 3.1 and 3.2.

oping countries for some time to come while the population of many industrialised nations will stagnate or even decline. Some of the problems that may be associated with assumptions of this kind are considered in the next section.

Population projections

We have already suggested how difficult it can be to obtain accurate data about population. Obviously any attempts to calculate the likely population of particular countries for the year 2020 as has been done in the last section or, indeed, for any date in the foreseeable future, are even more open to question. Even the estimates of population totals in the normal 10-year intervals between population censuses in economically advanced countries tend to be quite inaccurate at times. Inter-censal estimates of this kind are produced by amending the census totals to take account of changes resulting from natural increase or decrease plus changes occasioned by migration. Past experience in countries with relatively sophisticated methods of recording population change has shown that, however carefully records are kept, population estimates tend to become less reliable with each year that passes after a census. In countries where methods of recording appropriate data are much less effective, the problem of making accurate estimates is clearly much greater.

Many countries still lack efficient means of registering births and deaths, while information relating to migration is often unreliable or incomplete even in developed countries. Thus, even short-term estimates of population change may be inaccurate.

Long-term forecasts are obviously much less likely to be accurate. Estimates of population change over long periods of time are usually known as population projections and, although a detailed explanation of the methods used in making such projections is not appropriate here, it is useful to be aware of the bases on which they have been calculated. Most projections are now based on refinements of the component method devised in the late nineteenth century. This involves subdividing a population into a series of groups of males or females each within a relatively narrow age range (often either one or five years) and assessing likely changes in each of the groups (or cohorts) on the basis of certain assumptions concerning fertility, mortality and migration over a period of time. It is not usually considered satisfactory to use this method in stages of more than five years at a time. A projection of, say, 25 years would involve carrying out a series of calculations, each reflecting likely changes during periods of five years or less to particular cohorts.

The assumptions made concerning particular variables are clearly of fundamental importance, yet many possibilities exist and it is not surprising that population projections have become notorious for their inaccuracy. Recent changes in birth rates in the UK have led to drastic revisions of projections made in the mid-1960s. Some forecasts at that time anticipated a total UK population of 80 million by the year 2000. Later forecasts for that date have been much lower (see Fig. 3.3), reflecting the marked decline in birth rates that occurred in the period after the contraceptive pill was introduced in the 1960s (see Case Study 2A). In terms of national planning, inaccurate projections can cause major problems. This has been clearly apparent in the attempts to relate the number of trained teachers to the number of children in schools in the UK during the last 30 years or so.

(a)

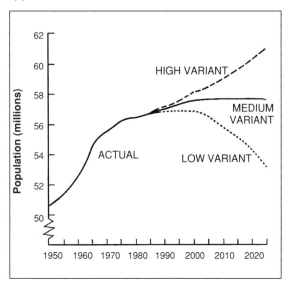

(b)

	Low variant	Medium variant	High variant
1985 (base population)			
0–14	10,927		
15–64	37,141		
65 and over	8,549		
All ages	56,618		
2000			
0–14	10,463	11,099	11,685
15–64	37,529	37,533	37,554
65 and over	8,870	8,856	8,894
All ages	56,862	57,509	58,133
2025			
0–14	7,411	9,941	11,868
15–64	34,336	35,972	37,430
65 and over	11,570	11,550	11,564
All ages	53,317	57,464	60,862

Fig. 3.3
(a) Variant population projections for the UK, 1985–2025.
(b) Variant population structure projections for the UK, 2000 and 2025.
Source: based on data from *World Population Prospects 1988*, United Nations 1989.

All data in thousands

Problems of both teacher unemployment and teacher shortages at different times have resulted, at least in part, from changes in birth rates not having been accurately anticipated by planners. Similar problems can also occur in, for example, the fields of housing provision and health services.

Because of the many problems inherent in population projections it is now usual for demographers to calculate a series of projections based on different assumptions rather than producing only a single projection. This series of projections, called variants, is not usually averaged out but is seen as indicating a range of possibilities. Recent population projections for Great Britain provide a good illustration of this approach. Projections of the population of Great Britain and of its constituent countries by sex and age were first produced in the 1920s. Since 1955, new projections for the United Kingdom have been made every year, using the component method. Until the mid-1970s these were based on a single set of

assumptions concerning the three components of population change: births, deaths and net migration. The strategy of drawing up a single projection was favoured up to that time on the grounds that it provided a common framework or a consistent starting point for all population-related planning. Despite warnings, however, false implications were read into the single projection, most notably that the future population could be determined with a high degree of accuracy.

Because of this problem there was pressure to publish a range of projections based on different assumptions concerning fertility, mortality and migration both from within the UK and from organisations like the United Nations, which requested countries to undertake 1970-based projections incorporating fertility at 'high' and 'low' as well as 'medium' levels as a contribution to new world projections. It was thought that the publication of variant projections would help users in two ways:

1 by giving some idea of the magnitude of the uncertainty in the population projection and hence enabling users to test the sensitivity of their plans to possible future population variations; and

2 by enabling users to assess the costs and implications if the birth trend, population growth, etc. were either above or below the central projection.

The use of variant population projections is now common, and recent variant projections for the UK are summarised in Fig. 3.3. The high and low variants have been relatively narrowly spaced in order to give a useful measure of the uncertainty to be attached to the medium projection. Very broadly spaced variants would, while covering more future possibilities, be of little value for educational planners, for users concerned with manpower issues and for those concerned with the provision of services for old people, all of whom need to devise a limited number of alternative plans.

The projections show that it is the fertility component that is surrounded by most uncertainty. The projected population aged 0–14 in the year 2000 varies by more than a million and by 2025 by almost 4.5 million. Further uncertainty is caused by the fact that by the latter date the various projected child populations of 2000 will have entered the adult group. Thus by 2025, according to these projections, the population of the UK may be as low as 53.3 million (more than 3 million below the base population of 1985) or may exceed 60.8 million. It is not just overall totals that are significant, however, and you are asked to consider also some aspects of age structure forecasts in Exercise 3.2.

Mapping population distribution and density

So far we have confined discussion of population distribution and density to a consideration of differences on a world scale and have made no attempt to map these, largely because maps on such a scale are so generalised as to be almost meaningless. The cartographic representation of

Exercise 3.2

United Kingdom: population projections

Summarise the information provided in Figs. 3.3a and 3.3b concerning the possible future population size and structure of the UK and briefly suggest some of the socio-economic implications for the UK should either the high or the low variant projection prove to be correct.

population data presents particular problems even when dealing with considerably smaller areas, largely because of the near impossibility of precisely locating populations on a map, even when detailed information is available from censuses or similar sources.

The most common type of population distribution map in which an attempt is made to pinpoint the location of population as precisely as possible is the dot map, though these are perhaps less frequently used than they once were. Figure 3.4 is a fairly typical example of such a map and can be used to illustrate the main problems involved in constructing dot distribution maps; that is, how many people should be represented by a single dot, where each dot should be placed, and what should be the physical size of the dots themselves. Clearly the map involves some compromise. The dot size has been kept small to allow for as much flexibility as possible – a larger dot size would have meant that dots would be more likely to overlap, which is clearly undesirable, or that their value would have had to be increased. Despite this, with a value of 10,000 people per dot, the location of particular dots must have been difficult, for at the date to which the map relates East Africa had very few agglomerations of 10,000 people. In the whole of mainland Tanzania, for example, there were only 14. Thus the location of dots is inevitably symbolic to some extent. Even if dots with a value of only 100 people had been used it would have been difficult to locate them accurately in some of the sparsely populated zones of northern Kenya, where the few perma-

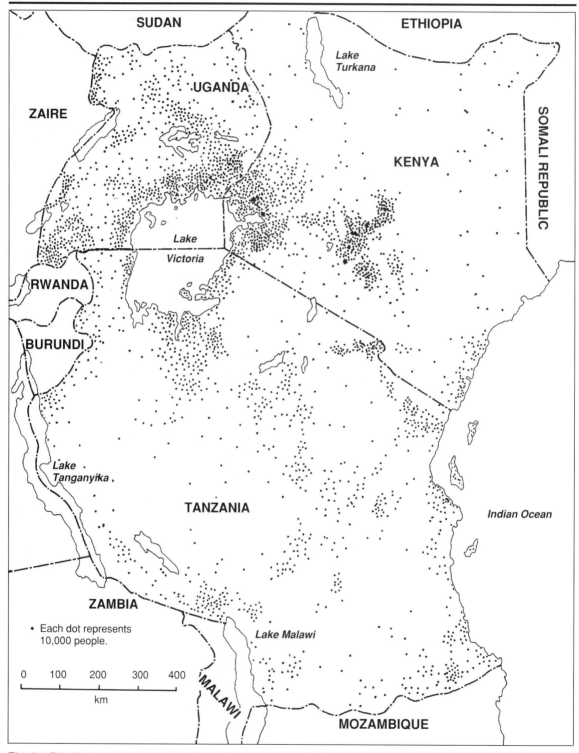

Fig. 3.4 Distribution of population in East Africa excluding the four largest towns.
Source: after Morgan, 1973, based on data published in national censuses, 1967–69.

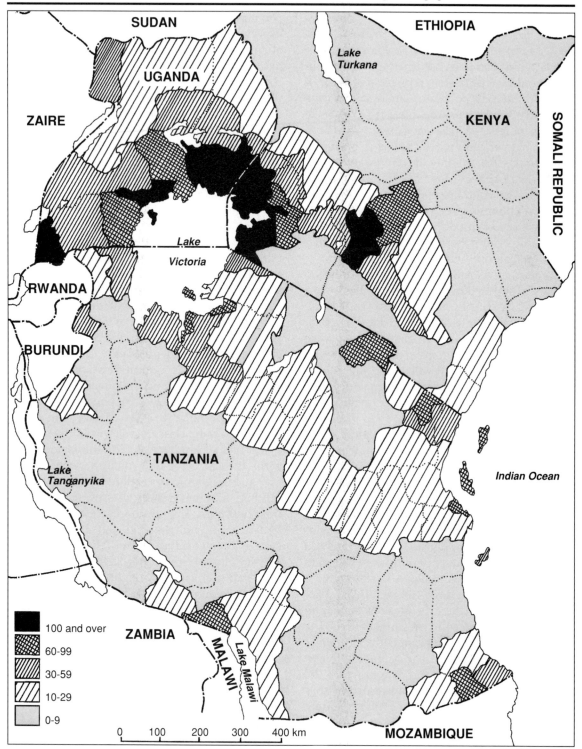

Fig. 3.5 Density of population per square kilometre in East Africa.
Source: after Morgan, 1973, based on data published in national censuses, 1967–69.

nent settlements are small and some groups are semi-nomadic and so have no permanent 'location'. Moreover, if dots of a lower value than 10,000 people had been used, cartographic problems would have arisen in representing some of the more densely populated areas such as the Kenya Highlands and the areas fringing Lake Victoria unless the basic map scale had been increased. Even with the dot values used, it was found impossible to show the four largest settlements (Nairobi and Mombasa in Kenya, Kampala in Uganda and Dar es Salaam in Tanzania). This is a common problem and cartographers often use such symbols as proportional circles, squares or even spheres to show larger settlements on maps of this kind.

An alternative to the population distribution map is a population density map. Figure 3.5 provides an example of this kind of map for the same area as is depicted in Fig. 3.4 and uses the same sources of population data. Though some population density maps relate population totals to the area of cultivated land, the inhabited area or similar measures, the majority (like Fig. 3.5) simply indicate the relationship between population and land area. The map suffers from the fundamental weakness of all density maps in that population totals have been related to units of area within which there was not a uniform distribution of population. The densities mapped thus represent averages for the particular units of area. Even where, as in Fig. 3.5, these units are relatively small, considerable variations in density are represented within each areal unit. For example, in Kigezi in south-west Uganda (A in Fig. 3.5), although the average density was over 100 per square kilometre, some quite extensive areas of forest and game reserve were almost uninhabited. The Bwindi forest area of approximately 300 square kilometres, for example, had a population of only about 100 people at the date to which the map relates, although some adjacent parishes had population densities of over 600 per square kilometre (Kagambirwe, 1972).

The smaller the units of area used, the more likely it is that density maps will give an accurate representation of reality but there are often problems in obtaining data for small areal units, especially in developing countries. Additionally, whatever size the units are, it is difficult to avoid the artificial visual impression created by the boundaries of the units. In Fig. 3.5, although there are quite marked changes in density between, for example, the Kenya Highlands and the areas to the south of these, largely as a result of distinct changes in physical character, the 'break line' between different areas is not quite as clearcut as the map implies. In cases where suitable data are available, some cartographers have mapped densities on the basis of grid squares of a particular size but, though this sometimes gives a better impression than using administrative areas as the basic units, it introduces a different kind of artificiality, for densities obviously do not alter in a formal pattern of squares. One other aspect of density maps is perhaps worth mentioning at this stage and that is the crucial importance of the class boundaries chosen. For example, it is easy to assume that any of the areas in central Tanzania shown in Fig. 3.5 as being within the density class 10–29 people per square kilometre had a density that was more similar to that of any other area within the same class than it was to the density of any area in another class. But this is not necessarily the case. Two units of area with densities of 9 and 11 people per square kilometre would fall into different density classes, even though their densities are much more similar than those of two units with, say, 11 and 28 people per square kilometre that would fall into the same density class. With this problem in mind, it is clear that very careful thought needs to be given to the division of density values into suitable classes if these are not to be misleading. This and the other problems involved in producing dot and density maps will have to be confronted in attempting Exercise 3.3.

Despite their shortcomings, both dot and density maps can provide a useful indication of spatial variations in the pattern of population distribution to anyone who is aware of the limitations of such maps. A useful graphic method of showing variations in population in a very different way is through the construction of

Exercise 3.3

Dot distribution and density maps of population

Select a predominantly rural area in the United Kingdom that contains approximately 4 to 6 parishes for which you have available a 1:25,000 Ordnance Survey map sheet. From the most recent census returns available for these parishes (obtainable from most large libraries), record the total population and area of the selected parishes. Then:

a) using the appropriate census data and information provided on the OS map sheet, construct dot distribution and density maps of the population of your selected area;

b) comment on the difficulties involved in the construction of the maps; and

c) discuss the relative advantages and disadvantages of the two types of map, paying particular attention to ways in which the maps might be misleading to anyone using them.

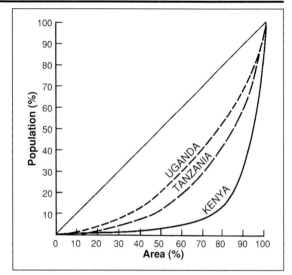

Fig 3.6 Lorenz curves for East African countries. *Source:* after Morgan, 1973, based on data published in national censuses, 1967–69.

Lorenz curves (see Fig. 3.6). This technique, originally devised to indicate concentrations of income or wealth, can be used when information about an area is available for equivalent areal units (e.g. for parishes or countries), and so can frequently be employed in dealing with population data. Units of area are ranked in order of density of population and then populations and areas of these units are totalled for each density class. Cumulative percentages of area can then be plotted against cumulative percentages of population on a graph and the points joined together to form a 'curve'. If all the units of area had similar densities this curve would follow the diagonal, indicating an even distribution of population throughout the total area concerned. Normally, of course, there is considerable deviation from this and the more 'bowed' the Lorenz curve, the greater is the unevenness of distribution of population.

Thus in Fig. 3.6 Uganda is shown to have the most evenly distributed population of the three East African countries, though even in Uganda 30% of the population occupied almost 60% of the total area, this being largely a reflection of the low densities in the more arid parts of the country. In Kenya, distribution was markedly more uneven, with the densely populated areas of the Kenya Highlands and Lake Victoria Lowlands accounting for the bulk of the nation's population and 80% of the total area containing well under 20% of the total population. As in Uganda, the most sparsely populated areas were mainly in the areas of low rainfall, in this case in the north and north-east of the country.

Urbanisation

The most striking examples of population concentration occur in urban areas. By 1990 approximately one in every four Mexicans – some 18 million people – lived in the 3,250 square kilometres of the dried-up lake beds 2,200 metres above sea level occupied by the urban built-up area of Mexico City. With an overall density of about 5,500 people per square kilometre, Mexico City is obviously a very crowded part of the world's surface but many other cities have much higher population densities. Some, as diverse in character as Paris, Manila, Cairo and Calcutta, have overall densities in excess of 20,000 per square kilometre. Like several other Indian cities, Calcutta has a particularly high population density (over 88,000 per square kilometre in the late 1980s). Localised densities exceeding 1,000 per hectare are not uncommon in cities of the developing world. Some areas of Bombay have densities in excess of 3,000 per

hectare while Jakarta's urban *kampungs* and the old walled sections of Muslim cities such as Ibadan in Nigeria and Fez in Morocco provide examples of areas with densities of over 2,000 per hectare. For many years densities in excess of 2,500 per hectare existed in parts of the old 'shophouse' core of Singapore (see Fig. 3.7) before the redevelopment programmes began in the 1960s, and similar densities were recorded in New York's lower East side in 1900. Today, densities approaching 1,000 per hectare are relatively rare in more developed countries as a result of urban renewal programmes, improved living standards and communication systems that allow people to live at a considerable distance from their place of work.

Although cities were already in existence more than 5,000 years ago, it is only in the relatively recent past that urban dwellers have comprised a substantial proportion of the total world population. As recently as 1800, probably only 3% of the world's people lived in settlements with a population of more than 5,000. By 1900 this proportion had increased four- or five-fold and by 1950 approximately 30% of the world's people lived in cities. Most estimates

Fig. 3.7 A typical street in central Singapore in the 1970s, shortly before redevelopment. Built in the mid-nineteenth century and consisting mainly of three-storey shophouses, streets like this housed very large numbers of people. Part of the ground floor of each building was occupied by a shop or small industrial concern but the remainder of the shophouse was divided into numerous small cubicles in which as many as 8 or 10 people might occupy an area only 3 metres square. Much of the area has now been replaced by high-rise flats.

suggest that urban dwellers will form the majority of the world's population from soon after the year 2000. In terms of actual totals, the 80 million or so urban dwellers of 1800 had increased to about 30 times that number by the early 1990s.

Comparison of the level of urbanisation (i.e. the proportion of the population living in urban areas, usually expressed as a percentage) between different countries is difficult because the definition of 'urban area' varies greatly and has also changed through time. In some cases urban areas are defined solely in terms of numbers, as in Ghana, where they are described as 'localities of 5,000 or more inhabitants', or in Venezuela and Malaysia where centres of 2,500 and 10,000 people respectively are regarded as urban areas. In Peru, urban areas are described as 'populated centres with 100 or more dwellings' and in several countries they are defined in administrative terms. Thus in Tanzania the urban population comprises the residents of 16 'gazetted townships' and in Ecuador urban areas are defined as 'capitals of provinces or cantons'. Some definitions are far more complex, however, taking into account a range of different factors. An interesting example of this type is provided by India where urban areas are defined as follows:

> 'towns (places with municipal corporation, municipal area committee, town committee, notified area committee or cantonment board); also all places having 5000 or more inhabitants, a density of not less than 1000 persons per square mile or 390 per square kilometre, pronounced urban characteristics and at least three-fourths of the adult male population employed in pursuits other than agriculture.'

Despite the difficulty of making accurate comparisons between countries with different definitions of urban areas, it has often been suggested that there are quite marked contrasts between developed and developing countries. In the former, urbanisation levels in excess of 70% are common although there is by no means a uniform pattern. In north-west Europe, for example, urbanisation levels in 1990 ranged from 95% in Belgium to only 56% in Ireland. In Africa and Asia, by contrast, urbanisation levels averaged about 30% but urbanisation levels in Latin America have increased considerably in the last half century and are now in many cases similar to those of Europe and North America. It has also been suggested that the more urbanised a country is, the higher is its wealth as measured by Gross National Product (GNP) per capita. Figure 3.8 illustrates the statistical relationship between GNP and levels of urbanisation in many countries, and Exercise 3.4 further investigates this idea.

Urbanisation in developed countries has been closely associated with industrial expansion, agricultural change and the development of modern transport networks. The evolution of the factory system encouraged the growth of larger settlements than had the earlier domestic industries, while improvements in agriculture and the development of new forms of transport enabled the concentrations of population in urban areas to be provided with the food, raw materials and other items they needed. These economic changes occurred first in Western Europe and were accompanied by the transfer of workers from agricultural to industrial and service occupations, which resulted in a transfer of people from rural to urban areas. Similar changes took place in North America (where the number of people employed in agriculture in the United States declined from over 70% of the total employed population in 1820 to below 40% by 1900 and has since fallen below 5%) and in other now economically advanced countries such as Australia (see Case Study 3A) and Japan. The extreme of urban development in such areas is to be seen in the great metropolitan centres such as London, Tokyo and New York, all of which have populations in excess of 10 millions and serve as centres of employment for extensive surrounding areas. The changing nature of employment is obviously a major factor influencing patterns of population distribution within individual countries, though various other factors may also be of significance, as Case Study 3B illustrates.

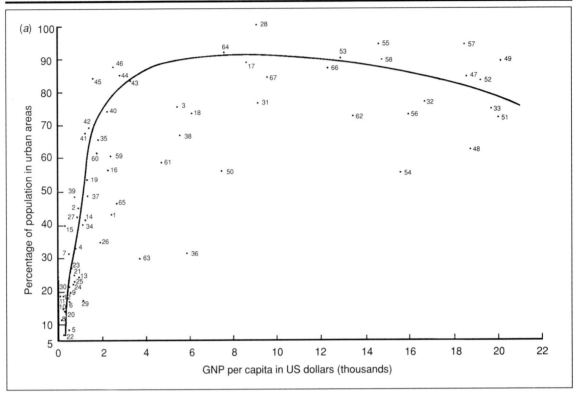

Fig. 3.8 The relationship between Gross National Product (GNP) per capita and the percentage of total population living in urban areas, about 1990: (a) a scattergraph to illustrate this relationship, and (b) the data from which the scattergraph was compiled.

Source: 1990 World Population Data Sheet, Population Reference Bureau, Inc.

Exercise 3.4

Spearman rank correlation between GNP and degree of urbanisation

a) Select at random 20 countries from those for which information is provided in Fig. 3.8b and use the Spearman rank correlation coefficient technique to obtain a measure of the degree of correlation between GNP per capita and the percentage of the population living in urban areas. The coefficient is derived from the formula:

$$R = 1 - \frac{6\Sigma d^2}{n^3 - n}$$

where R is the Spearman rank correlation coefficient, Σd^2 is the sum of the squares of the difference in rank of the variables, and *n* is the number of samples taken.

b) In the light of your calculation in part (a) and the evidence shown on the scattergraph (Fig. 3.6a), comment on the relationship between GNP per capita and the percentage of the population living in urban areas.

c) Discuss the nature and significance of increasing urbanisation in developing countries.

(b)

	Urban population (%)	GNP (US $ per capita)		Urban population (%)	GNP (US $ per capita)
1 Algeria	43	2,450	35 Mexico	66	1,820
2 Egypt	45	650	36 Cuba	32	5,990
3 Libya	76	5,410	37 Jamaica	49	1,080
4 Ghana	32	400	38 Puerto Rico	67	5,540
5 Burkina Faso	8	230	39 Bolivia	49	570
6 Mali	18	230	40 Brazil	74	2,280
7 Nigeria	31	290	41 Colombia	68	1,240
8 Ethiopia	11	120	42 Peru	69	1,440
9 Kenya	20	360	43 Venezuela	83	3,170
10 Malawi	14	160	44 Argentina	85	2,640
11 Mozambique	19	100	45 Chile	84	1,510
12 Tanzania	19	160	46 Uruguay	87	2,470
13 Zimbabwe	25	660	47 Denmark	84	18,470
14 Cameroon	42	1,010	48 Finland	62	18,610
15 Zaire	40	170	49 Iceland	89	20,160
16 Rep. of South Africa	56	2,290	50 Ireland	56	7,480
17 Israel	89	8,650	51 Norway	71	20,020
18 Saudi Arabia	73	6,170	52 Sweden	83	19,150
19 Turkey	53	1,280	53 United Kingdom	90	12,800
20 Bangladesh	13	170	54 Austria	55	15,560
21 India	26	430	55 Belgium	95	14,550
22 Nepal	7	170	56 France	73	16,080
23 Pakistan	28	350	57 German Federal		
24 Sri Lanka	22	420	Republic	94	18,530
25 Indonesia	26	430	58 Netherlands	89	14,530
26 Malaysia	35	1,870	59 Hungary	60	2,460
27 Philippines	42	630	60 Poland	61	1,850
28 Singapore	100	9,100	61 Greece	58	4,790
29 Thailand	18	1,000	62 Italy	72	13,320
30 China	21	330	63 Portugal	30	3,670
31 Japan	77	9,230	64 Spain	91	7,740
32 Canada	77	16,760	65 Yugoslavia	46	2,680
33 United States	74	19,780	66 Australia	86	12,390
34 Guatemala	40	880	67 New Zealand	84	9,620

Although urban population increases in the period between 1750 and 1950 occurred mainly in what are now economically advanced countries, such increases have more recently been of growing importance in developing countries. Some countries within this group, notably in Latin America, already have urbanisation levels similar to those of many European countries, as has been previously mentioned (see Fig. 3.8). The urban population of developing countries more than doubled in total between 1960 and 1980 with a rate of increase more than twice that of developed countries and current evidence suggests that the urban population of developing countries will double again between 1980 and 2000 while that of developed countries will probably increase by less than 20% during the same period. Moreover, with urbanisation levels still being relatively low in Africa and Asia, there would seem to be considerable scope for further growth. Thus as rates of urban growth in the more economically advanced areas decline, it seems certain that for the foreseeable future urban population increases will be concentrated very largely in developing countries.

It would be wrong to assume that the developing countries are merely following a pattern set at an earlier stage by the present industrialised countries. Between 1950 and 1990 the *average* urban population increase in southern Asia, Africa and Latin America was approximately 4% per annum and many individual cities are today increasing at rates in excess of 6% per annum. By contrast, most European countries during their period of most rapid urbanisation registered increases in urban population of little more than 2% per annum, though rates of growth in some North American and Australian cities, boosted by immigration from Europe, were closer to those of cities in developing countries at the present time. Figure 3.9 illustrates the different patterns of growth in what Haggett (1975) called 'Western' and 'non-Western' countries, typically representing the experiences of European and developing countries respectively. The former group has typi-

cally had a period of slow growth followed by a sharp increase in growth rate in the second half of the nineteenth century and a gradual levelling out thereafter. The typical curve for a developing country shows a later but much more rapid period of growth with little sign of any significant slowing-down overall, though rates of growth inevitably vary somewhat between different areas and between cities in particular areas.

The different rates of growth reflect other economic, social and demographic differences. The growth of cities in nineteenth-century Europe was very heavily dependent on migration from the countryside into the cities, as natural increase within the cities was limited by the high mortality rates that prevailed when sanitation was often poor, water supplies frequently polluted, malnutrition common and medical provision limited. In 1861, for example, Liverpool still had a crude death rate of 29.0 per thousand and a natural increase rate of only 0.5%. Substantial decreases in urban death rates in many cases did not long precede the falling birth rates that have been a feature of most European cities in the twentieth century.

By contrast, rates of natural increase in cities in developing countries in the second half of the twentieth century have often been high, with health standards and medical provision generally better than in surrounding rural areas. Death rates in many cases fell by as much in the period between 1950 and 1975 in cities in developing countries as during a period three times as long in the nineteenth and early twentieth centuries in European cities. There is some evidence of growing malnutrition and disease in the 1980s in a number of cities in developing countries, related at least in part to world economic problems and resultant employment difficulties and reductions in spending on urban services such as water and sewerage. Though devastating for particular groups, often those inhabiting the slums and squatter areas, this did not appear to have had a major effect on general trends in death rates by the early 1990s. Meanwhile, birth rates have tended to remain at a high level in the period since 1950, often

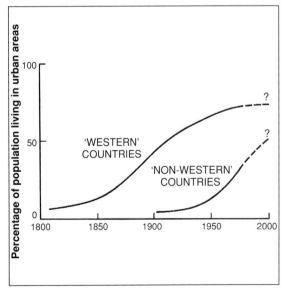

Fig. 3.9 Idealised urbanisation curves for 'Western' and 'non-Western' countries.
Source: after Haggett, 1975.

approaching and sometimes exceeding 30 per thousand per annum. The limited amount of research into desired family size in the urban areas of developing countries suggests that while in some cases five or six children still represent a desirable aim for parents, especially amongst the poorer and less well-educated groups, social attitudes to family size are beginning to change and in some cases have already done so. For example, in a number of Indonesian cities in 1990, one of the present authors found widespread acceptance of government policies favouring two-child families by young couples from very different social and economic backgrounds. It is still too early to be sure whether the pattern of decreasing family size in urban areas that occurred in developed countries will be followed in developing countries and, if it is, how long the process will take. Many cities still show a pattern of high birth rates and low death rates, sometimes described as a combination of pre-industrial fertility and post-industrial mortality, with natural increase rates exceeding 2% in many cases and reaching 3% in some.

To this rapid rate of natural increase is added the massive influx of migrants from rural areas. The migrants, despite the relatively limited industrial development in many cities, perceive the possibility of greater opportunities being available in the urban areas than exist in the often poverty-stricken rural areas where rapid rates of natural increase have exacerbated existing problems. The proportion of the urban population increase resulting from natural increase compared with that resulting from migration has varied. In the earlier stages of rapid urban growth, in-migration has normally been responsible for the majority of population increase. Thus, for example, between 1950 and 1970 about 70% of population increase in São Paulo is thought to have been attributable to migration, and of the 828,000 people living in Nairobi at the time of the 1979 census only 26% had been born in the city. Most of the latter were young children, with 95% of Nairobi's population aged 15 or over having been born elsewhere. This situation has been gradually changing as early

migrants have become permanent urban residents and, as already mentioned, have often had large families. Forecasts suggest that the majority of population increases in cities in developing countries between 1985 and 2000 will be a result of natural increase rather than migration. The pattern will be by no means uniform, however, with two-thirds of the total increase in many Asian and Latin American cities expected to be a result of natural increase while growth in many African cities may still depend more on migration than on natural increase.

The balance of world urban population between developed and developing countries is changing dramatically. In 1960 some 55% of the world's urban population lived in developed countries and 45% in developing countries. By 1980 these proportions had been reversed and by 2020 it is anticipated that almost 80% of the world's urban dwellers will be in developing countries (see Fig. 3.10). The forecasts on which Fig. 3.10 is based suggest that the world's urban population will increase by over 3.6 billion

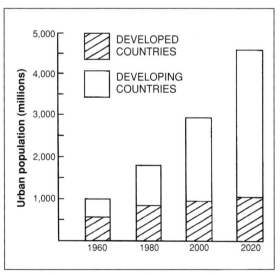

Fig. 3.10 Estimated world urban population growth, 1960–2020. The term 'Developed countries' here includes all the countries in Europe and North America, together with Australia, New Zealand, Japan and the former USSR. All other countries are classed as 'Developing countries'.
Source: data in *World Population Prospects 1988*, United Nations, 1989.

between 1960 and 2020 and that approximately 87% of that increase (more than 3.1 billion people) will occur in cities in developing countries. Figure 3.11 shows another dramatic aspect of these changes. In 1960 only three of the world's ten largest urban agglomerations were in developing countries and Shanghai was the only one of these with a population of over 10 million. By the year 2000, eight of the ten largest cities in the world are expected to be in developing countries and both they and a further ten cities in such areas will have populations in excess of 10 million. Clearly changes of this nature have massive implications for both governments and individuals. Most cities in developing countries already face major difficulties in providing for the needs of their populations in terms of housing, water supply, sanitation and other basic amenities. Such difficulties seem likely to be greatly exacerbated in the years ahead unless much better urban management strategies are developed than has generally been the case to date.

Since 1800 a major shift in the world's population distribution has clearly taken place, with the rapid growth in urban populations, first in the present industrialised countries and more recently in developing countries, where growth continues at a rapid rate. On a rather less spectacular scale, population distributions *within* cities have also tended to change through time,

again with some contrasts evident between developed and developing countries.

Within urban areas it is usually possible to differentiate contrasting functional zones that characteristically have different residential population densities. Examination of the pattern of residential populations has involved the use of a method known as *gradient analysis*. Investigations of residential population density gradients for 36 cities in different parts of the world by Clark (1967) showed that, in general, densities decline with increasing distance from the city centre, normally decreasing most sharply near the centre and less markedly as distance from the centre increases. Since the data used in plotting density gradients are based on the averaging of information available for administrative or census units which are approximately equidistant from the city centre, it is clear that the gradients as plotted may obscure differences that exist within particular concentric zones around the city centre. This is especially true of large urban agglomerations that incorporate subsidiary centres within the urban area. Factors like this should be borne in mind when drawing conclusions based on density gradients.

Figure 3.12 shows how the density gradient for London changed during a period of 160 years, largely as a result of changing transport facilities. The steep gradient for 1801 indicates a

The ten largest cities, 1960	Population total (millions)	The ten largest cities, 2000	Population total (millions)
1 New York	14.2	1 Mexico City	24.4
2 London	10.7	2 São Paulo	23.6
3 Tokyo	10.7	3 Tokyo	21.3
4 Shanghai	10.7	4 New York	16.1
5 Rhine-Ruhr	8.7	5 Calcutta	15.9
6 Beijing	7.3	6 Bombay	15.4
7 Paris	7.2	7 Shanghai	14.7
8 Buenos Aires	6.9	8 Tehran	13.7
9 Los Angeles	6.6	9 Jakarta	13.2
10 Moscow	6.3	10 Buenos Aires	13.1

Fig. 3.11 The world's ten largest cities, 1960 and 2000.
Source: Human Development Report 1990, UN Development Programme.

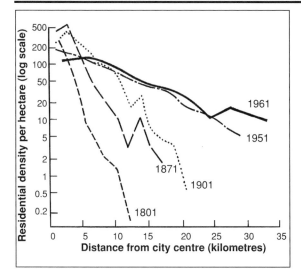

Fig. 3.12 Residential density profiles for London in selected years.
Source: after Clark, 1967.

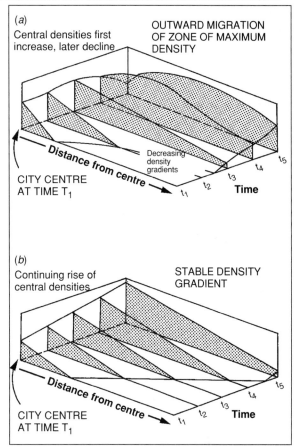

Fig. 3.13 Changes in urban density gradients through time for (*a*) 'Western' and (*b*) 'non-Western' cities.
Source: after B.J.L. Berry *et al.*, 1963.

stage when transport provision was limited and people had to live close to their place of work. Later stages indicate first an increase and later a decrease in city centre population densities together with an outward spread of settlement into suburban areas made possible by improved transport facilities and motivated by a wide range of social, economic and administrative changes. A generalisation of the changes in residential population gradients for 'Western' cities through time is provided in Fig. 3.13a. This shows three main features:

1 the initial rise and later decline in population density of the central part of the city;
2 the outward spread of the population through time; and
3 the consequent decrease in the density gradient through time.

By contrast, a similar generalisation for 'non-Western' cities (Fig. 3.13b) indicates a continuing rise of densities in the central area and the consequent maintenance of relatively stable density gradients as outward spread occurs. These differences largely reflect different types of functional zone and the limited development of transport networks in such cities. The central

areas of 'non-Western' cities tend to retain a major residential function as well as providing employment opportunities, as in the 'shophouse' core of most Malaysian cities and the *medina* of many Arab cities in North Africa and elsewhere. The suburban areas frequently include extensive, densely populated, informal settlements as well as better-quality housing at lower densities, giving rise to higher average population densities than in most suburbs of 'Western' cities. Additionally, the immature development of urban transport systems has tended to limit the general outward spread of settlement, thus giving rise to a more compact urban plan than that in a 'Western' city of comparable population, and to higher overall population densities. In time, the transport systems of urban areas in such cities may become more like those of 'Western' cities and there is already evidence of this in, for example, some cities in the Middle East and in newly industrialising countries in Asia where standards of living are above average and city authorities have more revenue available for investment in transport networks than is the case in most cities of the developing world. More generally in 'non-Western' cities financial shortages and continuing rapid population increases seem likely to restrict transport development for many years to come, so perhaps perpetuating the differences in population density gradients indicated in Fig. 3.13.

CASE STUDY 3A

Urbanisation in Australia

The Australian population is overwhelmingly coastal and conforms to the three generalisations concerning the distribution of population at the continental scale suggested by Fielding (page 39). Australia has also long been characterised by a high degree of urbanisation with the urban hierarchy dominated by the five state capitals of Sydney, Melbourne, Brisbane, Perth and Adelaide, all of which are now 'million cities'.

In 1940, the Australian geographer Griffith Taylor pointed out the very uneven population distribution of Australia in a simple but telling map, the essence of which is incorporated in Fig. 3.14. He divided the country into two parts which he called 'Empty Australia' and 'Economic Australia', the dividing line on his map being where the population density fell below one-eighth of a person per square mile. Within Economic Australia he identified five particularly attractive areas: eastern New South Wales, the greater part of Victoria, the south-east corner of Queensland, the southern Flinders Range in South Australia and the extreme south-western corner of Western Australia. He also commented on the remarkable degree of urbanisation in Australia at that time when only one-third of the population lived in rural areas despite the country's large dependence upon the export of primary produce.

Since the 1940s the Australian population has become even more unequally distributed, its coastal concentration has become more pronounced and it has become even more a country of urban dwellers. By 1950 three-quarters of Australia's population was urban and since 1970 the urban proportion has been just over 85% of the total population. In the first part of this period, until the early 1970s, the rural population fell in every state in absolute as well as percentage terms, affected by such factors as increased mechanisation of agriculture, the relative decline in rural incomes (especially in dairying areas), the lack of alternative employment opportunities in many rural districts, and a recession in the wool industry in the late 1960s which led to substantial out-migration from parts of rural New South Wales and Victoria. More recently there has been a slow increase both in absolute numbers and in the proportion of the population living in rural areas. This would seem to reflect a similar process of counter-urbanisation to that recognised in other developed

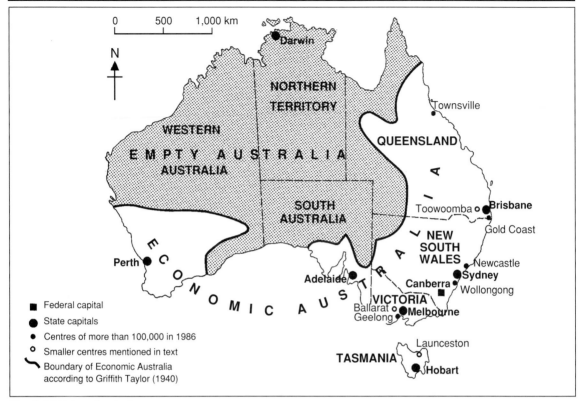

Fig. 3.14 Urban Australia.

countries (see, for example, Cloke, 1985, and Hornby and Jones, 1991) though as yet on a small scale. One notable aspect of this development is the rapid growth of small coastal settlements in Queensland and New South Wales based largely on the development of recreation, tourism and retirement facilities. The increase in the proportion of the population aged over 65 from 8.3% in 1971 to 11.0% in 1989 is a significant factor influencing this kind of development.

Despite these recent developments, Australia, as already suggested, remains dominantly urban. The five state capitals that are also 'million cities' are very much larger than any other cities in the continent. All but Brisbane contain over 60% of the population in their state (see Fig. 3.15). Sydney is approximately eight times as large as Newcastle, the next largest settlement in New South Wales; Brisbane is about five times as large as second-ranked Gold Coast in Queensland; Melbourne is

some twenty times larger than Geelong, the second largest settlement in Victoria; and both Perth and Adelaide exceed the second towns in their respective states by an even greater ratio. Canberra, the federal capital, and Hobart, the Tasmanian capital, fall within the second tier of cities in terms of population while Darwin, capital of Northern Territory, still has a population well below 100,000 despite a period of rapid growth following the granting of self-government to Northern Territory in 1978 (see Fig. 3.14).

The early domination of the larger state capitals was clearly related to the economic development of the continent as a whole. During the nineteenth century, as Europeans extended economic and political control over the interior of the continent, an export-based economy developed with sheep, cattle, wheat and mineral production geared principally to the British market. Short (1988) clearly expresses the nature of this development in his comment that 'Australia was a branch plant of an economic enterprise whose head office was in London'. By the same analogy, the 'regional office' was the main city in each of the then separate colonies, serving as the port, financial and government centre. As agricultural output and trade increased, so did the size of the cities. Increased wealth from these activities led to greater diversification with industrial and commercial activity concentrated in the same cities, each of which developed as a primate city serving the rest of the colony. Not until 1901 were the separate areas linked politically. The capitals of three of the present states formed the early foci of urban settlement in the continent: Sydney, in a New South Wales that then incorporated most of the eastern third of the continent, including Tasmania; Adelaide in South Australia; and Perth in Western Australia. In time, Tasmania, Victoria and Queensland were granted equivalent status to their mother colony of New South Wales and their present capitals began to develop more rapidly. Canberra, the federal capital, was eventually inaugurated as the seat of national government in 1927 but 30 years later still had fewer than 40,000 inhabitants. More rapid growth has taken place since 1960 but Canberra still ranks well behind the five major state capitals in population size (see Fig. 3.15).

Even after federation in 1901, patterns of economic development and urban growth changed only slowly with the state capitals continuing to dominate the urban hierarchy. Some medium-sized towns gradually emerged, however, including the industrial centres of Newcastle and Wollongong in New South Wales and Geelong in Victoria; Townsville, a port and market centre and Gold Coast, a resort centre in Queensland; and regional centres with light industry such as Launceston (Tasmania), Ballarat (Victoria) and Toowoomba (Queensland). The first five of these named above now have populations in excess of 100,000 and these, together with the state and territory capitals (including the national capital), accounted for over 70% of the Australian population in 1990. Almost 40% of Australians live in Sydney and Melbourne alone, but it is interesting to note that their proportions of the state populations of New South Wales and Victoria respectively showed a slight decline between the 1971 and 1986 censuses, though total numbers continued to increase (see Fig. 3.15).

An important element in the growth of Australian cities since 1945 has been immigration. At the time of the 1986 census about 3.25 million Australians were foreign-born, over one-third in the UK and Ireland, another third in other parts of Europe and over 16% in Asia. Almost 40% of the population increase since 1971 is accounted for by migration and in 1988 and 1989 net migration slightly exceeded natural increase. British

	1971		1976		1981		1986	
	(a)	(b)	(a)	(b)	(a)	(b)	(a)	(b)
Sydney	2,935,937	63.8	3,143,750	63.4	3,279,500	62.7	3,472,700	62.8
Melbourne	2,503,022	71.5	2,723,700	71.5	2,806,300	71.1	2,931,900	70.1
Brisbane	869,579	47.6	1,000,850	47.8	1,096,200	46.7	1,196,000	45.6
Adelaide	842,693	71.8	924,060	72.5	954,300	72.3	1,003,800	72.6
Perth	703,199	68.2	832,760	70.7	922,040	70.9	1,050,400	72.0
Hobart	153,216	39.2	164,400	39.9	171,110	40.1	179,000	40.1
Darwin	38,885	45.0	44,232	45.0	56,478	46.1	74,800	48.4
Canberra	142,925	99.2	206,550	99.4	226,450	99.5	257,850	99.6

(a) *Total population*
(b) *% of state/territory population*

Fig. 3.15 Australia: estimated resident population of capital cities of states and territories.
Source: Australia Yearbook 1990.

migrants remained the single most numerous group in the late 1980s at just under 20% of the total but New Zealand (about 15%), other European countries and, increasingly, South-east Asia are also very important sources of migrants. Progressive removal of immigration restrictions based on country of origin, race and colour between 1949 and 1972 and the increased acceptance of refugees in the post-war period, including many from East and Central Europe between 1947 and 1953 and from Vietnam from the late 1970s onwards, have been significant in changing the patterns of migration to Australia. Whatever their origin and background, the tendency has been for the vast majority of immigrants to settle in the large urban centres, especially in the state capitals with their greater range of employment opportunities, and this seems likely to continue.

Most recent projections suggest only limited changes in patterns of population growth in the foreseeable future. The 1988-based UN median projections suggested that the level of urbanisation may have reached 89.5% by the year 2025 following renewed urban growth from the late 1990s onwards. Sydney and Melbourne were expected to remain the two largest cities by a considerable margin but Perth, whose population exceeded that of Adelaide for the first time at the 1986 census, was expected to overtake Brisbane by 1991 to move into third place. A distinctive feature of Australian cities is the low density pattern of residential areas, with most Australians occupying single-family dwellings, many of them in sprawling suburbs. (Sydney covers something like ten times the surface area of Paris though having a considerably smaller population.) If growth continues along the lines suggested, especially in what seem destined to become the two huge urbanised regions of New South Wales and Victoria, this continued spread may give rise to considerable urban planning problems.

CASE STUDY 3B

Changing distribution of population in the United States

1790 –1870: westward expansion

When the first census of population was held in the United States in 1790 the population stood at 4 million. At that time the country was restricted to the 13 original states on the eastern seaboard together with a 'back country' stretching from the Great Lakes in the north to the northern boundary of Florida in the south, and as far west as the River Mississippi (Fig. 3.16). Less than a century later in 1870, as a result of purchases and the spoils of war, the country stretched from the 49th parallel in the north to the modern border with Mexico in the south, and from the Atlantic Ocean in the east to the Pacific Ocean in the west. It also included Alaska.

Those 80 years, which Borchert (1967) called the epochs of the sail and wagon (1790–1830) and the iron horse (steam locomotive) (1830–1870) saw the westward expansion of population at first from the seaboard states and their so-called *gateway ports*, principally Boston, New York, Philadelphia, Baltimore and Charleston, and from New Orleans on the Gulf of Mexico at the mouth of the Mississippi, and later from inland gateways such as Detroit and Buffalo on the Great

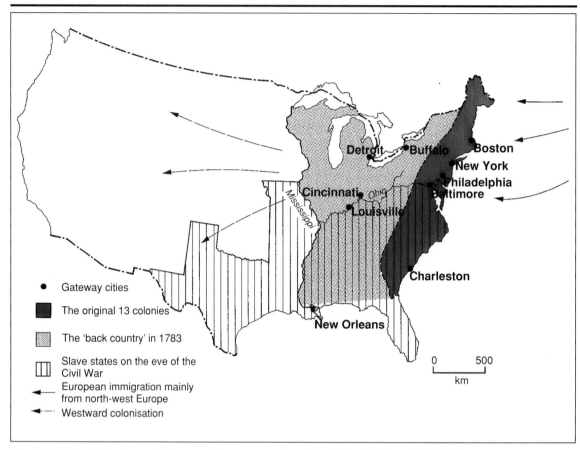

Fig. 3.16 Selected features of the population geography of the United States, 1790–1870. See text for explanation.

Lakes and Cincinnati and Louisville on the River Ohio to the west of the Appalachian barrier. The availability of agricultural land free or at low cost, discoveries of precious metals, and the expanding river, canal and railroad transport networks, stimulated the westward spread of population, drawing on native-born Americans from the eastern states and European immigrants alike. Between 1820 and 1880 about 7.3 million immigrants arrived from three major sources: Germany (3 million), Ireland (2.8 million) and Great Britain (1.5 million).

In the southern states a plantation economy based on slave labour had become firmly established by 1700 and it has been estimated that a million slaves were brought to the USA in the second half of the eighteenth century. Although the importation of further slaves was prohibited after 1808, by 1850 the Black population stood at 3.5 million, with more than 95% concentrated in a band of southern states stretching from Virginia and the Carolinas in the east to Texas in the west (Fig. 3.16).

1870 –1950: the growth of an industrial nation

This 80-year period saw the rise to maturity of the United States as an industrial nation, and this economic transition had profound effects on the size, distribution and ethnic composition of its population. Although there was a steady decline in the birth rate throughout the period, the population continued to grow rapidly (from 35 million in 1865 at the end of the Civil War to 151 million in 1950) because of the continued large influx of immigrants. Whereas just over 7 million immigrants entered the country in the 60 years between 1820 and 1880, the number of immigrants entering the country almost quadrupled to more than 26 million during the following half century. In the 1920s immigration declined sharply after the passage of the Immigration Act which set a ceiling on the number of immigrants who could enter the country and set quotas for individual countries. Immigration remained low in the depression years of the 1930s and the war years that followed. The national composition of the immigrant flow also changed after about 1870. Although the flow from north-west Europe continued it was augmented by massive flows from eastern and southern Europe and by increasing numbers from Asia and Latin America.

As industrialisation took place, the population not only expanded but became concentrated in the nation's industrial regions, mainly in urban areas. The immigrants went overwhelmingly to urban industrial regions. It has been estimated that in 1900, 75% of the populations of New York, Chicago, Milwaukee and Detroit consisted of immigrants and their immediate descendants (Bohland, 1988).

Rural–urban migration within the United States also made a significant contribution to population growth in the urban industrial regions. The most important of these rural–urban movements was that of Black Americans from the former plantation states in the south who had been freed from slavery at the end of the Civil War in 1865. What was at first a trickle of migration became a flood after 1910. Several factors combined to initiate and maintain the flow. Important push factors were the open discrimination practised against the Blacks and the grinding poverty of their lives. At the end of the Civil War many former slaves became share croppers or share tenants on smallholdings created out of the former plantations. Share croppers received land, seed, fertiliser and implements from the landlord and in return paid him up to half the value of the cash crop. Share tenants provided their own seed, fertiliser and implements, and paid a smaller proportion of the cash crop to the landlord. Neither category of tenant had much agricul-

tural education or capital, and in most cases successive generations of farmers fought a losing battle against the damage done by heavy rains on farms where no cover crop was grown, and against the ravages of the boll weevil if they were growing cotton. In the face of such difficulties many farmers continued to live on under- and unfarmed smallholdings and commuted to non-agricultural employment. Others gave up their tenancies and migrated.

These rural migrants were attracted in large numbers to urban centres within the South and in other parts of the country. Within the South the cities of the Gulf Coast of Texas and Louisiana were important magnets, as were the textile, timber-processing and tobacco-curing towns of the Piedmont and inner coast plain of Georgia and the Carolinas. Industrial regions outside the South also exerted a considerable pull, particularly the North East, the Great Lakes region and the west coast (Fig. 3.17). Between 1870 and 1950 Black Americans ceased to be predominantly southern and rural; they became increasingly urban and northern.

Figure 3.18 shows the changing distribution of manufacturing employment between 1870 and 1969. The New England, Middle Atlantic and East North Central divisions coincide generally with what had become known by about 1920 as the Manufacturing Belt (Fig. 3.17). This vast region possessed the combined advantages of fuel resources (particularly coal), raw materials (most importantly iron), markets, and a well-developed transport system. In 1870, 77% of the nation's manufacturing employment was concentrated there, and despite later relative decline, the region still contained 68.5% of manufacturing employment in 1940. By that date the Manufacturing Belt contained nearly half of the nation's population. Within the Manufacturing Belt the population was not only overwhelmingly urban, but was concentrated in the largest metropolitan centres. Outside the Manufacturing Belt the most important secondary concentrations of urban growth to have emerged between 1870 and 1950 were on the west coast, particularly in central and southern California (centred on San Francisco-Oakland and Los Angeles-San Diego respectively), in the oil-

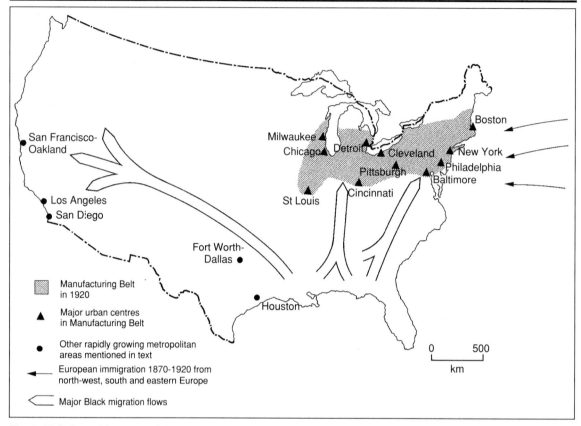

Fig. 3.17 Selected features of the population geography of the United States, 1870–1950. See text for explanation.

	1870	1910	1940	1969
New England	21.5	13.5	11.0	7.5
Middle Atlantic	35.0	31.5	29.5	21.5
East North Central	20.5	22.5	28.0	26.5
West North Central	6.5	8.5	5.0	6.5
South Atlantic	8.0	9.0	11.5	14.0
East South Central	4.0	4.0	4.0	6.0
West South Central	2.0	4.0	3.5	6.0
Mountain	0.5	2.0	1.0	2.0
Pacific	2.0	5.0	6.0	10.5

Fig. 3.18 Percentage of manufacturing employment change in the United States by census division, 1870–1969.
Source: Estall, 1972.

fields of western Texas and the western Gulf Coast (Dallas, Fort Worth, Houston), and in the coalescing resort and retirement towns and cities of Florida.

Change since 1950: towards a post-industrial society

Since 1950 the American economy has entered a new phase which has been called 'late capitalism' or 'advanced capitalism'. Some writers also refer to the later stages of this phase as the beginnings of a post-industrial society. The main economic characteristics of the post-1950 period that affect population distribution are:

a) The decline of employment in the manufacturing sector. The decline is most marked in what are sometimes called the 'smokestack' indus tries such as iron and steel, heavy engineering, and textiles, i.e. the industries that were the basis of the industrialising phase. This decline is offset to some extent by the growth of high-technology industries such as electronics, optics, pharmaceuticals and ordnance. Research and development activity (R&D) may outstrip factory floor activity in these industries.

b) A marked expansion of employment in service industries and their contribution to GNP. Employment in education, health care and government are areas of notable expansion.

c) The emergence of a smaller number of large and powerful organisations, many of which are multi-national companies.

Although in the last decade of the twentieth century the pattern of population distribution established by 1950 can still be clearly discerned, the economic transition outlined above is radically reshaping that pattern. Four important changes can be clearly distinguished. The Manufacturing Belt is in decline, many large cities are losing population, small- and medium-sized communities outside the large cities within and beyond the large metropolitan areas are expanding, and Americans are becoming increasingly concentrated in the South and near the coast.

The states comprising the Manufacturing Belt have consistently experienced population growth rates below the national average since the 1950s or 1960s. For example, as a whole the states of the Middle Atlantic division (New York, New Jersey, Pennsylvania) grew by 13.3% between 1950 and 1960 (national average 18.5%), by 8.9% between 1960 and 1970 (national average 13.4%), and declined by 1.1% between 1970 and 1980 when the country's population grew as a whole by 11.4%. The figures for the states of the East North Central division (Ohio, Indiana, Illinois, Wisconsin) for the same period were 19.2%, 11.2% and 3.5%. Growth has been much faster in the last 40 years in the South and West. In the period between 1950 and 1960 it was 55%, between 1960 and 1970 it was 61%, and between 1970 and 1980 a remarkable 89.9%. Growth has continued to be concentrated in the South and West since 1980. Between 1980 and 1983, for instance, more than half the

United States' population growth was concentrated in just three states: California, Texas and Florida (Bohland, 1988).

Not surprisingly, at the scale of individual cities and metropolitan areas (a metropolitan area in the United States is a conurbation made up of a large city (called a central city) and its surrounding satellite towns and villages (called suburbs); see Chapter 7 for further discussion of population decentralisation and commuting in metropolitan areas in the USA) there has been widespread stagnation and decline in the Manufacturing Belt, but urban decline has not been restricted to that region. Only in the South where generously bounded central cities still have room for expansion within their city limits, is central city growth a widely distributed phenomenon.

Figure 3.19, showing population change in metropolitan areas (i.e. central city plus satellite communities) between 1970 and 1980, illustrates graphically the decline of the northern states (often referred to as the Snowbelt or Frostbelt) and the population expansion in the southern states (the Sunbelt). The six most rapidly declining metropolitan areas between 1970 and 1980 were all in the Snowbelt: New York, Cleveland, Pittsburgh, Boston, Philadelphia and Buffalo. All their populations declined by at least 100,000. New York alone lost 854,000. By contrast nine metropolitan areas in the Sunbelt gained by at least 400,000 each in the same period.

There is a strong relationship between these growth rates and the changing nature and location of manufacturing industry. Between 1970 and 1980, New York State lost 318,000 jobs in manufacturing, Pennsylvania lost 197,000, Ohio 138,000 and Illinois 122,000. During the same period all the states in the South and West gained manufacturing jobs, the three largest increases being in California (433,000), Texas (307,000) and Florida (133,000). Most of these new jobs in the South and West were in high-technology industries which are not tied to fuel sources, raw materials, or ports and railways.

Another important component of population growth in the South and West is the migration there of retired people. In Florida, for example, the number of elderly people is twice the national

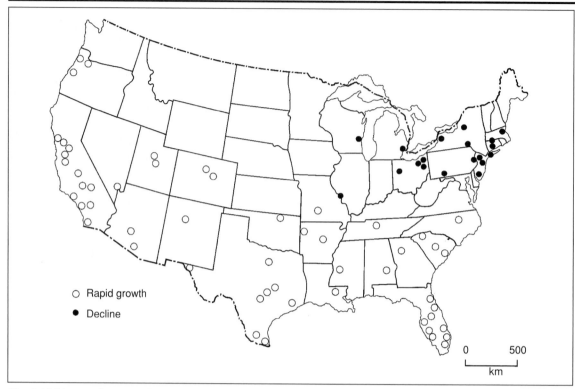

Fig. 3.19 Metropolitan population change in the United States, 1970–80.

average and not all of these are US citizens. Watson (1982) quotes a government source that revealed that more than one million Canadians owned winter or permanent retirement homes in Florida.

4

Population and resources

Fig. 4.1 Measuring out medicine for a malnourished child in a health centre at Rora Habab, Eritrea, during the Ethiopian civil war. Often during periods of drought and famine, medical help comes too late to save those being treated, despite all the efforts of the aid agencies and others who struggle to overcome problems of poor communications in difficult terrain, an unhelpful political bureaucracy, and military activities.

Malthus and after

We have already focused attention briefly on the problem of providing sufficient food and other resources to meet the needs of a growing world population. This is not a new problem. At a local level there have been many occasions in history when a particular community reached a stage where it was difficult or impossible to supply all its subsistence needs. Such situations have often helped to motivate migration, as in Ireland in the nineteenth century, when some 800,000 people left the country in the space of only five years or so after the potato crop failures of the 1840s. Additionally many people may die from starvation when food supplies are inadequate as has happened on a dramatic scale more recently in Ethiopia and several other African countries (see Fig. 4.1).

In the early nineteenth century there was some concern that the population of Great Britain was likely to grow to such an extent that it would exceed the capacity of the country to feed itself. People's ideas were strongly influenced by the writings of the Reverend T.R. Malthus who in 1798 published the first edition of his *Essay on the Principle of Population*. This essay and the author's subsequent writings were much discussed when first published and have continued to be a source of interest and argument in recent times. Basically Malthus suggested that whereas food production was likely at best to increase at an arithmetic rate (i.e. by the repeated addition of a uniform increment in each uniform interval of time), population

tended to increase at a geometric rate and was likely to double every 25 years or so unless certain checks were imposed on it. Thus, while food output was likely to increase in a series of 25-year intervals only in the progression:

1, 2, 3, 4, 5, 6, 7, 8, 9, etc.

population was capable of increasing in the progression:

1, 2, 4, 8, 16, 32, 64, 128, 256, etc.

On the basis of a supposed world population of 1,000 million in the early nineteenth century and an adequate means of subsistence at that time, Malthus suggested that there was a potential for a population increase to 256,000 million within 200 years but that the means of subsistence were only capable of being increased sufficiently for 9,000 million to be fed at the level prevailing at the beginning of the period. He therefore considered that the population increase should be kept down to the level at which it could be supported by the operation of various checks on population growth that he categorised as 'preventive' and 'positive' checks.

The chief preventive check envisaged by Malthus was that of 'moral restraint', which was seen as a deliberate decision by men to refrain 'from pursuing the dictate of nature in an early attachment to one woman', i.e. to marry later in life than had been usual and only at a stage when fully capable of supporting a family. This, it was anticipated, would give rise to smaller families and probably to fewer families, but Malthus did not advocate birth control *within* marriage and did not suggest that parents should try to restrict the number of children born to them after their marriage. He indicated that some consequences that he saw as undesirable might follow from the postponement of marriages, most obviously an increase in the number of children born to parents who were not married, but considered that any such consequences were likely to be less serious than those caused by a continuation of rapid population increase.

Malthus saw positive checks to population growth as being any causes that contributed to 'shorten the natural duration of human life'. He included in this category poor living and working conditions that might give rise to low resistance to disease as well as more obvious factors such as disease itself, war and famine. Some of the implications of Malthus's ideas had obvious political connotations and this partly accounts for the interest in his work and possibly for the misrepresentation of some of his ideas by authors such as Cobbett, the early English radical. Later writers modified his ideas suggesting, for example, strong government action to ensure later marriages and, indeed, such action was taken in parts of Germany in the mid-nineteenth century. Others did not accept the view that birth control should not be practised after marriage and one group in particular, called the Malthusian League, strongly argued the case for birth control within marriage, even though this was contrary to what Malthus himself had advocated.

Clearly any forecasts concerning future relationships between population and food supply, or the supply of other resources, are based on a number of assumptions concerning rates of consumption, production and population change. The problems of forecasting population change have already been considered in Chapter 3. In modern times, population growth has rarely been at an even rate for long periods and it is very difficult to anticipate even a few years in advance what growth rates will be. Similarly there are difficulties in forecasting rates of increase in food supply or how consumption will vary. Despite this, consideration of the future balance between population and food supplies has continued to attract interest, and gloomy predictions concerning this balance are still often described as 'Malthusian' or 'neo-Malthusian'.

One assumption in many discussions of the future situation has been that there is a definite ceiling to food production from any given area. Thus it can be argued that beyond a certain stage continued population growth will result in less food being available per person until ultimately some people have insufficient to eat. They will then die, either directly from starvation or from disease resulting from a lack of resistance brought about by malnutrition.

This increased mortality rate, it can be argued, acts as a 'Malthusian check' on population growth and might be expected to affect the fertility rate in at least two ways. First, the deaths of many women of child-bearing age and of their partners would be likely to have an immediate effect on the numbers of children born, and the deaths of younger people would reduce the numbers of those available to become parents in later years. Secondly, it is likely that the situation would encourage deliberate attempts to reduce the number of births because of the increasing awareness of the problems caused by continuing population growth. Thus a sequence of events might occur similar to that shown diagrammatically in Fig. 4.2, culminating in a decrease in the rate of population growth and possibly even a decline in total numbers. Migration, too, might become a significant factor in this decline. It is also possible that fertility would eventually decline

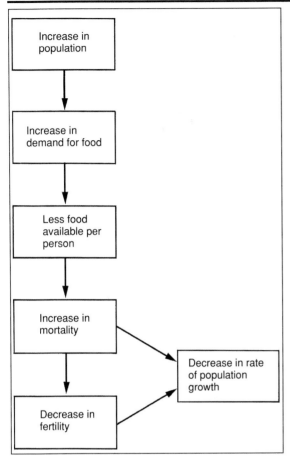

Fig. 4.2 A possible sequence of events envisaged by some Malthusians. See text for comment.

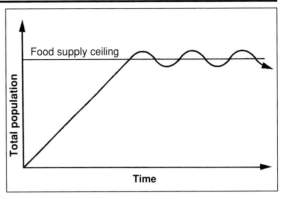

Fig. 4.3 The possible effect of a food supply ceiling on population growth. See text for comment.

as a result of a reduction in the physiological capacity to conceive in conditions of malnutrition. (This has happened in recent years during famine periods in Bangladesh and parts of Africa.)

Looking further ahead, if the decrease in population growth rate gave rise to a decline in total population to a level where food supplies were again more than adequate it would seem possible that checks on growth would cease to operate and population would again increase. If this were repeated, a cyclical pattern as illustrated in Fig. 4.3 might emerge, with fluctuations above and below a critical level determined by the food supply ceiling. This pattern of develop-

ment has been clearly observed in animal populations and the limited evidence available suggests that it has been a feature of some primitive human societies. Some countries, especially in Africa and southern Asia, have found great difficulty recently in providing sufficient food for their populations. The gloomy predictions made in the early nineteenth century about Great Britain were not realised, however, largely because some of the assumptions on which they were based proved to be invalid.

In fact, population continued to increase in Great Britain after 1800 and, though grave concern about food supplies was expressed by politicians and others for many years, living standards also improved in time. A series of developments based on new techniques in agriculture, industry and transportation revolutionised the economy of Great Britain and of much of the rest of the world, resulting in great increases in agricultural productivity and the output of manufactured goods in Great Britain. This made it possible for much of the food needed by the British population to be obtained from other countries in exchange for industrial goods and services provided by Great Britain. These changes were on a scale unprecedented in history and emphasise the difficulties of forecasting what is likely to happen in future concerning population growth, food supply and relationships between them. So far as Britain was concerned, the changes in economic structure and productivity meant that population growth was not limited by any food-supply shortages of the type envisaged by Malthus or others. The pattern of development that occurred in the nineteenth century may be outlined as in Fig. 4.4 though it must also be remembered that during this period many people emigrated from Great Britain and various internal adjustments in population distribution also occurred as a result of migration.

More recently there has been a reduction in the rate of growth of the British population (see Case Study 2A). The reasons for this are complex and incompletely understood but seem to be fundamentally related to changing social attitudes rather than resulting from direct physical controls such as food shortages.

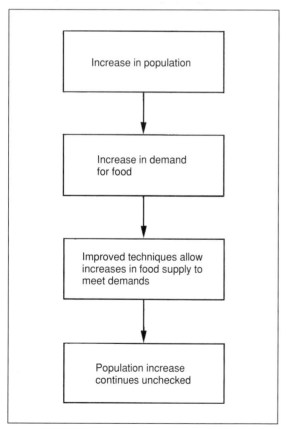

Fig. 4.4 Population increase and food supply in nineteenth-century Britain. See text for comment.

Boserup's hypothesis

An alternative view to that of Malthus has been developed by Ester Boserup, a Danish economist, who has experience as a research worker in several developing countries. She has pointed out (Boserup, 1965, 1987) that the Malthusian approach to the relationship between agriculture and population growth is 'based upon the belief that the supply of food for the human race is inherently inelastic and this lack of elasticity is the main factor governing the rate of population growth'. Thus population growth is seen as being dependent upon preceding changes in agricultural productivity. These changes are themselves seen as occurring in response to various other factors that occur largely by chance, such as particular technical innovations.

Boserup asserts that it is more realistic to suggest that population growth is a major factor in determining the nature of agricultural developments than that it is controlled by them. Her views have sometimes been summarised in the phrase 'necessity is the mother of invention', because she argues that in many pre-industrial societies population growth served as the main stimulus to change agricultural techniques and so increase food production. She supports her views with evidence from developing countries, and states that few people would wish to suggest – in line with what she sees as the essence of Malthusian thinking – that rapid population growth in these areas in recent years can be explained by reference to changes in the conditions for food production. She goes further to claim that in agricultural development generally, and not merely in the experience of developing countries in the twentieth century, 'agricultural developments are caused by population trends rather than the other way round'.

Her investigations were based on a range of land-use systems that she classified on the basis of their intensity of production, measured in terms of cropping frequency. In an admittedly simple classification, she identifies five different intensities of agricultural land use recognisable in many parts of Latin America, Africa and Asia:

1 *Forest-fallow cultivation*, in which plots of land are cleared in the forest each year, cropped for a year or two and then left fallow long enough for forest to re-colonise the cleared areas. This implies a fallow of at least 20 to 25 years and possibly as long as a hundred years.

2 *Bush-fallow cultivation*, in which the process is similar to forest-fallow but the fallow period is much shorter (normally 6 to 10 years) so the vegetation that develops on cleared land is not forest but bush with possibly a few young trees. These first two groups are sometimes jointly described as long-fallow or shifting cultivation systems.

3 *Short-fallow cultivation*, in which the fallow period is only 1 or 2 years so that only wild grasses are likely to colonise the cleared area.

4 *Annual cropping*, in which land is usually left uncultivated for several months between harvest and planting – a period that can be viewed as a fallow period though it is not usually so described.

5 *Multi-cropping*, in which plots bear two or more successive crops each year so that cropping is virtually continuous.

Boserup points out that during the twentieth century, as population has increased, there has been a change from less intensive to more intensive systems of cropping in many parts of the developing world. Thus in some areas forest-fallow cultivation has gradually changed to bush-fallow cultivation or even more intensive systems, and in parts of Asia in particular, the growth of population has stimulated the rapid spread of multi-cropping systems.

Related to these changes have been changes in technique that, in Boserup's view, have developed because of the changes in land use. She points out that forest-fallow cultivation normally involves the burning of trees and other vegetation on a plot before planting or sowing directly into the ashes left after burning. A digging-stick is an adequate tool to make a hole for planting in these conditions and no hoeing is required because the soil is relatively weed-free and of suitable texture for planting. When the vegetation burnt off is more sparse, however, as in bush-fallow cultivation, hoeing is usually necessary before planting and so the hoe is introduced not just as a technical improvement on the digging-stick but because an additional operation is needed when the more intensive bush-fallow system replaces forest-fallow. A further change to short-fallow cultivation would be greatly helped by the use of a plough, for burning is less efficient as a means of preparing land for cultivation when the vegetation is mainly grass and so roots tend to be left largely intact. Boserup emphasises that in cases where a plough is not available at this stage, short-fallow cultivation is often avoided altogether by lengthening the period of cultivation in a bush-fallow system so that the land is cultivated year after year for perhaps as much as 8 years. This restricts grass growth and the plot is then left fallow for a further 8 or 10 years so a bush rather than dominantly grass vegetation develops. If population density continues to increase there may be a 'jump' directly from bush-fallow to annual cropping without an intervening period of short-fallow cultivation.

Boserup suggests that similar patterns of change operated much earlier in Europe as population was increasing. She argues that, unless population increases, intensification of agricultural production and associated technical changes are unlikely and thus population change has stimulated agricultural development in many areas. Her ideas tend to assume that the techniques required for new agricultural systems are known to the societies undergoing population growth and she recognises that if this is not the case then the agricultural system is likely to regulate population size. She also accepts that various other circumstances may restrict agricultural development even when rapid population growth is occurring. She has pointed out, for example, that land tenure systems may mean that farmers have little incentive to improve agricultural techniques because increased production will be of little or no benefit to them, and she has suggested that this situation was to be found in some parts of India in colonial times. Clearly, interactions between population change, agricultural techniques and socio-economic factors are complex and Boserup's hypothesis has been criticised as being too simplistic from several points of view. For example, even the description and classification of agricultural systems in terms of intensity of production is over-simplified as, in reality, a variety of agricultural types can be recognised at any given intensity. Nevertheless, Boserup's work is a useful and interesting contrast to that of Malthus and obviously casts doubt on some of the basic tenets of Malthusian theory. Findlay and Findlay (1987) make the interesting point that it might be at the level of national governments that Boserup's ideas come closest to being applicable in the modern, increasingly market-oriented world food production system since governments of the developing world, faced with large food import costs to meet the demands of their growing populations, have often been motivated to encourage changes in their agricultural systems. Such changes have often not been as beneficial as they might have been, however, and have tended to promote cash cropping for export rather than improved domestic food production.

Despite the criticisms by Boserup and others of Malthusian ideas, much recent comment on relationships between population growth and food supply has been comparable in some ways to that of the early Malthusian era. Various forecasts have predicted doom for either the world as a whole or for individual countries such as India or China as population has continued to increase and threatened to outrun supplies of food or other resources. Additionally, there has been a growing awareness in the later part of the twentieth century of the potential damage to the environment of further increases in population and of various economic activities that have resulted in the rapid consumption of certain of the world's resources to supply the needs or demands of people who seek ever higher standards of living. Issues such as the destruction of the tropical rainforests, high levels of energy and mineral consumption, global warming and the 'greenhouse effect', and inequalities in living standards between and within different communities, have all been seen as relevant in one way or another to the debate about the relationships between population and resources in recent years.

The nature and use of resources

The provision of adequate resources for future populations is clearly as crucial a consideration now as it was in the time of Malthus. The term 'resource' can itself be a source of confusion. One fundamental division is between *human resources*, which can be taken to incorporate the skills and abilities of particular groups of people as well as their total numbers, and *natural resources*, which people derive from the physical environment. Basically this latter group includes the supply of any items that are regarded as necessary or useful to humanity but it is helpful to differentiate, as does Haggett (1975), between stocks and resources. He suggests that 'all the material components of the environment, including both mass and energy, both things biological and things inert can be described as total stock'. By contrast, resources are seen as a cultural concept, with a stock becoming a resource only when it is utilised by people to meet their needs for food or other purposes. Factors affecting this transformation might be technical, economic or social and clearly change through time. Thus many minerals have been transformed from stocks into resources in relatively recent times as people have perceived a use for them and developed a technology capable of providing them in a form in which they are needed at a cost that someone is prepared to pay.

Natural resources fall into two main groups: those that are not renewable and those that are. Non-renewable resources are those that cannot effectively be replaced once they have been worked out except in terms of a geological time-scale (though some can be recycled for future use). Most minerals belong to this first category and recent technological developments have been instrumental in these being used at an extremely rapid rate in modern times. Increasing demands from the more advanced industrial nations are the cause of most of this consumption and this has led to considerable concern about what might happen as living standards continue to rise in such countries, provoking even greater demands for resource development, and as developing countries endeavour to industrialise too. In an early but still widely quoted study commissioned by the 'Club of Rome', an international group concerned about problems of resource use, Meadows *et al.* (1972) calculated that in 1970 the population of the United States was consuming resources at a rate per capita seven times that of the world average. They also suggested in their report *The Limits to Growth* that as the rest of the world developed economically it was likely to follow a pattern of increasing output similar to that followed by the United States (see Fig. 4.5) and so also increase the rate of resource utilisation. This suggestion, of course, is based on assumptions concerning future development that may not ultimately

prove to be justified. Other nations may follow different patterns of economic development from that implied, while technological changes may substantially alter some current relationships between industrial output and resource utilisation (e.g. through recycling of some resources). The scale of the problem, however, is indicated by the fact that the quantity of most minerals used in the present century has far exceeded the total amounts of those minerals used in the whole of humanity's previous existence.

Renewable resources, as the name implies, are not used up in the same way. This category includes soil and biotic resources (i.e. resources derived directly from living things) that provide, directly or indirectly, much of the world's food supply and many raw materials for industrial processes. It also includes a group, sometimes separately described as flow resources, that includes running water, ocean tides, winds and solar energy. Although the resources in this category are renewable or re-usable in different ways or, in some cases (e.g. wind), available continuously but at a variable level, their economic value is clearly related to the level of technology and management skills of those wishing to use them. Most biotic resources can be utilised at such a rate that they are effectively destroyed. Examples include the rapid clearance of forest in areas such as Amazonia and much of western North America, and the overfishing of areas such as the North Sea in recent years. Soil resources can also be harmed by poor management. In many tropical areas, where shifting cultivation has traditionally been practised, fallow periods that allow for land to recover from cultivation have been progressively shortened in attempts to increase output, so soil quality has worsened. Over-grazing is another major problem in such areas – sometimes leading to desertification. In more developed countries, agricultural intensification in recent years has caused extensive soil erosion and the US Department of Agriculture has estimated that at the beginning of the 1990s the world was losing 24 billion tonnes of soil annually. Moderate to severe soil erosion was esti-

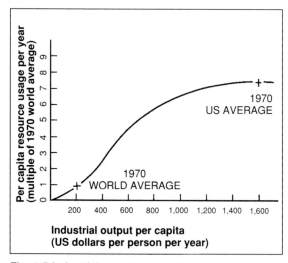

Fig. 4.5 Industrial output per capita and resource usage (after Meadows *et al.*, 1972). This postulated model suggests that as industrial output increases, non-renewable resource consumption rises rapidly, gradually levelling off at a high rate of consumption, as has happened in the United States. See text for comment.

mated to affect approximately 30% of the arable land in the USA and Western Europe and at least 40% of such land in Africa and Asia.

Technological innovation can greatly alter the value of flow resources. For example, the opening of the Rance power station in France in 1966 marked a major advance in the use of tidal energy, which had previously been used mainly for very small projects such as the operation of corn mills on the ebb tide. In a different way, supplies of running water can be greatly affected by human management systems. On the one hand, careful control of rates of flow by the construction of dams and irrigation systems can markedly improve the value of water resources as, for example, in Bali where intricate irrigation systems have been developed to provide three crops per year from spectacularly terraced padi fields. On the other hand, the consumption on a massive scale of groundwater supplies tapped through boreholes can seriously deplete groundwater reserves and so reduce availability of surface water supplies, a problem recently encountered in the area south of the River Humber largely as a result of increased water usage by industrial consumers in the Grimsby–Immingham area. People's quality of life and, indeed, their very survival are obviously related to the development of these different types of resources. It is also evident, however, that changes in technology may make 'new' resources available or may result in present resources being used in different ways from those now common. The scale of such changes is something we cannot truly comprehend – you can get some idea of the problem if you try to imagine a medieval peasant farmer envisaging the kind of technology that we almost take for granted today – yet it is something that any assessment of future development should take into account.

It is perhaps helpful at this stage to return to a consideration of the work of Meadows *et al.* (1972) in what is still probably the best known attempt to assess the world situation with regard to population growth and resource utilisation. In *The Limits to Growth*, they expressed particular concern about what they perceived to be the finite nature of the world's food supplies, the depleting reserves of non-renewable natural resources, and rapidly rising levels of pollution. Their major conclusions, based on the development of computer models, were these:

1 If the present growth trends in world population, industrialisation, pollution, food production and resource depletion continue unchanged, the limits to growth on this planet will be reached sometime within the next hundred years. The most probable result will be a rather sudden and uncontrollable decline in both population and industrial capacity.

2 It is possible to alter these growth trends and to establish a condition of ecological and economic stability that is sustainable far into the future. The state of global equilibrium could be designed so that the basic material needs of each person on Earth were satisfied and each person had an equal opportunity to realise his or her individual potential.

The first of these statements has been widely criticised, largely on the grounds that it is based on a range of assumptions and generalisations that are not considered to be valid. A review of the book in *The Economist*, March 1972, sums up the attitudes of many critics, suggesting that the authors have based their computer analysis on 'many dear, dead assumptions' especially in terms of assuming that existing exponential growth in resource use would continue but failing to make sufficient allowance for changes in technology that could affect resource availability and provision in many ways. In illustration of this criticism, *The Economist* article suggests:

'In 1872 any scientist could have proved that 1972's quantum of urban transport and travel within London was impossible (and therefore a city the size of London was impossible), because where were Londoners going to stable all the horses and how could they avoid being asphyxiated by the manure?'

Others have criticised the nature of the model in other ways, e.g. because of its very general nature and because of the lack of consideration of social variables.

The second statement raises various issues concerning the ways in which people can regulate the use of resources, and hints at the fact that access to the world's resources as a means of satisfying basic human needs is far from equitable at present and that changes are necessary if human beings are all to have the opportunity for full personal development.

Despite the various criticisms of *The Limits to Growth*, the issues raised by its authors are obviously still matters of concern. People everywhere have basic needs for food, water, fuel and shelter and in many parts of the world these are not being adequately met at present. The relationship between population size and natural resources is rarely simple. In the past, even where numbers have been low, resources have often been damaged or destroyed by poor management. In many areas today, ways of life are based on very high levels of resource usage, often coupled with high levels of wastage. Some poorer communities have major difficulties in meeting their basic needs for food and other commodities and yet are locked into a world trading system that encourages them to use their land and other resources to provide food and raw materials that mainly satisfy the demands of their more wealthy counterparts. Rapid exploitation of resources in some areas, especially within the tropics, is tending to destroy such resources without having a significant effect in improving the quality of life for most people who live in such areas. This kind of exploitation in some cases, as in the tropical rainforest areas of Amazonia, may also be resulting in increased pollution of the atmosphere and in a dramatic reduction in biological diversity as species unique to particular areas are destroyed, possibly in the process disposing of biotic resources with a potential to contribute to improvements in agriculture, health or industry of which we are not yet even aware. Against this kind of background, the likely population increases of the next century or so are seen by some people as a threat to the future with their potential for increased resource demands, while others argue that with better management of the world's resources and appropriate technological advances, the Earth is capable of supporting a much larger population than at present at a reasonable standard of living. The remainder of this chapter examines various issues relating to this situation.

The concept of optimum population

Many discussions of relationships between population and resources have involved reference to the concepts of optimum population, over-population and under-population. There is an attractive simplicity in the idea that for any area there is an optimum population (i.e. a total population that is the ideal size to live and work in such an area) and that a higher total population would result in that area being over-populated and a lower total in it being under-populated. Unfortunately, when considered in more depth, this concept is seen to be of much greater complexity. It is easy to appreciate the concept of a population optimum in a general way, but it is impossible to define it precisely in a manner that is universally acceptable, or to suggest a specific number that is the optimum population for a particular area. Moreover, it is clearly not realistic to consider an optimum population as a static feature, for changes in technology, as already suggested, can have a major impact on the capacity of a population to support itself at an acceptable level. For example, the application of modern technological methods to the tapping of underground water, oil and natural gas supplies in the Saharan region since 1950 could perhaps be seen as increasing the optimum population of the region by enabling food production to be increased in some areas and by providing new economic opportunities in others.

This kind of example suggests that measurement of the optimum population might have an economic basis. Indeed, the concept has most frequently been considered largely in economic terms as in Petersen's (1975) definition of optimum population as 'the number of people that, in a given natural, cultural and social environment, produces the maximum economic return'. But, as Petersen points out, this is not an entirely satisfactory definition. The basic size of a population is a very crude indicator of its economic potential, for the abilities, health and age structure of a population can greatly affect its value as a workforce. If we consider only age structure, it is obvious that a population with more than half its members aged over 60 or under 15 has a very different economic potential from one in which fewer than a third of the people are in these age categories. The 'maximum economic return' is also difficult to define. It has often been measured simply in terms of the Gross National Product (GNP) per capita (a measure that attempts to represent in monetary terms the total product of a country, including both goods and services). A high GNP does not, however, reflect a situation in which all members of a society necessarily obtain even the basic necessities of life. Many economists would argue that the 'maximum economic return' is not very meaningful unless some attention is also given to the spread of economic benefits throughout the population.

The relationship between demographic variables and the economy has been examined in some detail by Wrigley (1967, 1969) with regard to both primitive and more advanced societies. It is not possible to consider much of Wrigley's work in depth here but some aspects of it are particularly helpful in illustrating graphically the concept of an optimum population defined in economic terms. Wrigley developed a series of models based on presumed demographic changes in a society assumed to be at a comparatively primitive level of material culture in a situation where that culture is static 'so that it is not possible to secure a steady increase in the production of food in the community by taking advantage of technical advances in agriculture'. This implies that the population could not exceed a ceiling determined by the potential food production of the area at the stated level of material culture.

Wrigley suggests, however, that it is wrong to assume that the population would necessarily increase to that ceiling, arguing that an equilibrium level of population might be established at one of several points below the ceiling, in accordance with changing fertility and mortality levels. He indicates three possibilities (see Fig. 4.6) to illustrate this. In Fig 4.6a the population increases at a uniform rate until point A, with the levels of fertility and mortality remaining constant. Thereafter both mortality and fertility are affected as a critical population density is reached, with mortality increasing and fertility declining until at point B these two are in balance and the population neither rises nor falls. In Fig. 4.6b mortality changes in the same way as in the previous example, rising steadily beyond point A when the critical population density is reached, but fertility is affected much later and to a lesser extent. In this situation the population increases to C, a considerably higher point than B in Fig. 4.6a, before fertility and mortality are in balance. In Fig. 4.6c a further case is illustrated where the pattern of mortality change is again the same as in Fig. 4.6a but fertility declines much more rapidly beyond point A than in the two previous cases, so that fertility and mortality are in balance at a total well below that reached in Fig. 4.6a or 4.6b.

The final graph, Fig. 4.6d, shows the implications of these three situations in terms of living standards as indicated by real income per head. Clearly, given the assumptions of a limited resource base and a fixed level of material culture, there will be some population total at which real income per head will be at a maximum. Wrigley suggests that it is reasonable to suppose that mortality levels will begin to rise sometime *after* this optimum level has been reached. If the fertility and mortality levels intersect before mortality begins to increase then an optimum level of population might result, 'enjoying the highest standard of living possible in the cultural and environmental context of the day and place'. Points D, B and C in Fig. 4.6d all represent later stages of population growth than this optimum, with D (taken from Fig. 4.6c) representing a more advantageous equilibrium level of population than B (from Fig. 4.6a) and B a more advantageous equilib-

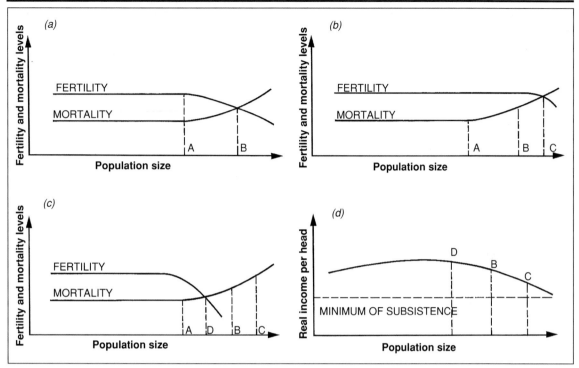

Fig. 4.6 Some simple models of population change.
Source: after Wrigley, 1967.

rium level than C (from Fig. 4.6b) – always assuming that the optimum population is that in which real incomes are at the highest level.

These models of demographic development are based on a series of stated assumptions and Wrigley goes on to examine a range of possibilities related to different assumptions and more complex situations (e.g. cases where the land area worked by a group is extended at a particular stage of development and different techniques are utilised to provide a more intensive use of resources). The introduction of such possibilities means that the population ceiling is no longer fixed and attempts to define an optimum population involve much more complex problems – even if such an optimum is considered capable of definition in terms of real incomes or some such economic measure.

Fundamental questions might be posed, how-

ever, concerning whether the concept of an optimum population should be seen solely in economic terms. Can a population be the optimum for an area, no matter what economic returns it achieves, if it is using up resources in such a way that it is causing massive pollution or depleting soil and biotic resources in a manner that is likely to cause problems for future populations? Is there a population level for an area at which social and psychological stresses become significant factors to be considered, as can happen with some animal populations? Or should the concept of optimum population be considered more in terms of Southwood's definition (quoted in Taylor, 1972): 'the optimum population ... is the maximum that can be maintained indefinitely without detriment to the health of individuals from pollution or from social or nutritional stress'?

Clearly, no simple definition of optimum population is likely to be entirely satisfactory and the terms under- and over-population should be used with care, if at all. These concepts are extremely complex, involving consideration of a wide variety of factors, many of which are difficult to assess objectively and may well change through time as a result of technological or cultural developments that are themselves difficult to anticipate. Despite this, many national population policies are implicitly based on the concept of an optimum population. Thus attempts to reduce birth rates in China (see Case Study 4A) imply that the Chinese government considers that either the country is over-populated now, or is likely to be so in future. Similarly, the opposition of some governments to family planning policies suggests that they may believe their countries to be under-populated, though their attitudes may also have religious and/or political overtones in some cases, as in Brazil.

Population and food supply

We have already suggested that the population/resource relationship that was uppermost in the mind of Malthus almost 200 years ago still gives rise to controversy and concern today. Food is one of the basic needs of people everywhere yet food supplies are still inadequate in many parts of the world – at least periodically – and food consumption varies greatly between different areas. Moreover, some people in even the richest countries are under-nourished. Figure 4.7 gives an indication of contrasts in food consumption between different countries, expressed in terms of calorie intake.

The basic calorie intake necessary for a person to live in normal health is a matter of disagree-

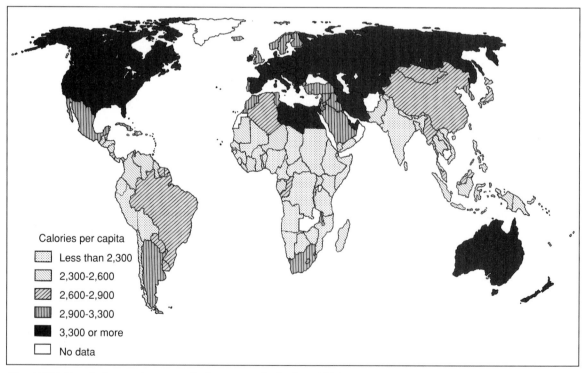

Calories per capita

- Less than 2,300
- 2,300-2,600
- 2,600-2,900
- 2,900-3,300
- 3,300 or more
- No data

Fig. 4.7 Daily calorie supply per capita by country in the late 1980s.
Source: World Bank Atlas, 1989.

ment between nutritionists and, of course, differs between individuals on the basis of such variables as age, physique, type of employment and general living habits. It is usual to suggest, however, that for most communities an average daily intake of at least 2,300 calories per capita is necessary for healthy life. Some experts would suggest a considerably higher figure. An examination of Fig. 4.7 makes it clear that many of the world's people live in countries where the average calorie intake was below 2,300 calories in the late 1980s and, even allowing for variations in consumption within individual countries, it is apparent that many people do not receive sufficient food for normal health to be maintained. The United Nations Food and Agricultural Organisation (FAO) recently estimated that one in every ten human beings suffers from chronic hunger, receiving fewer than 1,500 calories per day. Children under 10 years old make up 40% of those suffering from chronic hunger and one estimate suggests that as many as 40,000 children die every day from hunger or from disease related to hunger. Much publicity is given in the countries of the developed world to famine situations such as those that have affected Ethiopia, Sudan and other African countries on several occasions since the 1970s but it is important to recognise that, for many people, hunger is a continuing part of everyday life and in the words of Robinson (1989), 'Death from hunger is not a media event but a constant, unpublicised reality'.

The total number of people who are regularly undernourished is difficult to calculate. FAO estimates in the late 1980s suggested that perhaps 520–550 million people fell into that category but other organisations have suggested that the total may be considerably higher. While most of the nations with average daily calorie intakes per capita of under 2,300 are in Africa and it is in Africa that the worst levels of malnutrition are to be found, only some 30% of the world's undernourished people live in Africa; whereas approximately 55% are in Asia. FAO data suggest that India has a far larger number of undernourished people than any other country despite the massive increases in food output

associated with the technological changes of the so-called 'Green Revolution' that began in the mid-1960s. Annual production still fluctuates considerably but in a good year India has a surplus of food grains (over 24 million tonnes of wheat and rice in 1985, for example). Here, as in many other countries, people go hungry for reasons other than national food production shortages.

Indeed, the world produces enough grain in a normal year to provide every one of its inhabitants with about $1\frac{1}{2}$ times their basic calorie requirements – if it were distributed evenly. But, of course, it is not. About 40% of the world's grain is fed to livestock, much of it to provide food for the people of North America and Europe where calorie intakes are particularly high (see Fig. 4.7). It is sometimes suggested that dietary changes in such areas could lead to reductions in grain consumption on a scale sufficient to resolve most of the food shortage problems of other areas. While this may be true in theory, the situation is in reality much more complex. The fact that more food is produced or is available on the markets of the world does not mean that those most in need of extra food supplies will necessarily be able to obtain them. At the household or individual level, poverty is the basic cause of hunger. This may mean in some situations that families have insufficient land and other resources to produce the food they need to feed themselves. In other situations, it may mean they have insufficient income to buy the food they need. Often it is a combination of both.

Because population growth and hunger often occur together in a particular area, it has frequently been suggested that the first causes the second. It is perhaps more accurate to suggest that they are often linked by a complex web of factors, one of the most important of which is the insecurity brought about by poverty. Thus when parents are reliant on children for support in their old age and when they can expect that some of their children will die before reaching adulthood because of their poor living conditions or uncertain food supplies, they often seek what they see as the security of a large family and birth rates are high. In parts of the developing world where food supplies for poor families are more reliable and attempts have been made to provide effective social services that provide support in times of need, population growth has tended to decline. The state of Kerala in India provides one example of this with population growth rates there declining much more rapidly than in neighbouring states in the recent past. In the light of this kind of experience it is now widely argued that the best way to reduce population growth and to eliminate hunger is to combat poverty. We shall return to this theme later.

Food and health

One of the major consequences of food shortages in developing countries is the presence of nutritional diseases such as kwashiorkor (Fig. 4.8), beri-beri and pellagra. Children tend to be amongst the worst sufferers and many die from under-nourishment when still young, while those who survive may be permanently affected, either physically or mentally, as a result of dietary deficiencies in their early years. A growing body of evidence suggests that in periods of acute food shortage, of the kind suffered by several African countries since the 1970s, nutritional deficiencies can directly affect population change not only as a result of increasing death rates but also as a result of a decline in fertility through a reduction in the physiological capacity to conceive. Such changes could clearly be of major significance to particular communities in periods of prolonged or repeated food shortages.

As well as giving rise to specific diseases, under-nourishment makes individuals more susceptible to a range of other diseases. This is particularly true of many tropical areas where climatic conditions encourage insect vectors and where poor hygiene and limited medical facilities tend to make the problem worse. In such circumstances, diseases like malaria, typhoid, cholera and dysentery are common. Particular outbreaks of disease may be related to a complicated web of causes that include under-nourishment, contaminated food and/or water sup-

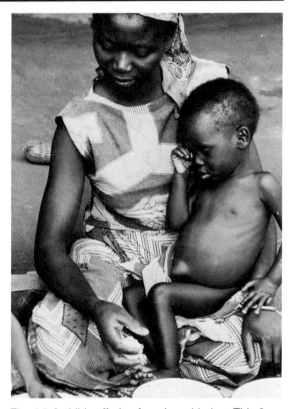

Fig. 4.8 A child suffering from kwashiorkor. This 2-year-old in Malawi was being fed on maize porridge, the staple diet in much of the country. He was so weak from under-nourishment that he was unable to stand. Recent research suggests that what were sometimes seen as purely nutritional diseases may have more complex origins. Kwashiorkor, a major killer disease of under-nourished children, is now thought to be associated with the eating of food contaminated by a fungus known as *Aspergillus flavus*. It is hoped that this discovery will help in developing treatment for the disease.

plies, poor medical facilities and general poverty. A major cholera outbreak in Peru and neighbouring countries in 1991, for example, mainly affected poor people with inadequate or marginally adequate calorie intakes, using contaminated food and water supplies resulting from a lack of basic hygiene, and with limited access to medical facilities. Ministry of Health instructions to boil all water for 10 minutes and not eat uncooked food, especially fish that was considered likely to be contaminated, were often ignored by those who felt they could not afford kerosene to heat water or cook food. Cholera gives rise to violent diarrhoea in which people can lose as much as 24 litres of body fluid in a day and death results from extreme dehydration leading to kidney and heart failure. Children are particularly vulnerable. Oral rehydration therapy is often successful in saving lives in such circumstances but, although this is relatively cheap and simple to administer, some Peruvians were unable to reach medical posts where this was available or did not realise how necessary it was.

The widespread prevalence of ill-health in tropical areas and in developing countries elsewhere is thought to have a major effect on the capacity of many people to work effectively. A low work input is likely to affect productivity and, where most of the population are farmers, can give rise to a shortage of food and hence to continuing under-nourishment and low resistance to disease. Thus a circular causation system can occur (see Fig. 4.9), aptly described by one writer as a 'misery-go-round'. It is extremely difficult for this circle to be broken in many communities and one of the major problems is that a worsening of the situation in any one element tends to have cumulative effects so that the total situation can also rapidly worsen.

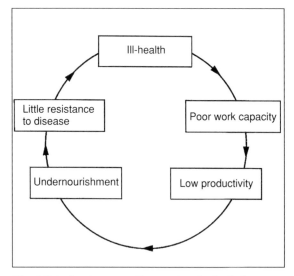

Fig. 4.9 A circular causation system typical of many developing countries.

Hunger, food production and food aid

As we have seen earlier, considerable progress has been made in recent times in reducing disease through medical programmes that have resulted in declining death rates. This, in turn, has often given rise to marked population growth that has increased demands for food. In general terms, the world's farmers have responded to these demands by increasing food production at a rapid rate, especially in the period between 1950 and 1980. On a world scale, grain production increased by 34% in the 1950s, 30% in the 1960s and 31% in the 1970s. These spectacular increases were based on such factors as new grain varieties, massive increases in fertiliser and pesticide inputs and dramatic changes in farming methods. In the 1980s production increased more slowly, by 17%, and some forecasts suggest that in the 1990s growth may fall to below 10%, well below likely increases in demand, though others are more optimistic.

Increases in production have varied considerably between different parts of the world during this period of expanding output and there has been varying success in meeting demand in the areas where production took place (see Exercise 4.1). For example, food production in Asia increased at an annual rate of 3.5% between 1960 and 1985 while population increased on average at only 2.1%. In Africa, by contrast, food production increased at 2.0% and population by 2.8% in the same period. Thus in several African countries food production per capita showed a decline in this period. Even in Asia uneven distribution of food meant that not everyone benefited from the overall increases in per capita production. Additionally, as production varies from year to year so will problems of meeting food needs. In the difficult year of 1987, for example, 25 out of 43 African states for which data were available had a per capita production below the average for 1979–81, as had 9 out of 28 Asian and 17 out of 23 Latin American countries.

While problems of hunger and famine in developing countries often dominated news-

Exercise 4.1

World food production (by regions)

a) Examine the information concerning food production provided in the table below. Describe the regional variations highlighted by the table and suggest why such variations have occurred.

b) Discuss how changes in output in North America and Europe would be likely to affect food producers and consumers in other parts of the world.

c) Outline the major problems faced by one selected developing country in its attempts to increase food production per capita and explain how such problems have been (or might be) overcome.

Indices of food production by regions (1979–81 = 100)

For each region A = total food production
B = food production per capita

		1980	1981	1982	1983	1984	1985	1986	1987	1988	1989
World	A	99.2	102.4	105.8	105.7	111.2	114.1	116.1	116.3	117.6	121.2
	B	99.3	100.6	102.2	100.2	103.7	104.6	104.6	103.0	102.3	103.6
Africa	A	99.9	103.1	104.5	101.5	103.3	111.8	116.6	114.9	119.5	121.7
	B	99.9	100.1	98.5	92.9	91.8	96.5	97.7	93.4	94.3	93.2
North & Central America	A	96.1	105.3	105.3	91.8	103.4	108.6	105.2	102.8	96.6	106.9
	B	96.1	103.8	102.3	88.0	97.7	101.3	96.8	93.3	86.5	94.5
South America	A	99.6	104.1	108.1	105.6	109.3	115.6	113.4	118.3	125.1	125.2
	B	99.6	101.8	103.4	98.9	100.1	103.6	99.5	101.7	105.3	103.3
Asia	A	99.9	103.7	107.6	114.4	119.6	123.0	126.2	127.9	133.0	136.2
	B	99.7	101.8	103.6	108.1	111.0	112.1	112.9	112.4	114.7	115.4
Europe	A	101.1	99.6	104.8	103.3	109.7	107.4	110.0	109.6	109.0	108.8
	B	101.0	99.2	104.0	102.2	108.3	105.7	108.0	107.2	106.2	105.7
Oceania (incl. Australasia)	A	94.7	100.8	94.0	110.0	106.4	107.2	108.2	106.0	110.7	106.8
	B	94.7	99.2	90.9	104.8	100.0	99.3	98.7	95.4	98.2	93.5
Former USSR	A	99.6	97.4	105.0	110.0	110.6	110.3	118.3	119.0	118.8	122.8
	B	99.6	96.6	103.3	107.2	106.8	105.5	112.1	111.6	110.3	113.0

Source: FAO Yearbook (Production), 1990.

paper headlines in the 1970s and 1980s, in Western Europe and North America food surpluses rather than shortages were seen as a problem. In the European Community (EC), for example, modernised farming methods made substantial production increases possible and EC rules encouraged farmers to maintain high levels of production by offering them the opportunity to sell some of their products into state intervention stores at guaranteed prices rather than having to sell them cheaply on the open market. As a result, so-called 'food mountains' of stored products such as cereals, butter, milk-powder and beef, and even a wine 'lake' had developed by the early and mid-1980s. Great publicity was given to these in periods of famine such as that of 1984–85 in Ethiopia and other African countries with pressures being exerted on the EC to use some of its food surplus to provide 'food aid' to people in famine areas.

Food aid has been a significant feature of world trade since well before the 1980s, however. The USA has had a food aid programme since the mid-1950s and the EC since the late 1960s. Motives for providing food aid have varied and have often been marked by self-interest on the part of the donors, perhaps most notably as a means of maintaining political influence in recipient countries. Food aid falls into three main categories. *Programme aid*, usually over half the total, goes direct to governments who may use it in various ways, e.g. selling it on local markets or using it as payment in kind to government employees. *Project aid* is, as the name suggests, related to specific projects and may be used, for example, on 'food for work' schemes where workers are paid in food rather than money for work on projects such as road or reservoir construction, or as one element in schemes designed to improve nutrition and health. *Emergency aid* tends to receive most publicity, with food aid being provided after disasters or during periods of famine, but this normally accounts for the smallest proportion of food aid. In 1987–88, for example, emergency food aid amounted to only 19% of world food aid, with programme aid accounting for 54% and project aid 27% of all food aid.

There has been widespread criticism of food aid. Its use as a means of securing political influence has been greatly resented but it has also been blamed for having adverse effects on agriculture in recipient countries by lowering prices for food on local markets (and so reducing profits made by indigenous farmers) and by lessening the likelihood of governments carrying out reforms in indigenous agriculture. In areas where food aid or cheap food imports become a regular feature of a country's economy this may cause further problems for local farmers and governments. Nigeria and Indonesia, for example, now import wheat to supply demands for bread that developed as an urban elite was created during and after the colonial period although other grain crops can be more easily produced locally. Changes in recent years have seen attempts to use food aid more sensitively and to link it effectively with general development programmes in agriculture. 'Triangular' food aid operations have also become more common whereby, for example, a European donor might pay for surplus food in one developing country to be used to overcome shortages in a neighbouring country instead of supplying food aid direct from Europe. Thus Kenyan maize has been used to help famine situations in Mozambique and rice from Thailand provided for Vietnam. Such triangular operations help farmers in developing countries by improving regional trade and may also mean that food provided in an emergency reaches those in need more quickly and is more suited to local diets. Similar operations have also been helpful within particular countries, as in Sudan where aid agencies have bought food from farmers in one part of the country to supply those in shortage areas elsewhere in the country. Such operations may encourage farmers in developing countries to increase output whereas other forms of food aid may discourage production by lowering prices.

A decline in the late 1980s in the size of the European and American 'food mountains' reflected to some extent deliberate attempts to reduce over-production and stored surpluses in Europe and North America and pressure from environmental groups concerned about high levels of fertiliser and pesticide use and resultant pollution. Other factors affecting the situation have been the continual rise in consumption (see Fig. 4.10) and some particularly poor harvests resulting from droughts and crop failures in several areas, such as the drought that affected many North American wheat-producing areas in 1988. Between 1987 and 1989, the world used about 150 million more tonnes of grain than it produced (roughly equivalent to half the US annual production), giving rise to some forecasts of major food supply problems in the near future. Most commentators saw this as only a temporary phenomenon based on short-term fluctuations, and efforts to reduce output continue. This kind of situation does, however, focus attention on the potential of populations in developing countries already affected by food shortages to improve their own food supplies and ensure that they reach those in need.

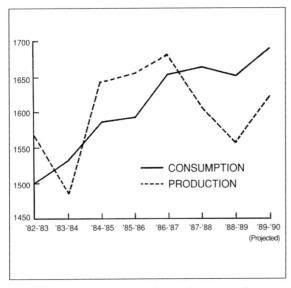

Fig. 4.10 World food production and consumption (wheat, rice and coarse grains, million tonnes) during the 1980s. Note the steady rise in consumption in comparison with the marked fluctuations in production during this period.
Source: US Department of Agriculture.

Population and food supplies in developing countries

The most obvious way of ensuring food supplies in developing countries is by increasing food production within these countries themselves. Some of the problems associated with this have already been mentioned but it is useful to examine the agricultural situation in such countries in a little more detail, as this is clearly so crucial an element in world food supplies. The use of terms like 'developing' or 'Third World' countries (the latter a term coined in the 1950s to contrast such countries with the other two 'worlds' of the 'western democracies' mainly situated in North America and Western Europe and the then communist world of Eastern Europe and the USSR), tends to suggest a degree of uniformity that can be misleading. Obviously there are many differences between developing countries in terms of their physical character, social organisation, levels of income and political attitudes, and these differences are perhaps tending to become more marked as economic and social development occurs at different rates in different areas.

Nevertheless, there are also some broad similarities. Many such countries, for example, are characterised by widespread poverty; relatively low levels of technological development, education and literacy; limited development of modern manufacturing industry and related low levels of energy consumption; and a poorly developed transport system in comparison with the more developed countries. Many, too, have a high proportion of their working population in agriculture (sometimes over 70% of the total) though this is usually decreasing. Agriculture is also often affected by particular physical difficulties, especially in tropical areas where soils are often low in plant nutrients, climates unreliable and disease widespread.

Traditionally, agriculture in developing countries has tended to be labour-intensive with little use made of machinery. Seeds have been of low quality, fertilisers little used and attempts at pest and disease control limited. The labour force, in addition to being affected by frequent ill-health (see earlier), has often also been limited in quality by low levels of literacy, lack of technical knowledge and poverty, which impose constraints even when the knowledge needed to make improvements is available. Organisational problems have also limited agricultural development, ranging from the small size and fragmented nature of many landholdings to storage difficulties, lack of rural credit facilities and poor marketing systems.

In recent years, most developing countries have undergone agricultural changes of one kind or another. Many have undertaken some kind of land redistribution or land consolidation programmes. The former have often been more significant in terms of social and political development than in economic terms and the value of land consolidation schemes such as those in Kenya in the 1950s and 1960s, though probably helping to increase production, have not always been easy to assess because political and other economic changes have been occurring simultaneously with them. In any case, re-organisation of landholdings is perhaps most significant when seen as part of a broader suite of changes as in China (see Case Study 4A).

In Latin America, several countries have achieved moderate but steady increases in food production per capita mainly by increasing the area under cultivation in sparsely populated parts of the interior. Thus between the mid-1960s and the mid-1980s, cropland in Latin America increased by about one-third and cereal output by just over 40%. In the same period in Asia cropland increased by less than 5% but cereal production expanded by almost 80%. This rapid increase in agricultural production was largely due to the so-called 'Green Revolution' involving Western-based agricultural techniques, especially the use of new high-yielding varieties (HYVs) of wheat and rice. The new varieties offer the twin advantages of higher yields than traditional varieties and a shorter growing season, so that double-cropping has become possible in several areas.

The adoption of HYVs, beginning in the mid-1960s, has thus resulted in major increases in output and has helped in much of south and east Asia to increase food production at a rate above that of population growth. The impact of the HYVs has been far from uniform, however. In India, for example, in the wheat-producing district of Ludhiana in the Punjab, where most cultivators had holdings in excess of 6 hectares, the benefits of HYVs were apparent from the 1960s onwards with rapid increases in production and individual wealth, though some smaller landholders benefited only marginally. In many rice-growing districts, where numerous landholdings were too small to be economically viable (often less than one hectare) farmers found it difficult to fund the Green Revolution because HYVs required more expensive inputs than more traditional varieties in the form of additional fertilisers and pesticides and carefully regulated water supplies. Those with access to larger areas of land thus tended to benefit most and also quickly took advantage of mechanisation of production, so that in many areas although production increased and average income levels rose, there was greater inequality.

In the north-west of Peninsular Malaysia, the development of rice production under the Muda Scheme (see Fig. 4.11) saw output increase by 140% between 1966 and 1974. This was made possible by the widespread adoption of double-cropping using HYVs with their shorter growing season. The scheme also involved major investment, funded largely by the World Bank and the Malaysian government, to provide reliable water supplies for irrigating a second annual crop, training and education for farmers, an efficient advisory service, better banking and credit facilities, improved marketing systems, a good transport infrastructure, and various kinds of subsidies to provide cheaper agricultural inputs and maintain high prices for the rice produced. In the Muda area, formerly an area of widespread poverty, living standards rose considerably and the number of households below the official poverty line halved between 1972 and 1982, though about 30% of families in the area still fell into that category and an estimated 7% were worse off in the early 1980s than they had been when the scheme

Fig. 4.11 Harvesting rice on the Muda Scheme, north-west Malaysia. This photograph was taken in the early period of the 'Green Revolution'. It indicates the intensive labour input needed for harvesting which, like transplanting, was traditionally undertaken by women in this area. Double-cropping, although increasing incomes, also increased the pressures on many women already burdened with heavy domestic and agricultural duties. Mechanisation, especially the introduction of combine harvesters after 1977, reduced the demand for labour, freeing many women from a major work burden but also often adversely affecting their incomes and encouraging many younger women to seek new forms of employment in the growing urban areas. In this and in many other ways, the Green Revolution often brought about a major upheaval in people's lifestyles.

began. Although the scheme has been criticised because benefits that accrued were not evenly shared (and it is clearly necessary to endeavour to resolve the problems of those who remain poor in this area), it is worth emphasising that over 90% of the population in the area would appear to have benefited economically from the scheme.

Many early assessments of the Green Revolution were highly critical (e.g. Frankel, 1971). It was suggested that benefits accrued almost entirely to more wealthy farmers able to afford the range of inputs required to guarantee high yields. It was noted that in several areas landlessness increased amongst the poor as larger landowners chose to work their own land rather than rent it out and to acquire more land where this was possible. Increasing inequality was emphasised rather than improved living standards. More recent analyses (e.g. Farmer, 1986; Rigg, 1989) have often taken a more favourable view of the changes, suggesting that some of the earlier criticisms were based on exaggerated expectations and that, as time has passed, poorer, smaller landholders have frequently followed the example of richer farmers in reaping the benefits of the Green Revolution. Government extension schemes have often helped in this. Rigg suggests that variations in adoption of the new techniques are more marked between regions than within them, relating this to issues of land availability and environmental conditions. Referring to Boserup's theory that farmers are more likely to innovate when they are under pressure from population growth, he suggests that HYVs are more likely to be adopted when land is in short supply and so pressure to increase yields is high. Recent evidence also suggests that in several areas inputs of fertiliser and pesticides are now highest on the smaller farms and Rigg again suggests that this may reflect the fact that those working such farms are often under the greatest pressure to increase yields. Whatever problems may have resulted from the Green Revolution in certain areas of Asia, the overall increases in food supply have certainly benefited many in this region and it seems probable that without it much greater problems in resolving the population–resource balance would have occurred.

The increased food production of many Asian countries and the more moderate increases in Latin America have not generally been matched in Africa where food output per head declined in the 1970s and 1980s in a situation where food production faced severe problems and population continued to rise rapidly in many areas. Some countries, notably Ethiopia (see Case Study 4B), Somalia, Sudan, Angola and Mozambique have seen agricultural efforts repeatedly hampered by civil war. Political mismanagement has affected several other states, with agricultural development rarely given a high priority even where most of the population are directly dependent upon it. Environmental problems, especially severe droughts in sub-Saharan Africa, have resulted in major famines, particularly in the countries also affected by political strife. At the same time, desertification and deforestation have increased, largely because of poor land management and the lack of positive policies to help the growing number of poor people living on desert and forest margins, leaving a legacy of even more difficult environmental conditions for future generations.

There have been few attempts in Africa to develop grain-production systems similar to those brought about by the Green Revolution in Asia. The introduction of HYVs of wheat or rice has been limited by the paucity of effective irrigation systems and the accompanying need for governmental assistance through funding of training schemes, infrastructural improvements, marketing facilities and the like. There has been some improvement in maize yields brought about by the use of hybrid maize varieties in Kenya, Zimbabwe and one or two other areas but attempts to develop higher-yielding strains of other traditional food crops in Africa have not as yet had much success and have tended to take a low priority in world research.

Finally, perhaps more than in any other continent, the production of food in Africa – like so many other tasks – is in the hands of women and this has rarely been acknowledged in agricultural modernisation or training schemes. Political changes as well as modifications of economic and social organisation are needed if present food supply problems are not to worsen in many African countries – but it is important to remember that change is needed outside Africa too, for example in the attitudes of developed countries to their relationships with the developing world. The relationships between population and food supplies are clearly dependent on a very complex range of issues. The final part of this chapter examines three significant current issues in a little more depth.

Some current background issues

There is clearly no simple solution to many of the problems involved in feeding the world's people. Any survey of the kind attempted in this chapter must inevitably be incomplete and to some extent over-simplified, with certain background issues of considerable significance in the changing pattern of relationships between population and food supplies being touched upon only incidentally. Some relatively brief further comments on three disparate areas of current concern – debt problems in the developing world, female–male inequalities, and rising levels of pollution – may help to emphasise the complexity of these relationships.

Within the range of contacts between developed and developing countries that influence food production in the latter, concerns about trade (involving issues such as commodity prices and restrictions by developed countries on their imports from developing countries) and aid (whether as food or in other forms), have long loomed large. To these concerns has recently been added the issue of debt. The debt problems of many developing countries had their origins in the 1970s and early 1980s when 'Western' banks and international lending agencies made large loans, initially at low rates of interest, to many governments in the developing world which were attempting to expand their economies and improve social provision through investment in industry, agriculture, health, education and the like. Massive rises in oil prices in the 1970s caused further borrowing by non-oil producers and, as world recession gave rise to falling commodity prices and higher interest rates in the late 1970s and 1980s, debt burdens increased. Within 20 years the total debts of developing countries increased approximately 10-fold (see Fig. 4.12).

During the 1980s, debt burdens were a major factor behind the stagnation of the economies of many such countries, with investment in economic development and in social services such as health and education often declining drastically. The impact on food production has varied but many problems have been created by such factors as falling government investment in agriculture, affecting subsidies to farmers for seeds, fertilisers, and pesticides as well as many planned development projects and training schemes; attempts to encourage production of export crops to pay off debt interest rather than

food crops for home needs; and falling health standards that can result in lower productivity. Lower health and education standards may also have affected the success of family planning schemes. Attempts have been made by lending agencies to ease repayment situations or even write off loans but there is little evidence to suggest that the debt burden will be removed from developing countries in the near future. Their efforts to increase food production and improve the living standards of their people will almost inevitably be constrained by this (see Exercise 4.2).

This situation may well impinge more heavily on women than on men in developing countries if past experience is repeated. The United Nations *Human Development Report 1990* states that:

'Women have shouldered a large part of the adjustment burden of developing countries in the 1980s. To make up for lost family income, they have increased production for home consumption, worked longer hours, slept less and often eaten less – substantial costs of structural adjustment that have gone largely unrecorded.'

It seems unlikely that this situation will change significantly for the better in the 1990s. Gender inequality is apparent in many aspects of life in the developing world, usually to a greater degree than in developed countries. For example, despite the fact that higher female literacy is now generally acknowledged to be associated with lower infant mortality, better family nutrition and reduced population growth rates, female literacy rates in the developing world average less than three-quarters of male rates and fall well below half the male rate in some countries (e.g. Chad, Afghanistan, and Oman).

Harrison (1987) has emphasised how the low status of women in much of Africa aggravates the difficulties involved in food production. Work tasks have traditionally been segregated on the basis of gender in most communities, with women doing much of the heavy work. In agriculture, women are estimated to do 70% of the hoeing and weeding, 60% of the harvesting,

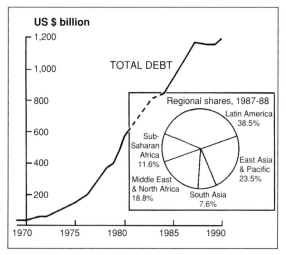

Fig. 4.12 The debts of developing countries, 1970–90.
Source: United Nations Development Programme, *Human Development Report 1990.*

Exercise 4.2

International debt

Examine the table below concerning the international debts of selected countries of the developing world.

Country	Population estimate, mid–1990 (millions)	Natural increase rate, *c.* 1990 (%)	Total debt outstanding, 1988 (US$bn)	Ratio of debt to GNP, 1987 (as %)	Ratio of debt interest to value of exports, goods & services, 1987 (as %)
	(1)	(2)	(3)	(4)	(5)
Bolivia	7.3	2.6	5.7	133.7	44.4
Brazil	150.4	1.9	120.1	39.4	28.3
Chile	13.2	1.7	20.8	124.1	27.0
Costa Rica	3.0	2.5	4.8	115.7	17.5
Ecuador	10.7	2.5	11.0	107.4	32.7
Ivory Coast	12.6	3.7	14.2	143.6	19.7
Jamaica	2.4	1.7	4.5	175.9	14.2
Mexico	88.6	2.4	107.4	77.5	28.1
Morocco	25.6	2.6	22.0	132.4	17.3
Philippines	66.1	2.6	30.2	86.5	18.7
Venezuela	19.6	2.3	35.0	94.5	21.9

Sources: Columns (1) & (2) *1990 World Population Data Sheet*, Population Reference Bureau, Inc. Columns (3), (4) and (5) World Bank's World Debt Tables (in R. Evans, 1989).

a) Comment on the patterns of debt indicated by the data provided.

b) Suggest what influence the patterns of debt indicated are likely to have on:

i) any attempts to increase agricultural production in the countries concerned; and

ii) relationships between population growth and food supply.

80% of the work involved in transporting and storing crops, and 90% of food processing. In eastern and southern Africa, as many as half the households may have a single woman or the wife of a migrant worker as their head. Such women do virtually all the farm work with the aid of their children. If firewood is in short supply and water sources distant, women may also be required to spend an hour or more each day collecting firewood (with loads weighing up to 500 kg) and, in some cases, two or three hours fetching water. Providing essential daily needs of fuel and water may use up 400–500 calories a day out of an energy intake that is already inadequate and this can be a major contributor to malnutrition problems. As fuelwood and water become increasingly scarce, a range of other problems may develop (see Exercise 4.3).

Exercise 4.3

Environmental degradation cycle

1 Examine the diagram of a degradation cycle provided below. Discuss what this suggests about the effects of increasingly scarce supplies of fuelwood and water in a developing country on:
a) the economic activities of women
b) the social and economic situation of families

c) health
d) the environment.

2 Make a critical assessment of the diagram, suggesting any modifications you think might be appropriate.

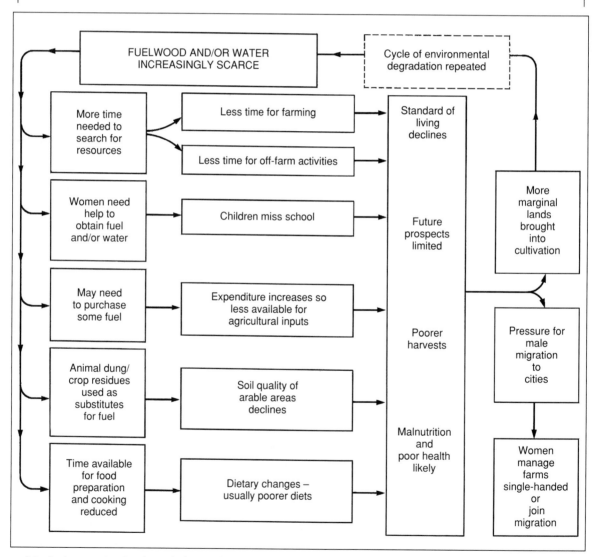

A typical example of a degradation cycle originating from scarcity of fuelwood and/or water in a developing country.
Source: adapted from FAO, 1989.

Although women have such a major input into farming activities, men usually control farm planning. Women often have little say in how money is spent on farm inputs or whether it is used in this way at all. Men frequently give priority to cash crops (and receive the income from these to use as they wish) rather than to subsistence food crops that would better serve the needs of their wives and families. Women, too, have rarely been much involved in training schemes until relatively recently. Increasingly the formation of women's groups and their involvement in land conservation or similar schemes in countries such as Kenya is demonstrating the potential for agricultural improvement that can be released by their fuller involvement, though there is still great scope for further developments of this kind.

Many more changes are needed, however, if the role of women is to be properly acknowledged and the enormous burden of domestic work imposed on them at present is to be significantly reduced. Changes in traditional male attitudes, improved educational and training opportunities for women, the development of easier access to fuelwood through tree-planting schemes, the provision of more fuel-efficient stoves and better food-processing equipment, the development of improved water supplies, and a better transport technology to carry water where this is still necessary – all these could help to open up new opportunities for women in Africa and other areas of the developing world and in so doing also probably increase food production and lower population growth rates.

A very different issue from those discussed so far in this section relates to the concern about environmental pollution. This concern has increased considerably since the 1972 report of the 'Club of Rome', which emphasised the need for sustainable development (i.e. development that meets the needs of the present without compromising the ability of future generations to meet their needs). Much attention has been focused on ways in which both industry and agriculture are adversely affecting the environment. In the developed world, recent growth in

agricultural output has been achieved largely through massive increases in the use of fertilisers and pesticides that have eventually penetrated and polluted water supplies. Current attempts to reduce agricultural production in North America and Europe are motivated in part by a desire to limit such damage in future. Concern about similar developments in the developing world has to date been more muted but in a situation where up to 40% of food production in some countries is lost to weeds, pests and disease, where increases in output are desperately being sought, and where environmental awareness is increasing, this is likely to be an issue of growing importance. Many developing countries have also tried to increase food production through extending irrigation. Today about one-fifth of the world's agricultural land is irrigated, accounting for almost three-quarters of the global use of fresh water (*Third World Planning Review*, 1989). Sadly, many irrigation projects have had undesirable side-effects, in particular through salinisation and water-logging of irrigated areas, rendering agriculture in such areas difficult or impossible. About a fifth of the irrigated lands of India and Pakistan and perhaps as much as a quarter of Iraq's irrigated areas suffer in this way.

Alongside attempts to intensify agricultural production by the use of fertilisers, pesticides, irrigation, etc. have been attempts to extend the area under agriculture. This is especially marked in tropical areas at present and although sometimes aimed at increasing subsistence food production, it is more frequently directed towards satisfying demands from consumers in more affluent areas. The development of new farming areas has often involved clearance of tropical rainforest as in Indonesia to produce palm oil, or for cattle-ranching in Brazil. Such development may lead indirectly to some increase in food supplies for people in Indonesia or Brazil but has been criticised because, amongst other things, clearance of such areas by burning is a significant contributor to atmospheric pollution. The emission of carbon dioxide, the major source of global warming via the so-called 'greenhouse effect', is one result of such burning and the longer-term effects of this on world farming are a matter of current debate (see, for example, deFreitas, 1991) but may have considerable effects on world food supplies in future.

These three brief examples, as suggested earlier, do little more than hint at the complexities of likely future social, economic, political and environmental influences on world population and food supply. They do, perhaps, serve to emphasise the danger of suggesting simplistic solutions to any problems arising from attempts to feed the world's people.

Population and food supply in China

The year 1949 marked a major turning point in China's development, as a new, communist government initiated a whole range of social, economic and political changes destined to bring about radical alterations to the lives of people in the world's most populous country. We shall focus here on changes in agricultural and population policies but it is important to remember that these form part of a much wider suite of changes. Until 1949 most agricultural land was in the hands of a relatively small number of people, with most Chinese farmers renting their land at crippling cost, often paying more than half their harvests as rent in kind. Farmers struggled on from year to year with inefficient methods, little equipment, poor seeds and few incentives to improve the land they worked. With a population of some 500 million, 80% of whom lived in rural areas, the new govern-

ment of China faced problems that many thought were insuperable. Most notable of these was the basic problem of adequately feeding this large and growing population.

Within a decade, major agricultural reforms took place. First, land was taken from existing landlords and redistributed so that all heads of families in each rural area held similar amounts of land. Though owning their own land was seen by many rural Chinese as the fulfilment of their dreams, this redistribution solved few agricultural problems and, as it neared completion in 1953, other changes leading to a more 'socialist' form of agriculture were already under way. These occurred at different rates in different areas but generally moved through a series of stages progressively involving: joining together to work individual landholdings through the pooling of labour, equipment and draught animals in *mutual aid teams*; working the land as a unit through the inclusion of landholdings in the pooling system but with some recognition of private ownership in that people's incomes were related to their inputs of land, equipment and animals as well as labour in *elementary co-operatives*; and eventually moving to a stage where all the means of production – land, animals and equipment – were collectively owned and payment was solely in terms of labour inputs in *advanced co-operatives*. By 1957 about 90% of Chinese farms were advanced co-operatives with all land in them being co-operatively owned and farmed except for members' small-holdings on which they could grow a few vegetables and raise one or two pigs and some poultry. There was, inevitably, some opposition to these changes but re-organisation appears to have led to increased production and this, together with strong government propaganda, helped to limit such opposition. Official Chinese figures for 'food grain' production (i.e. for most basic food crops expressed in terms of grain equivalents) showed an increase from 160 to 200 million tonnes for the period 1953–57 and although, like much statistical data emanating from China, these figures may not be entirely accurate, most experts agree that there was a substantial increase in that period.

The advanced co-operatives, usually involving 100 to 200 families, were run by elected management committees and were concerned almost entirely with agriculture. In April 1958 one group of co-operatives combined to form a much larger unit, later to be called a *commune*. By December 1958, 700,000 advanced co-operatives had been re-organised into about 26,500 communes. Communes took over responsibility for all economic activity, not just agriculture, as well as for education, social welfare and local government. Usually involving 2,000 to 12,000 families, communes were subdivided into production brigades of some 150 to 500 families and these, in turn, were subdivided into production teams of about 15 to 30 families (often corresponding to a small village). Strong control was exercised by the state over all aspects of production, and at each level of the hierarchy production quotas had to be met.

The introduction of communes coincided with the 'Great Leap Forward' of 1958–60, a period of rapid, often ill-founded, social and economic changes that was followed between 1960 and 1962 by a series of droughts and floods that induced a massive famine. Jowett (1986) has estimated that China's population fell by 13.5 million in 1960 and 1961 in the face of this disaster and it seems unlikely that food production rose above 1957 levels until about 1965. Surplus labour from the communes was used, however, to develop irrigation schemes, communications, schools, clinics, etc. and these were the basis for many later improvements in production and living standards.

In spite of the further upheaval caused by the so-called 'Cultural Revolution' (1966–76) with its anti-capitalist political campaigns and frequently mis-guided interference in agricultural production systems, total food grain production increased by over 30% in the decade following 1965, i.e. from about 210 to 280 million tonnes. In the same period, population appears to have increased by some 27% from an estimated 725 to 920 million, though it must be remembered that all these figures are subject to some doubt. Communes in some cases were extremely successful, increasing production through better organisation of labour, mechanisation, more scientific farming and improved irrigation. Others were less effective because of poor policies (e.g. attempting to grow grain in areas unsuited to it; restricting the planting of vegetables and fruit in some areas where there were good local markets for such products; and forbidding the marketing of surpluses for cash). Many such policies were based on an antipathy to any kind of 'capitalist approach' and even private ownership of a few hens or a pig was often criticised during the Cultural Revolution.

Fears of a slowing rate of increase in output, opposition to the constraints of the commune system and changes in political leadership led to rapid agricultural changes after 1978. Since then family farming under the contract or responsibility system has largely replaced collective farming, with the communes' administrative role being taken over by townships. In general, families have been allocated land on a lease of 15 years or more. In return they have to sell to the state at a fixed price an agreed quantity of grain or other crops but can dispose of any output above their quota as they wish. The state has facilitated the development of trade by abandoning most of its monopolies in agricultural produce, and local markets have been encouraged. The effects of these new policies have been variable, with farms near to urban markets perhaps benefiting most, but production has risen considerably with food grain production exceeding 400 million tonnes by the mid-1980s. Living standards have improved for many rural dwellers and many new rural enterprises based on trade or manufacturing have come into being with an estimated 60 million people now employed in rural industry. Despite this last development, it is often suggested that perhaps 35–40% of the farm labour force (about 150 million people) are surplus to requirements and the size of the Chinese rural population in relation to employment possibilities is a matter of major concern. Food grain production is forecast to reach 500 million tonnes by the turn of the century but some stagnation of output in the late 1980s has caused concern and led to suggestions of further reforms, including increases in farm size, greater specialisation and mechanisation, and a reduction in the labour force per farm. This has again emphasised the significance of the continued population growth of the country.

Between 1949 and 1990 China's population more than doubled, from 540 to 1,134 million. With an annual increase of some 17 million by 1990, it is perhaps not surprising that China's population policies have changed from optimistic, pro-natalist approaches in the 1950s, implying that China could feed her population however rapidly it increased, to the strongly anti-natalist one-child-per-family policy of the 1980s and 1990s. In this period, as Jowett (1989b) has indicated, China appears to have moved through the demographic

transition (see Fig. 4.13). Major improvements in food output and distribution, sanitation and medical care helped to reduce mortality, especially of children, quite dramatically from about 38 to 18 per thousand between 1949 and 1957. The famine of the early 1960s dramatically increased mortality, especially amongst the young, and also had a major effect on fertility with the pre-famine number of births almost halved in 1961. A brief post-famine baby boom in 1963–65 when food supplies returned to normal was followed by a marked reduction in birth rates which more recently have fluctuated at about half the level of the early 1950s. In the same period mortality rates have declined and then levelled off at below 10% (see Fig. 4.13).

Urban fertility declined first, in the 1960s, and rural birth rates fell in the 1970s under strong government encouragement both through publicity, stressing maternal and child health benefits as well as economic and ecological advantages, and through greatly expanded, community-based, family planning services. The slogan 'later, longer, fewer' implying later marriage, a longer interval between births and fewer children, was widely used and by the end of the 1970s later marriages,

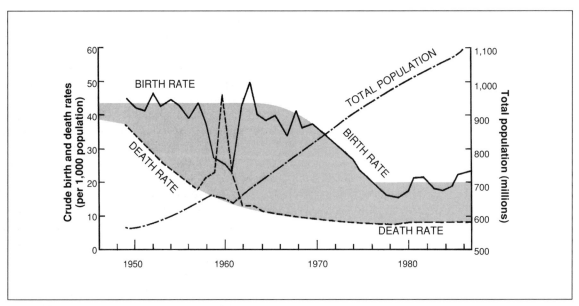

Fig. 4.13 Demographic transition in China, 1949–87. The data on which this diagram is based were calculated by the US Bureau of Census because original Chinese data (especially in the 1950s) were considered unreliable.
Source: Jowett, 1989b.

the use of modern contraceptives and widespread abortion had greatly reduced fertility. These changes were accompanied by improvements in health, education, standards of living and an improved status for women that also played a substantial part in the fertility decline. A more distinctively Chinese feature has been the way in which the government 'socialised' decisions concerning age of marriage, size of family, etc. so that individual couples have been pressurised by their community into accepting officially promoted norms. This has been even more marked since 1979.

Despite the substantial success of family planning policies in the 1970s, the youthful population structure seemed certain to result in very substantial increases if further action was not taken. In 1979 a policy of one-child families was introduced, offering specific incentives for parents only having one child and penalties for those who have more than two children. Much-publicised 'Glory Certificates' entitled a couple and their child to various financial, employment, educational and other benefits in exchange for a promise to have no further children after the first-born. By raising the proportion of one-child families and preventing families from having more than two children, the government hoped to reduce the natural increase rate to zero by the year 2000 and avoid the population growing beyond 1,200 million. The single-child policy has had mixed success, however, and it is now clear that population will continue to grow well into the twenty-first century and probably exceed 1,500 million before 2025.

In some urban areas during the late 1980s over 90% of births were the first-born in a family but in some rural areas the proportion was below 40%. Problems of female infanticide have occurred, again mainly in rural areas where the traditional preference for sons is strongest, and fears that a one-child policy will create a society with too many dependent old people and too few working young have also been voiced. In many rural localities the single-child policy has never been strongly enforced and there was a more general relaxation in applying the policy in the late 1980s. Government planning would seem to have reduced the average size of families below what it might have been but not to the level originally intended. The clear need for further increases in food production will probably entail further significant re-organisation within agriculture to intensify yields. Only time will tell how successful the Chinese people have been in their attempts to balance food supply and population growth but the enormous changes that have taken place since 1949 perhaps help to make the outlook more hopeful than some neo-Malthusian forecasts have suggested.

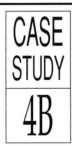

Politics, people and famine in Ethiopia

For many people outside Africa, Ethiopia has come to epitomise that continent's struggle to provide food for its population. Some 250,000 Ethiopians died in the famine of 1972–74, possibly 1 million in the 1984–85 famine and more recently many thousands have died or had their lives disrupted by further times of famine as droughts have periodically affected this area. But drought does not necessarily give rise to famine and the reasons for Ethiopia's difficulties involve other factors besides environmental ones.

Prior to 1974 Ethiopia was ruled by an emperor under a complex feudal system. In the south a few landlords owned most of the land and were allowed by law to take as much as three-quarters of their tenants' produce in rent. In much of the north, including Tigray, Gondar, Gojjam and parts of Wollo and Shewa (see Fig. 4.14) there was a form of communal ownership but land was unevenly shared and, as population increased during the twentieth century, fragmentation of landholdings grew and many became too small to adequately support a family. Most farmers were also subject to various taxes and customary dues that imposed further pressure on them, and in much of the highlands tenurial systems discouraged farmers from investing effort in long-term improvement schemes of any kind. Already by 1974 environmental degradation was widespread and continued population growth has since tended to increase pressures on the land. About 70% of Ethiopia's 52 million people now live in the highlands which rise to over 4,500 metres and where some three-fifths of all land has a slope of over 16%. Harrison (1987) states that annual top-

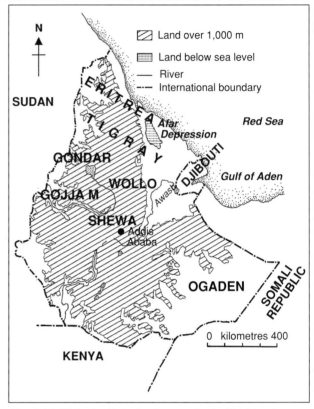

Fig. 4.14 Ethiopia. Note the large extent of highland, much of which is steeply sloping, causing agricultural difficulties. Only those provinces mentioned in the text are shown here.

soil losses average 70 tonnes per hectare with losses of almost 300 tonnes per hectare having been recorded on sloping fields ploughed for the traditional cereal crop, teff. Dramatic deforestation has also occurred with an estimated 40% of Ethiopia being forested in 1940 but only 4% by 1990. This is partly related to a shortage of fuelwood but also to commercial exploitation and to attempts to cultivate former forested uplands, many of which have proved unsuitable for cultivation and have since been rapidly eroded. The shortage of fuelwood also results in animal dung and stubble being used as fuel rather than to improve land quality. Land thus deprived of organic matter yet cultivated every year loses its water retention qualities and becomes increasingly prone to drought and erosion. Even in years of good rainfall, yields tend to be low and heavy rains accelerate erosion on the steep slopes.

In the hot, dry lowland areas, the Afar people traditionally lived as pastoralists, grazing their herds on the floodplain areas of the Awash River as part of their annual circulatory pattern of movement. Recently their way of life has been badly affected by a series of droughts and they suffered more than most in the 1972–74 famine when thousands of people and hundreds of thousands of their animals perished. Their problems have not, however, been related solely to the difficult environment. In the 1960s many of their traditional grazing areas were taken over by the government to create irrigation schemes producing sugar, cotton and other cash crops. The Afar found themselves forced to move north into more difficult areas where over-grazing became common. This in turn often led to erosion, loss of pasture and more pressure on the land. Attempts to move into adjacent highland areas led to conflict with cultivators, themselves moving into more marginal areas as pressure on their farmland increased. The military group, known as the Dergue, who overthrew the Emperor in 1974, showed no greater concern for the Afar, some of whom have been forced to abandon their traditional life to find work on the irrigated farms, while most struggle to survive in a worsening environment in which a slight decrease in rainfall can lead to disaster.

The Dergue aligned itself politically with the Soviet Union and adopted Marxist–Leninist policies. The revolution was supposed to remove some of the internal disagreements existing within the country but armed conflict with Eritrea (see Fig. 4.14), which was forced to become a part of Ethiopia in 1962, continued after 1974 and soon several other liberation movements had developed in Tigray and the South. There was conflict, too, in the Ogaden region which Somalia had never recognised as being part of Ethiopia rather than Somalia. With much of the country in a state of armed conflict, attempts by the Dergue to reform the landholding system since 1975 have had only limited success. The Land Reform Act displaced the old feudal landlords and gave land to the state. Peasants' associations were created

and some redistribution of land to small-holders took place but implementation was uneven throughout the country. Some land reforms were also carried out in areas like Eritrea and Tigray over which the liberation movements had control. Government efforts to introduce collective farming had little success and in the mid-1980s over 90% of cultivated land was in small-holdings. Villagisation schemes introduced from 1984 onwards – and intended in time to involve the whole of Ethiopia's rural population – probably had the long-term objective of introducing more collective farming but by the time the Dergue was overthrown in 1991 by the Ethiopian People's Revolutionary Democratic Front this had not been achieved, although by then some 15 million people were already in the new villages.

In addition to limiting the government's power to introduce new agricultural approaches, the military conflicts created a situation in which almost half government spending was on defence and internal security, leaving little for investment in the economy. Inevitably, too, it is difficult for agricultural production to be maintained while fighting is in progress. Given the physical and human constraints on production already outlined, it is not surprising that food production per head has shown little evidence of improvement in the 1980s (see Fig. 4.15). In such circumstances a marginal worsening of the situation can result in famine and the political situation can worsen the effects of such a famine.

In 1972–74 the pre-revolutionary government persistently denied reports of famine and starvation and this attempt to hide the situation was possibly aided by some Western countries who saw the Emperor as a political ally. Information about the situation in the mid-1980s and the early 1990s has also been restricted in various ways. Some governments would appear to have limited or delayed the aid they have provided because of their opposition to the Ethiopian government in power or because of concern about providing either goods such as lorries or food to groups (whether the government or the various opposition movements), who might use them for purposes other than those intended, e.g. to transport or feed their troops. In addition to the physical problems

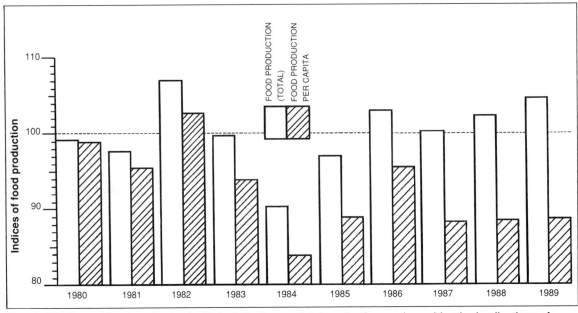

Fig. 4.15 Indices of food production in Ethiopia in the 1980s (1979–81 = 100). Note the proportionately greater change in food production per capita than in total production, and consider the implications of this.

occasioned by a very poor transport network, especially in the highland areas, there have been enormous logistical problems in actually delivering aid to those who needed it most because of the fighting that has restricted movement of vehicles, the unwillingness of particular factions within Ethiopia to provide help or information that might benefit their enemies, and the sheer confusion that exists in a country at war. Despite the massive wave of public support generated in many countries in the mid-1980s by 'Live Aid' and similar organisations, there have been suggestions that potential aid donors have since been discouraged by the recurrence of problems they thought they were helping to solve earlier and the fact that, in the kind of circumstances outlined, the media can easily highlight things that go wrong with the aid process – these often being more 'newsworthy' or dramatic than ventures that are successful.

However, as Kebbede and Jacob (1988) have pointed out: 'Ethiopia needs all the aid it can get to develop more permanent solutions to some of the underlying physical causes of famine such as the large-scale problems of environmental rehabilitation and land use improvement.' Emergency aid does little to help with such developments, geared as it must be to saving lives in the short term, but aid for longer-term projects (see Fig. 4.16) may be crucial if Ethiopia is to avoid a recurrence of recent problems. The new government, hopefully in a more peaceful situation, working where necessary with relief agencies and aid-providing groups, needs to build on recent schemes that have attempted to provide better water supplies; develop afforestation schemes; improve agricultural techniques, seed quality and livestock; implement terracing and other land improvement projects; and so provide a situation in which the Ethiopian people can themselves begin to resolve the difficulties they face. This may involve other changes, for example in landholding systems, but it must now be clear that these need to be developed with the agreement of those involved rather than being imposed from above. The future is uncertain but it need not be as gloomy as some reports have implied.

Fig. 4.16 A project in Ethiopia, supported by Christian Aid, in which trees have been planted and terraces built to conserve water in one of the many drought-affected areas. Schemes of this kind represent an attempt to safeguard food production by bringing about long-term improvement of agricultural land in a very difficult area.

PART Two:
POPULATION MIGRATION
AND CIRCULATION

5

Introduction:
Definition of terms

Fig. 5.1 A Bakhtiari family group during the annual migration from the Zagros Mountains to the coastal plain in Iran.

In its widest sense, human movement may be defined as a temporary, semi-permanent or permanent change of location. In this definition no restriction is placed on the distance of the move, its duration, or the voluntary or involuntary nature of the act, and no distinction made between movements within countries and movements between countries. Thus a move across a landing from one apartment to another would count as an act of population movement just as much as the seasonal wanderings of the Bakhtiari peoples of Iran (Fig. 5.1) or the journey of a Pakistani family from Karachi to a permanent home in Leicester, England – though, of course, the backgrounds and consequences of such moves are vastly different. Another group of human movements includes the continual moves of migratory workers such as the wheat-cutting combine harvester crews who, each year, travel progressively northwards across the United States, starting in Texas in May and reaching the Canadian border in Montana or North Dakota in September – a distance of some

2,800 kilometres. Itinerant construction gangs, such as those who build and maintain Britain's motorway system, provide another example of this kind of movement. The daily movement of workers from their homes in the suburbs and surrounding countryside to their urban work-places is yet another kind of movement that is of interest to geographers.

It is plain from the examples given above that it is unsatisfactory to include the great diversity of human movement under the one umbrella term of migration, and that it is unwise to label all movers as migrants. Mindful of this, the United Nations in 1958 published a multi-lingual demographic dictionary in which a wide range of terms used in the study of population geography, including studies of human movement, was defined. It is important to know the meaning of the most widely used of these now internationally recognised terms, but it will become clear that in practice it is not always possible to draw a sharp distinction between one type of movement and another.

Mobility, circulation and migration

The term *mobility* is all-embracing and includes both circulation and migration; all the cases cited above, therefore, are examples of the spatial mobility of population. *Circulation* has been defined as 'a great variety of movements usually short-term, repetitive or cyclical in character, but all having in common the lack of any declared intention of a permanent or long-standing change of residence' (Zelinsky, 1971). Thus the movements of the Bakhtiari, the American wheat-cutting teams and the motorway construction gangs, as well as of daily commuters, are generally considered to be examples of circulation rather than migration. *Migration* is a much more restricted term than circulation in that it is normally used only to describe a movement from one administrative unit to another that results in a permanent change of residence. There is, however, no agreement about the lowest level of administrative unit that should be considered for the purposes of migration studies. In developed countries it is possible to obtain data for very small areas, such as enumeration districts in England and Wales and census tracts in the United States, the former often containing only a few hundred people, but such detailed information is rarely available in developing countries. Whatever level of administrative unit is considered, the apartment dweller mentioned in the opening paragraph cannot 'officially' be called a migrant. Such a person is generally called a *mover*. But are distance and the crossing of an administrative boundary the most important criteria? An American geographer, Zelinsky, re-stated the problem in this way: 'Which family is more migratory, the one transferred 3,000 miles across the continent by an employer to be plugged into a suburb almost duplicating its former neighbourhood, or the black family that moves a city block into a previously white neighbourhood?'

There is yet another practical problem connected with the application of the term migration. The United Nations definition of permanent change of residence is 'having a duration of one year or more'. In practice, many geographers and other social scientists pursuing migration studies in regions where census data are unreliable or unavailable have been forced to collect their own data in the field and have often ignored official definitions of permanence. In any case there are many examples of long-term circulation involving absence from home for a period of longer than one year. In such circumstances individuals and groups may, despite their prolonged absence, maintain very close links with their home areas. Cases of this kind can be found, for example, in the Republic of South Africa (see Fig. 5.2), where several million 'migrants' of this type work in mines and factories and on plantations.

Migrations involve interactions between peoples and the displacement of populations. There is a whole host of terms related to these characteristics. Persons moving across internal administrative boundaries are either *in-migrants* (and the process is called *in-migration*) or *out-migrants* (*out-migration*). *Immigrants (immigration)* and *emigrants (emigration)* are persons who cross international boundaries. Migrations are embarked upon from an area of *origin* and are completed at an area of *destination*. Migrants sharing a common origin and destination form a *migration stream* or *migration current*. Normally wherever there is a migration stream there is a *counter-stream*, which is the reverse of the stream at a lower volume. Where a study is solely concerned with migration between two areas, whether at the inter-regional or international level, the aggregate of stream and counter-stream is termed the *gross interchange* between the two areas, and the difference between the two is called the *net interchange* or *net stream*. In investigations restricted to the effects of migration on a single area it is usual to refer to the total movement of population (in-migration plus out-migration or immigration plus emigration) as the *gross migration*, whereas the difference between in-migration and out-migration

Fig. 5.2 A 'migrant' worker in a gold mine in the Republic of South Africa. The gold mines have traditionally recruited labour on short-term contracts from neighbouring countries such as Botswana and Malawi as well as from most parts of the Republic.

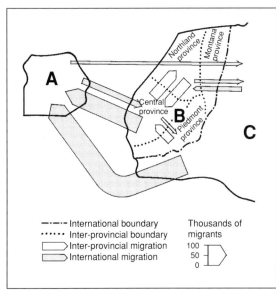

Fig. 5.3 Migration patterns for three hypothetical nation states. See text for comment.

(or immigration and emigration) is the *net migration* or *balance of migration*. This may be a positive or negative amount. The relationship between gross and net migration is expressed in terms of the *efficiency of migration*.

Migration patterns for three hypothetical nation states

An attempt is made in Fig. 5.3 to illustrate quantitatively a number of these terms in the context of three hypothetical nation states. Island nation A is separated by a narrow sea from continental nations B and C which are themselves separated by a high mountain range. State B is composed of four provinces whose boundaries are shown. The map shows selected migration streams for the most recent five-year period. For the purposes of the accompanying analysis it is assumed that migration between the three nations and other nations is negligible and can therefore be ignored.

Internal migrations in nation B

Montana province is mountainous and sparsely populated. There is little in- or out-migration. Piedmont province has witnessed heavy depopulation during the past decade. It is a region of marginal farms and declining mineral resources. Some hydro-electric power schemes have been initiated during the past five years. The map shows a migration stream of 40,000 out-migrants from Piedmont province, who have become in-migrants of Central province. There is a counter-stream of 10,000 from Central to Piedmont province. The gross interchange between the two provinces is thus 50,000 persons and the net interchange is 30,000. The efficiency of the migrations between the two provinces is relatively high in that the ratio of stream to counter-stream is 4:1 and there has been a net re-distribution of 30,000 people.

Turning next to migration between Central and Northland provinces we see a rather different picture. Both of these provinces are relatively affluent industrial regions with a high degree of urbanisation. Migration levels between the two provinces are high. The gross interchange is 100,000 persons, but the net interchange is zero. Migration has not been efficient in that the ratio of stream to counter-stream is 1:1 and the net re-distribution of people effected by the two streams is again zero. Low efficiency is a usual occurrence if the conditions in the areas of origin and destination are similar.

It should be noted that at a provincial level, gross migration and net migration figures are calculated by taking into account both inter-provincial and international migrations. For example, gross migration figures for Central province would be:

a) the gross interchange between Central and Northland provinces (100,000); plus
b) the gross interchange between Central and Piedmont provinces (50,000); plus
c) those emigrants from country B to countries A and C originating in Central province; plus
d) those immigrants to country B from countries A and C settling in Central province.

International migrations between countries A, B, and C

The migration streams are uneven. Nation A, which has undergone a period of spectacular economic growth in the last five years, accompanied by chronic labour shortages, has received 100,000 immigrants from nation C and 80,000 from nation B during that time. In the same period 15,000 persons have migrated from nation A to nation B and 10,000 from nation A to nation C. Migration between nation states B and C is at a low level with a gross interchange of about 30,000. If we consider the migrations between nation A and nation C (a relatively undeveloped and densely populated country) we can see that there is a major migration stream from C to A and a relatively small counter-stream from A to C. (It is interesting to speculate about the nature of the counter-stream. A good proportion of the 10,000 persons migrating from A to C may, in fact, have originated in C and be taking part in long-term circulation rather than international migration.) The gross interchange between A and C is 110,000 persons and the net interchange is 90,000. From the point of view of nation A the balance of migration is 90,000, and from the point of view of nation C it is -90,000. The efficiency of the migration between the two states is high in that the ratio of stream to counter-stream is 10:1 and there has been a net re-distribution of 90,000 people.

Exercise 5.1 offers an opportunity to use, in their appropriate context, some of the terms defined and illustrated in this chapter. The remainder of the second part of the book examines in more detail issues relating to migration (Chapter 6) and circulation (Chapter 7) and attempts to classify such movements through the use of migration typologies (Chapter 8).

Exercise 5.1

Use of terminology

Study carefully the table below which shows migration in the United Kingdom in 1988 (in thousands) between Wales, Scotland, Northern Ireland and the standard regions of England.

To read the table, first read the names along the top row. These are the areas *from* which the migrants are moving. Then read the names in the left-hand column. These are the areas *to* which the migrants are moving. Thus 90,000 people moved from the East Midlands to the rest of the United Kingdom in 1988. Of these, 28,000 moved to the South East.

a) How many people migrated in 1988 from:
   i) East Anglia to the South East?
   ii) Wales to the North West?
   iii) Yorkshire and Humberside to the South West?

b) i) From the point of view of the *area of origin*, which of your answers to (a) refer to out-migrants and which to emigrants? Justify your answer in each case.

ii) From the point of view of the *area of destination*, which of your answers to (a) refer to in-migrants and which to immigrants? Justify your answer in each case.

c) i) How many people migrated in 1988 from:
   –the South East to the South West?
   –the South West to the South East?
   ii) Which of your answers to (i) is the migration stream and which is the counter-stream?
   iii) Calculate the gross interchange and the net interchange between the South East and the South West.

d) If there had been no migratory movement *from* the North region to foreign countries in 1988 and no movement from foreign countries *to* the North region in 1988 (i.e. ignoring any migration not shown on the table), what would be:
   i) the gross migration total for the North region in 1988?
   ii) the balance of migration for the North region in that year?

Internal migration in the United Kingdom in 1988 between Wales, Scotland, Northern Ireland and the standard regions of England (in thousands)

Area of destination	United Kingdom	North	Yorkshire and Humberside	East Midlands	East Anglia	South East	South West	West Midlands	North West	Wales	Scotland	Northern Ireland
United Kingdom	:	55	88	90	54	320	110	95	105	49	64	17
North	51	:	9	4	2	14	3	3	7	1	6	1
Yorkshire and Humberside	95	10	:	16	5	28	7	7	14	3	5	1
East Midlands	108	4	15	:	8	42	7	13	10	3	4	1
East Anglia	70	2	4	7	:	42	4	3	3	1	3	0
South East	265	17	26	28	24	:	53	30	35	16	27	8
South West	145	3	6	8	5	86	:	14	9	8	5	1
West Midlands	88	3	6	11	3	31	12	:	10	7	3	1
North West	103	9	15	9	3	31	8	11	:	8	7	2
Wales	65	1	2	4	2	23	11	9	11	:	2	0
Scotland	50	5	5	4	2	19	4	3	5	1	:	2
Northern Ireland	9	0	1	0	0	4	1	1	1	0	1	:

Source: Bulusu (1989).

6

Processes and patterns of migration

One of the characteristics of modern geography is the quest for models to represent or predict human spatial behaviour. Such models are well represented in the field of migration studies. Two of the most widely quoted and used conceptual reference points are the 'push–pull' concept and Ravenstein's 'Laws of Migration'. The first is concerned with reasons for migration and the second with the selection of migrants and the development of migration patterns. These two generalisations, although they have been subject to criticism and have been continuously modified and refined, have provided the stimulus for much modern research and writing on migration.

Reasons for migration: the decision-making process

The push–pull concept

The push–pull concept simply states that for any individual the decision to migrate results from the interplay of two forces: pressures at the permanent place of residence (pushes) and inducements from a number of destinations (pulls). Examples of push factors are low wages, unemployment, political, racial and religious oppression, and natural disasters such as drought, famine and flood. Pull factors include employment offers and opportunities, better medical and social provision, and political and religious tolerance. It is clear that in some cases only pushes will be of major significance (for example when unforeseen disasters occur, as in the case of the nuclear accident at Chernobyl in the Ukraine in 1986 or the civil uprising and subsequent flight of the Kurds from northern Iraq to Turkey and Iran in 1991). In other situations, pulls will be of overwhelming importance, as in the case of a professional person who may find great job satisfaction in one place and then suddenly be confronted by a challenging new opportunity elsewhere – like many of the highly skilled professional and managerial migrants discussed in Chapter 7 and Case Study 8A. Yet other situations will arise where there are both strong pushes and pulls as in the case of Puerto Rican migrants who have been pushed from their homeland by poverty, unemployment, overcrowding and poor living conditions and pulled towards the United States by a favourable migration policy, the wide range of employment opportunities and better levels of living.

Two further dimensions of the basic push–pull theory are worth noting. First, migration is selective: in certain circumstances and at certain times particular persons or groups are more likely to migrate than others. Such *migration selectivity* is sometimes known as *differential migration*. Important differentials are age, gender and socio-economic status. For example, large numbers of the migrants to coastal resorts in England are retired persons. People of pensionable age (who comprised 18% of the total UK population in 1981) represented more than 30% of the populations of the south coast towns of Worthing, Eastbourne, Christchurch, Hove and Bournemouth (Warnes and Law, 1984). Modern migrations are overwhelmingly of an economic nature, however, and in the vast majority of these, persons in the young adult age group of 20–34 years are predominant. Sex selectivity appears to vary according to the stage of development of the society concerned. In the very broadest terms, studies seem to suggest that in advanced industrial countries females are predominant in short-distance migrations while males are predominant in long-distance migrations. Conversely, in developing countries males are normally in the majority in short- and long-distance internal migrations and in international migrations. There are indications that this pattern in developing countries is beginning to change, however, with increased short-distance female migration apparent in many countries and especially in the newly industrialising countries of Asia – creating a pattern increasingly similar to that of more developed countries. In the case of socio-economic (occupational) selectivity, professional people are proportionately far more migratory than skilled or unskilled workers.

Another aspect of differential migration is that the age, sex and occupational structures of migration streams vary in response to changing conditions in the area of origin and at potential destinations. In certain conditions (e.g. specific labour requirements in another region) only particular age groups may elect to migrate. In others (e.g. in times of earthquakes or floods) whole communities may move. In the former case the migrants may be said to be *positively selected*, in that they move to a particular destination in search of betterment, whereas in the latter the migrants may be said to be *negatively selected* in that there may be little choice involved in the decision to move and in the selection of their destination in the first instance. Figure 6.1 describes some aspects of the migrations from Ireland in the mid-nineteenth century following the 'Great Famine', associated with the failures of the potato crop for a number of years without respite after 1845.

A second important corollary of the push–pull concept is *migration elasticity*. This concept acknowledges the fact that individuals react differently to the pressures and inducements that lead to the decision to migrate. In some cases very little stimulus is required before an individual migrates; in other cases pushes and pulls have to be exerted either with great intensity or for a long time before a migration takes place. Cases have been recorded of disappointed migrants from the United Kingdom to Australia who, after a short stay, have returned to the UK, and then, after another unsettled period, have embarked upon a second migration to Australia. In such cases the attractions and drawbacks of the two places must

The *New York Times* said that in Kilkenny even the dogs had deserted: also the legal profession had been annihilated, because where there were no people left, there could be no litigation. In 1841 the population of Ireland had been 8,175,124, and Disraeli said it was the most thickly populated country in Europe. According to the 1851 census the population was only 6,552,385. The commissioners of the census remarked that at the normal rate of increase the population should then have been over nine millions, so the real loss was about two and a half million people in ten years. And in the years between 1851 and 1854 another 822,000 left.

Many sailed directly from Irish ports. In starving Limerick most ships were advertised as sailing not just for New York or Quebec but 'for the flourishing city of New York'; 'for the flourishing city of Quebec'. But most people went first to England and sailed from Liverpool. Others stayed in England, not because they had any love of that country but because they had no money to go further. They were not welcome. One family got as far as Cheshire and camped near the house of Thomas Murdoch, chairman of the emigration commissioners. The moment his servants noticed the Irish they considered them a pestilence to be driven away. Murdoch went down to the camp and found a poor family of four children, and their mother, father, and grandmother. The mother said they used to live fifteen miles from Athlone. They had brought over a tattered blanket with them, took sticks out of a hedge and propped the blanket up like a tent, and slept under it on the bare ground. Murdoch saw smoke, and a kettle boiling, and asked what they had there. They said nettles. For three years before this, they had existed on three acres of potatoes in Ireland, but this year they had none to plant, the workhouse was overflowing, so their master said there was nothing for them but to leave, and if they did leave he would give them a pound note. With this they begged their way to Dublin and paid their fare to Liverpool, and then walked to Murdoch's place, thirty-six miles from Liverpool.

Fig. 6.1 An account of the emigrations from Ireland following the 'Great Famine'.

have been under constant review before the final decision was made.

Refinements of the simple push–pull concept

In 1966, E.S. Lee re-stated the basic push–pull concept in the terms outlined in Fig. 6.2. Instead of isolating the pressures and stimuli confronting particular individuals or groups, Lee presents a situation in which a particular place of origin is characterised by a particular mix of attributes. Lee states that each individual at that place will perceive these attributes differently according to, for example, age, gender, education or marital status. A particular individual will see some of these factors as advantages and these will discourage migration (plus factors at origin) while others will be seen as disadvantages and will encourage migration (minus factors at origin). The same individual will be indifferent towards a third group of factors (neutral factors at origin). A similar picture of positive, negative and neutral factors is present at a potential destination.

To translate this into individual terms, consider the case of a middle-aged bachelor, working as a relatively poorly paid farm labourer (minus factor at origin) in a declining rural area. He may view relatives living locally and his wide circle of friends as important reasons for staying there (plus factors at origin), while at the same time being attracted by offers of well-paid factory employment in a nearby industrial region (plus factor at destination). The fact that

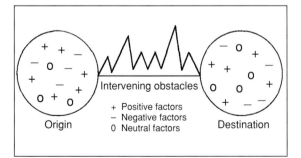

Fig. 6.2 E.S. Lee's theory of migration.
Source: after Lee, 1966.

flexible shift work to fit in with domestic commitments will be available for wives of employees will not enter his calculations (neutral factor at destination). Another farm labourer living in the same area but with few family ties there, with a grown-up family, and a wife keen to supplement her husband's income, might see the situation in a rather different light.

A study of male migration from rural northern Nigeria to the oil towns in the south of the country at the beginning of the 1980s (Hocking and Thomson, 1981) considered the factors influencing migration at the origin and destination in the terms of Lee's theory. For example, the authors suggest that the plus factors at destination were better jobs, higher wages, the ability to buy more consumer goods, the possibility of acquiring capital to establish a business in the area of origin, better facilities (e.g. medical facilities, schools, water supplies), better entertainment, and the freedom to develop a more sophisticated way of life. However, these advantages were offset by a number of negative factors: the complexities of the rules and regulations of urban life, bad housing, the relatively low numbers of women, the danger of being corrupted and the anonymity of urban life.

Having established the idea of the evaluation of perceived advantages and disadvantages at the place of origin and a potential destination, Lee then introduces a further component: the potential migrant is confronted by one or a number of real or perceived obstacles that must be overcome before migration can take place. These may be, for example, physical (the former Berlin Wall, the Rockies), financial, medical, academic or legal (immigration quotas, work permit regulations) or some combination of these and others as in the Canadian points system illustrated in Fig. 6.3. Thus Lee sees migration in terms of four related groups of factors: factors associated with the area of origin, factors associated with the area of destination, intervening obstacles, and personal factors.

At much the same time that Lee was developing his theory of migration, Julian Wolpert was publishing his concept of *place utility*. Place utility is an individual's degree of satisfaction or dissatisfaction with a place (Wolpert, 1965, 1966). It is assumed that the place utility of any given place will vary between different individuals because different people will consider different variables, and for any given variable they will assign to it different degrees of satisfaction or dissatisfaction. Another aspect of the place utility concept, which is shared with Lee's theory of migration, is that whereas the evaluation of the utility of the place in which the individual lives is based on first-hand experience, for other places the evaluation may be based only on short-term visits or entirely on second-hand information. This is clearly apparent from the material provided in Exercise 6.1 which provides an opportunity to consider further some of the ideas of Wolpert, Lee and others in a Kenyan context.

Brown and Moore (1970) used the concept of place utility as the starting point for their decision-making model concerning *intra-urban residential mobility*. They see the intra-urban migration process in two phases: first the decision whether or not to seek a new dwelling and, second, the search for and choice of a new dwelling. The first decision involves a household in recognising a state of dissatisfaction (what the authors call *stress*) with the existing dwelling. The stress may be generated by internal factors (e.g. the quality of the dwelling in relation to the household's changing self-esteem or the size of the dwelling in relation to family size) or external factors (e.g. noise, neighbours, access to schools). A particular household may remove the stress either by improving the dwelling (e.g. by adding extra rooms) or by

---

The Canadian Immigration Act of 1976 became law in 1978. There is no discrimination under this Act on the grounds of race, national or ethnic origin, colour, religion or sex, but because the number of applicants greatly exceeds the number of places available (which is set by the Prime Minister on an annual basis) a processing system has had to be established.

Close relatives of Canadian citizens, such as parents, grandparents, wives and children, may be sponsored by their Canadian relative and do not have to be assessed under the points system. Refugees and other persecuted and displaced people are also assessed separately. Other prospective migrants must submit themselves to the points system of assessment. This is out of 100 and the minimum score allowed is 50. There are exceptions in the case of entrepreneurs who intend to employ at least 5 Canadians who need only score 25, and 'other' relatives who have to score between 20 and 35 depending on their relationship with the Canadian who is sponsoring them.

The Points System headings and points allocations are as follows:

1 Education: One point for each year up to a maximum of 12.

2 Specific vocational preparation for a chosen occupation: Up to 15 points.

3 Experience on the job: Up to 8 points.

4 Occupational demand: Up to 15 points on the basis of employment opportunities available in the applicant's field of work.

5 Arranged employment or designated occupation: 10 points if the applicant has a job to go to or if the applicant is prepared to work in an occupation in which there is a shortage of adequately qualified personnel.

6 Plus 5 points for a person going to an area where new people are positively in demand, e.g. smaller towns, more remote areas. Minus 5 for a person going where they are not, notably the major cities to which most new arrivals normally flock.

7 Ten points for being between 18 and 35 years old. One point less for every year over 35, until zero points at age 45 and older.

8 Up to 5 points for fluent English and the same for French.

9 Personal suitability: Up to 10 points for likelihood of becoming established successfully in Canada (determined at interview with immigration official and based on such qualities as adaptability, motivation, initiative, and resourcefulness).

10 Relative: If someone comes into the assisted relative category but cannot provide the necessary documentation to prove it, he or she may get 5 points at the discretion of the immigration officer.

Fig. 6.3 The Canadian points system for assessing prospective immigrants.

Exercise 6.1

Rural–urban perceptions in Kenya

The tables provided on pages 108–109 are a summary of the mental images held by students at village polytechnics (VPs) in Kenya of their home areas in rural parts of the Kenya Highlands and of Nairobi, the capital of Kenya, based on a survey by Barker and Ferguson (1983). Although the students are from different parts of the Highlands, they form a relatively homogeneous group of 14–18 year olds whose formal education ended with primary school and whose families belong to the majority rural class of small subsistence farmers. In the VPs they are learning basic craft skills in, for example, building, textiles and car maintenance. Most live within three hours' travel time of Nairobi and had visited the city at least once but their first-hand knowledge of it is very limited. Each of 176 students was asked to state the three best and three worst things about Nairobi and about their home area, and the responses listed represent their replies, the uneven totals indicating that some students did not give a full set of responses to each section.

1 Examine the tables provided and summarise the perceptions held by the students
  a) of Nairobi and
  b) of their home areas
organising your comments into three sections relating to
  i) economic aspects
  ii) social aspects and
  iii) other aspects of the different areas.

2 Indicate the extent to which the comments on Nairobi might be used to illustrate
  a) Lee's theory of migration and
  b) Wolpert's concept of place utility
in terms of rural village polytechnic students contemplating the possibility of migrating to Nairobi at the end of their course.

3 From your more general reading on Kenya suggest
  a) how the rural control subsystem identified by Mabogunje might influence the propensity to move to Nairobi of students at a village polytechnic; and
  b) what intervening obstacles (as identified by Lee) might affect such movement.

improving the neighbourhood (e.g. by gaining improved access to schools). Another household may find the stress intolerable and begin to search for a new home. This is the second phase of the process which, after a search and further evaluation, may lead to the household in question either changing residence or coming to terms with the existing dwelling and/or neighbourhood.

A systems approach to rural–urban migration

Thus far migration has been viewed as a one-way, start and finish relationship between an origin and a destination. Mabogunje (1970), an African scholar writing with particular reference to his home continent, has approached rural–urban migration from another point of view: that of a system which is undergoing continued modification as events in one part cause repercussions elsewhere. (In the simplest terms a 'system' may be defined as a complex of interacting elements.) Mabogunje's ideas are summarised in Fig. 6.4. This shows the African rural–urban migration system operating within an economic, social, political and technological environment. This environment is one of change: of increasing degrees of commercialisation and industrialisation, of rising health and education standards, of changing government policies and of better transportation links and increased mechanisation. The system and the environment act and react upon each other continuously. Improving economic conditions in urban areas will stimulate migration from rural areas; a downturn in the urban economy will reduce the migration flows from such areas.

Perceptions of Nairobi

Best things		Worst things	
Image attribute	No. of responses	Image attribute	No. of responses
Good economic/employment prospects	103	Thieves, robbers, pickpockets	101
Tall, beautiful buildings	53	Motor car accidents	57
Good (cheap) communications	43	Thugs, beating, fighting	54
Good public utilities (water, electricity, hospitals)	24	Housing problems	41
Smart, clean people	20	'Things' (e.g. food) expensive	40
Centre of Kenya	20	Killings, murders	22
Recreational facilities	20	No place to grow food	18
Good shopping facilities	19	Bad employment/economic prospects	16
Many (different kinds) people	16	Unemployed people	12
Landmarks (airport, railway station, etc.)	14	Easy to get lost	11
Self-advancement/learn more things	12	If you have no job/money, difficult to survive	11
Social life enjoyable	12	Beer drinking/changa/bangi	7
High salaries/richer people	10	General anti-social behaviour	7
If you can get a job/house you can be happy	9	Police harass/arrest jobless people	6
Town is more developed than our area	8	Prostitution	6
Good climate	8	Social life/bad/too many amenities	4
Good housing	7	People forget homes/do not visit home	4
Many fantastic things (e.g. gold mines)	7	If you do not have a job you can become a robber	4
Large market	7	Crossing the road	4
Source of good (cheap) equipment	6	City is crowded/densely populated	3
Work is less arduous	6	Cripples, beggars	3
Educational facilities	4	Climate not good	3
People/children know more than us	4	Town is dirty, unhealthy, polluted	3
Good people	2	If state is in chaos, Nairobi people suffer	3
People are independent of neighbours	2	Problems with water and electricity	3
People to borrow money from	1	Vanishing from one's area (depopulation)	2
People co-operate at work	1	It is far from my district	1
No people to harass others at night	1	Selling without receipts	1
Agricultural Show	1	Selling uncooked food	1
Not far from my district	1	All types of food can be bought	1
		Girls can be easily misled	1
		Many non-believers	1
		Tall building spoilt by earthquakes	1
		If you have children they can be spoilt	1
Total	441	Total	455

Perceptions of home area

Best things		Worst things	
Image attribute	No. of responses	Image attribute	No. of responses
Good farms/agriculture/food crops	86	Excessive beer drinking/fighting	50
Good educational facilities	70	Bad communications	46
Livestock	42	Bad public utilities (water, electricity, hospitals)	37
Cash crops	39	Not safe to go out at night	34
Peaceful/calm	36	Stealing/thieves/robbers	32
Good economic/employment prospects	35	Agricultural problems	30
People are united/work in co-operation	32	Climate/environment	20
Climate/topography is favourable	29	Quarrelsome people	17
Trade/business is good/nearby	23	Reasons related to village polytechnic	16
Good communications	21	Bad economic/employment prospects	15
Public utilities (water, hospital)	19	Educational problems	15
No food problems/cheap/abundant	10	Reasons related to behaviour of young people	12
Social life interesting	6	Unemployment	10
No housing problems	6	Backward place/undeveloped	9
Religious reasons	5	Food/goods expensive	8
Friendly place	5	Diseases are common	6
Can earn a living farming if no job	5	People do not know how to make farms profitable	6
People are active/hard working	2	Antisocial behaviour	6
Goods are cheap	2	No big towns nearby	5
Recreational	2	Poisoning, killing, suicides	4
Not densely populated	1	People are not united	3
No idle people	1	Housing problems	3
One does not go far	1	Police harass those not at school; corrupt	2
Land demarcation	1	Rape, prostitution, fornication, adultery	2
It's where my parents live	1	No shops	1
People try to find money to help themselves	1	Digging the land	1
Not much work	1	Difficult to survive without a job	1
		Motor accidents	1
		Diet of people is unbalanced	1
		Place is not well known	1
		Attacks from Turkanas	1
		Nothing	6
Total	482	Total	401

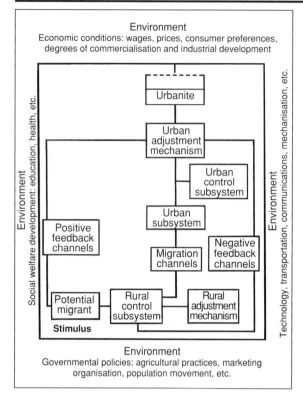

Fig. 6.4 Mabogunje's rural–urban migration system.
Source: after Mabogunje, 1970.

Having been stimulated to move by the environment, the potential migrant then comes under the influence of what Mabogunje calls the rural control subsystem, which in the African context is the family and rural community, whose attitudes will determine the volume of rural–urban migration. These attitudes will in turn be influenced by the ability of families and communities to adjust to migration loss. When migration takes place the rural dweller passes from the rural control subsystem to an urban subsystem with its own control subsystem (e.g. housing and job opportunities) and adjustment mechanism (e.g. an expanding labour market) which may transform the rural dweller into an urbanite. If the migrant maintains contact with his home area as the adjustment to urban life takes place, he sends back

information which modifies the system. This information may be of difficulties, setbacks and frustrations (negative feedback) that will discourage further migration, or of successes and opportunities (positive feedback) that will encourage further migration.

Although this system's approach is specifically related to African rural–urban migration, it is relevant to the study of migrations in general. Besides highlighting the self-modifying nature of a migration system, Mabogunje's study emphasises the threefold impact of migration: on the area of origin, on the area of destination, and on the migrant personally. This is an aspect of migration that is further considered in the case studies that form part of this chapter.

One further aspect of Mabogunje's work is also worth noting. He differentiates between what he calls *active* and *passive migrants*. The active migrants are the pioneers, the trailblazers who take the psychological, physical and financial risks, make the contacts and set up the networks that make the migration journey for others (the passive migrants) less arduous and their settling in at the destination less problematic. Once these networks exist, so-called *chain migration* can take place with relatives, friends and neighbours following on behind. Desai (1963) has shown the importance of such migration among Gujaratis from western India living in Birmingham.

Who migrates where? The generation of migration patterns

As long ago as the 1880s, in a study based on the birthplace data in the 1881 census of England and Wales, E.G. Ravenstein formulated what he called seven 'Laws of Migration' and, as was noted earlier, these have remained remarkably useful as starting points for the investigation of modern migrations. Ravenstein's laws are as follows:

1 We have already proved that the great body of our migrants only proceed a short distance and that there takes place consequently a universal shifting or displacement of the population, which produces 'currents of migration' setting in the direction of the great centres of commerce and industry which absorb the migrants . . .

2 It is the natural outcome of the movement of migration, limited in range, but universal throughout the country, that the processes of absorption go on in the following manner: the inhabitants of a country immediately surrounding a town of rapid growth, flock into it; the gaps thus left by the rural population are filled up by migrants from more remote districts, until the attractive force of one of our rapidly growing cities makes its influence felt, step by step, to the most remote corner of the Kingdom. Migrants enumerated in a certain centre of absorption will consequently grow less with the distance proportionately to the native population which furnishes them . . .

3 The process of dispersion is the inverse of that of absorption and exhibits similar features.

4 Each main current of migration produces a compensating counter-current.

5 Migrants proceeding long distances generally go by preference to one of the great centres of commerce and industry.

6 The natives of towns are less migratory than those of rural parts of the country.

7 Females are more migratory than males.

The fourth generalisation has already been noted in the discussion of stream and counter-stream (see Chapter 5). Similarly, Ravenstein's sixth and seventh laws refer to migration selectivity which is discussed elsewhere. The remaining generalisations (1, 2, 3 and 5) are important in explaining patterns of migration and their essence is embodied in the modern concepts of distance-decay, intervening opportunities and stepwise movement.

Distance-decay

On the influence of distance on migration, Ravenstein was very explicit in the last sentence of his second law. He argued that the volume of migration is inversely related to distance in that areas adjacent to a centre of absorption will normally provide more migrants than distant areas. On a graph with arithmetical scales, this relationship between volume of migration and distance produces a reverse-J curve (Fig. 6.5a), thus showing that the volume of migration does not fall off regularly with increasing distance but tends to decline at a decreasing rate. This is called a *negative exponential relationship* and when plotted on logarithmic graph paper it appears as a straight line (Fig. 6.5b). The rela-

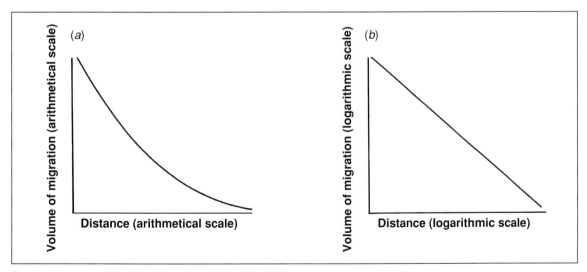

Fig. 6.5 The concept of distance-decay.

tionship is called distance-decay and is analogous to Newton's law of universal gravitation; it is therefore an example of a *gravity model*. The basis of the gravity model in a geographical context is that two places interact with each other in proportion to the product of their 'masses' and inversely according to some function of the distance between them. The 'mass' of a place may be expressed in various ways according to the problem under investigation. It may, for example, be the population of the place, or the number of its retail outlets, or the number of job opportunities. An example of the distance-decay relationship is illustrated in Fig. 6.6 using birthplace data from the 1861 census of England and Wales. The table and graphs show the number of migrants enumerated in Sheffield in that year who had been born in five increasingly distant counties to the south of Sheffield. The graphs show a falling off by a multiple of the

County	Greatest distance from Sheffield (km)	Number of persons born there and enumerated in Sheffield in 1861
Derbyshire (Dy)	72	13,329
Warwickshire (Wk)	144	1,890
Gloucestershire (G)	195	330
Wiltshire (Wt)	272	107
Dorset (Dt)	317	35

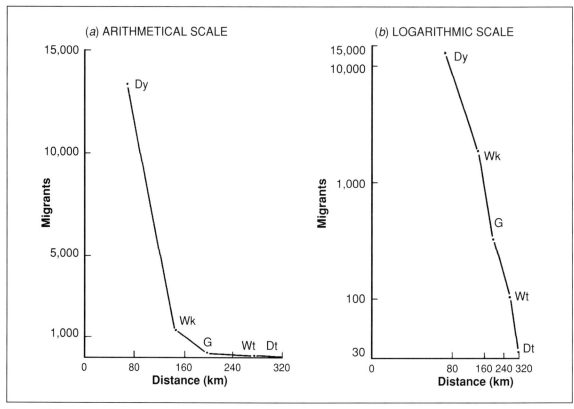

Fig. 6.6 Migrants in Sheffield in 1861 who were born in Derbyshire, Warwickshire, Gloucestershire, Wiltshire and Dorset.

distance rather like the gravity model, but they must be treated with some caution. The simple relationship shown in the graphs did not obtain in every direction. If the 'slopes' of decreasing numbers of migrants in all directions from the centre of absorption are seen, in the mind's eye, as a cone, with the centre of absorption at the peak, then small subsidiary cones may appear on the slopes. In the case of Sheffield in 1861, London formed such a cone. Although smaller in area than Warwickshire and more than 90 km further away from Sheffield, it furnished 227 more migrants. Plainly, migration does not just fall off with distance; it is also necessary to take into account the population of the places concerned. The volume of migration between two large towns is likely to be greater than the volume of migration between one of the towns and a sparsely populated rural area as distant as the other town. Thus, if account is also taken of population levels, the gross migration between two places may be expressed by a gravity model in the form:

$$Mij = \frac{Pi\,Pj}{dij}$$

where Mij = gross migration between places i
           and j
   Pi = population of place i
   Pj = population of place j
   dij = distance between places i and j.

Clearly this is still a simplification of reality and the equation needs to be further modified and refined if it is to be used to predict accurately migration flows between places. In its basic form it assumes that all potential migrants have perfect information about all other places, that transport costs are equal in all directions and, most importantly, that actual physical distance is the most important factor governing all decisions. Among modifications made to the basic model are the substitution or addition of economic variables such as unemployment rates, persons in the economically active age range and per capita income levels. Exercise 6.2 provides opportunities to explore this and other concepts in greater detail.

Exercise 6.2

Surrey: in-migration and out-migration, 1966–71

Study the graph below showing migration to and from Surrey 1966–71, according to distance travelled.

a) Describe carefully what the graph shows using specific percentages and/or proportions in your description.

b) State which of the following concepts is/are illustrated by the graph, justifying your answer in each case: distance-decay, intervening opportunities, stepwise migration.

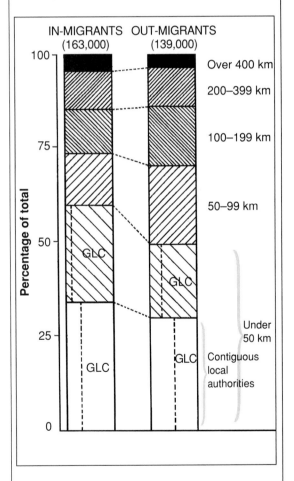

Surrey's migrants, 1966–71, analysed by distance.
Source: Craig, 1981.

Intervening opportunities

So far two factors that influence the generation of migration patterns have been isolated: first, distance between an area of origin and a potential area of destination, and second, population levels, which determine the number of potential migrants in one area and the number of opportunities at a potential destination. At this point a third factor must be recognised, that of intervening opportunities between an area of origin and a potential destination. This concept was introduced by an American scholar, Stouffer, in 1940 and refined by him in 1960. In his original article, Stouffer wrote that 'the number of persons going a given distance is directly proportional to the number of opportunities at that distance and inversely proportional to the number of intervening opportunities'. A reconsideration of the nineteenth-century Sheffield example will illustrate this concept. It was noted earlier that only 35 persons who had been born in Dorset were living in Sheffield in 1861 and this is partly explained in terms of distance and the relatively small population of Dorset. What then were the destinations of the other people leaving Dorset in the first half of the nineteenth century who were not enumerated in Sheffield in 1861? In fact, many of them moved to Bristol and the industrial towns of the Midlands. In terms of opportunities, Sheffield did not differ markedly from Bristol or the Midlands towns, but the latter were nearer to Dorset than Sheffield and, other things being equal, a Dorset migrant was less likely to consider Sheffield as a potential destination than similar places nearer to Dorset. Thus, viewed as opportunities, Bristol and the Midlands towns intervened between Sheffield and the Dorset migrant.

A study completed in the United States in the 1950s (Rose, 1955 in Jansen, 1970) took the concepts of distance-decay and intervening opportunities a step further by testing the hypothesis that persons of higher status (in occupational terms) seeking better positions (opportunities) must move further to find them than persons of lower status. The author recorded the previous place of residence and the new address in the city of a sample of 1,221 people who moved to

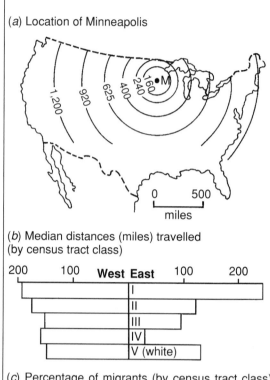

(a) Location of Minneapolis

(b) Median distances (miles) travelled (by census tract class)

(c) Percentage of migrants (by census tract class) originating from within 240 miles of Minnesota

	West		East
I	26.08	I	24.20
II	29.44	II	30.56
III	34.69	III	28.38
IV	38.65	IV	36.20
V (white)	28.81	V (white)	47.62

Fig. 6.7 Distance of direction travelled by 1,221 migrants to Minneapolis, Minnesota, 15 March to 1 July 1955.
Source: after Rose, 1955.

Minneapolis, Minnesota, between the middle of March and the beginning of July 1955. Previously he had compiled a map of Minneapolis in which each census tract was ranked from I to V according to the social status of its population. Tracts in the first rank were those that contained the highest aggregate scores based on four indicators of social class. The tracts ranked fifth had the lowest aggregate scores based on these characteristics. Having compiled the map it was possible, by plotting the new addresses of the sampled population, to assign the migrants to one of five socio-economic groups (Class I to Class V). The places moved from were classified into concentric rings centred on Minneapolis (Fig. 6.7a). In addition each place of origin was classified into east or west of the Mississippi (on which Minneapolis stands). The southern states were classified separately. The findings of the study were as follows:

1 The distance moved decreased steadily as the status of the neighbourhood declined. Thus the original hypothesis that higher-class migrants move further than those migrants of lower class was generally confirmed (Fig. 6.7b and c).
2 Class V migrants proved to be an exception. This was partly accounted for by the number of Black Americans in this class who had migrated greater distances than other migrants in the same class.
3 While most migrants in Class I were from the east (professional people moving from large cities in the industrial Midwest), the opposite was increasingly true in Classes II to IV where most migrants originated from the west – from rural areas in Minnesota and neighbouring North and South Dakota.

In terms of Stouffer's concept, this study suggested that people in low-status occupations were finding many more intervening opportunities in a given distance than people with high-status occupations and that geographical location has an important influence on opportunities for migration. Although Rose's assumptions and techniques have been criticised, few studies of this type have been attempted and his work does throw interesting light on the related concepts of distance-decay and intervening opportunities.

Stepwise movement

The germ of this concept is incorporated in Ravenstein's second generalisation where he states that 'The inhabitants of a country immediately surrounding a town of rapid growth flock into it; the gaps thus left . . . are filled up by migrants from more remote districts, until the attractive force . . . makes itself felt, step by step, to the most remote parts of the Kingdom'. Figure 6.8 shows, in its simplest terms, the type of hierarchical stepwise movement hinted at by Ravenstein and since investigated by others.

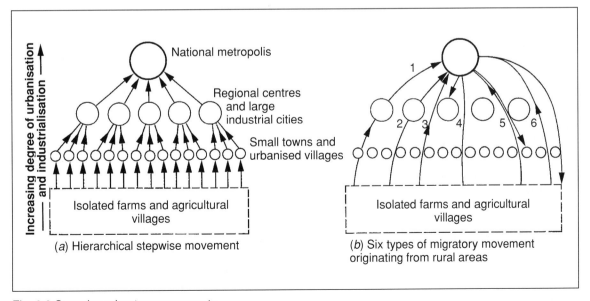

Fig. 6.8 Stepwise migratory movements.

Johnson (1990) in a study of migration in nineteenth-century Ireland, for example, claims that a form of stepwise migration was common in more remote areas at that time. A boy might find work through a hiring fair for a farmer elsewhere in Ireland; later he might find temporary work in England or Scotland, possibly as a so-called 'harvest migrant', and finally, after gaining experience and accumulating some savings, he might emigrate to London, New York or one of the mining towns in Canada or Australia. The difficulty of fully assessing the validity of the concept of stepwise migration lies in the problem of obtaining longitudinal migration case histories. Even where such data are available or have been obtained through questionnaire surveys, the evidence is often conflicting. Perhaps all that can be safely concluded is that stepwise movement up a hierarchy from a rural farm environment to the national metropolis is just one of many types of movement which include short-circuits of the hierarchy and reverse movements (Fig. 6.8b).

A rare example of the case-history type of study, completed in New Zealand (Keown, 1971), in which migrations in the predominantly rural western Southland region of South Island were investigated, shows that the stepwise model failed to account for all the migrations that had taken place. Instead the study suggested that a stepwise movement up the urban hierarchy is just one of three types of movement, each of which is related to occupational characteristics (Fig. 6.9).

The author recognised three groups of migrants in western Southland as follows:

1 A group of migrants who worked in farming, forestry and mining in the study area and who moved over short distances within the area.
2 Another group of persons who were changing their occupation. They were generally leaving farming, forestry and mining and seeking different types of employment in larger towns and cities. Their movements fitted the stepwise concept of movement up the urban hierarchy.

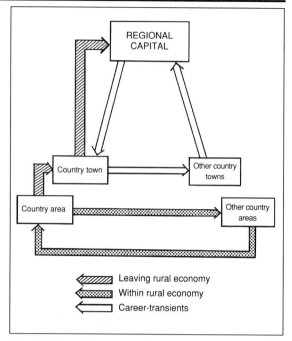

Fig. 6.9 A model of rural migration for western Southland, New Zealand.
Source: after Keown, 1971.

3 A third group termed *career-transients*, who moved through the area for promotion within a regional or national context and whose moves were in no way related to distance or a stepwise progression. Such migrants included government officers, post-office workers, bank and railway officials and teachers. Whether they were moving up or down the urban hierarchy or laterally within it depended to a great extent on whether they began their careers in a large city or country town, and on the location of opportunities for promotion within their chosen careers.

This chapter has ranged widely over a large field of study and a substantial number of concepts and models has been introduced. These concepts and models are explored further in Case Studies 6A and 6B.

Exercise 6.3

Districts in England and Wales experiencing rapid population increase or decrease, 1971–81

Read Case Study 6A, paying particular attention to the final section. Then consider carefully the information provided below which shows the 12 districts in England and Wales with the largest population increases 1971–81 and the 12 districts with the largest population decreases in the same period. Out-migration or in-migration was a major factor in producing the changes shown in each case.

a) Decide in which of the categories of district 1–11, as shown in Fig. 6.12, each of the 24 districts belongs.

b) For each category to which you assign a district or districts, name and discuss:
  i) the main reasons that have attracted migrants to that category of district in the case of those categories that experienced rapid growth, and
  ii) the main reasons that induced migrants to leave in the case of those categories that experienced rapid decline.

Largest relative population changes in England and Wales, 1971–81, by district

Largest increases		Largest decreases	
District (name and county)	**1971–81 population increase (%)**	**District (name and county)**	**1971–81 population decrease (%)**
Milton Keynes (Buckinghamshire)	85	Kensington and Chelsea (London)	26
Redditch (Hereford and Worcester)	63	Hammersmith and Fulham (London)	21
Tamworth (Staffordshire)	60	Islington (London)	21
City of London (London)	39	Westminster, City of (London)	20
Wimborne (Dorset)	32	Lambeth (London)	20
Forest Heath (Suffolk)	31	Southwark (London)	19
Bracknell (Berkshire)	28	Hackney (London)	18
Huntingdon (Cambridgeshire)	27	Manchester (Greater Manchester)	17
The Wrekin (Shropshire)	27	Camden (London)	17
Halton (Cheshire)	27	Liverpool (Merseyside)	16
Blyth Valley (Northumberland)	26	Wandsworth (London)	15
Breckland (Norfolk)	26	Haringey (London)	15

Regional and local migration in England and Wales since 1851

The growth of population in England and Wales during the nineteenth and twentieth centuries has already been described in Case Study 2A in Part One. As this growth took place there was a substantial re-distribution of the population, and it is the aim of this case study to outline the broad migratory trends at regional and local levels since 1851. Obviously this will involve some over-simplification of what were, and continue to be, exceedingly complex processes and patterns. In large areas over relatively short periods of time the trend has not been one of either continuous net in-migration or out-migration but one of fluctuation, as stagnation has succeeded growth and expansion has been followed by decline. The study is in four parts: the period from 1851 to 1911, which was one of rapid rural loss and urban gain; the period from 1911 to 1951, which saw a reversal of some of the earlier trends; the period between 1951 and 1971 in which certain of the trends of the first half of the century accelerated and other trends appeared for the first time; and the period since 1971 in which selective out-migration from the largest urban areas has been a major contributory factor in population growth in small towns and rural districts in the accessible countryside and more remote areas.

Migration 1851–1911

During the second half of the nineteenth century the rural areas suffered almost universally from prolonged and heavy depopulation, and gains by migration were recorded only in those rural areas which lay very near to growing urban areas and which became suburbanised. Figure 6.10, based

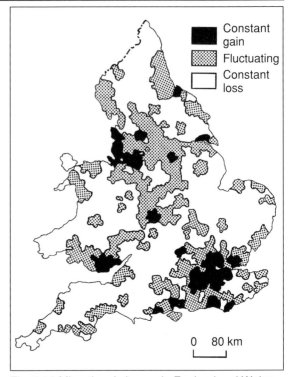

Fig. 6.10 Migrational change in England and Wales, 1851–1911.
Source: after Lawton, 1967.

on aggregates of migrational changes by decade between 1851 and 1911, shows large areas of severe out-migration stretching across South-west England into the South Midlands, occupying much of East Anglia, covering Wales outside the coalfields and including large areas in Lincolnshire, the Yorkshire Wolds, the Vale of York and the northern Pennines.

The causes of this heavy out-migration were varied and included both push factors in the rural areas and pull factors at potential destinations. One very important push factor was the decline in the demand for farm labour. During the late eighteenth century and the first half of the nineteenth century, acts of enclosure, reclamation schemes and the more intensive use of farmland actually increased rural population in some areas and kept it stable in others, but after the 1840s the demand for labour for hedging and draining declined. After the 1850s, increased mechanisation further reduced the need for manual labour, though ironically, after 1870 when rural depopulation reached particularly high levels, more mechanisation was called for because of labour shortages.

Continuously declining rural populations and the penetration of factory-made products into rural areas also caused the out-migration of rural craftsmen, tradesmen and professional people, not only from the villages but also from small country towns. The decline of rurally based trades and professions increased the isolation of the farm labourers among the residual rural population and this provided a further stimulus for out-migration, particularly among the young.

The net result of the prolonged presence of these negative factors was that the number of agricultural labourers (including shepherds) aged over 20 fell (according to calculations made by Lawton, 1967) from 809,000 in 1861 to just over 498,000 in 1911. During the same period the total rural population fell absolutely and proportionally from 9.1 million (45.4% of the total population) to 7.9 million (21.9% of the population).

The areas which attracted the rural migrants were London, the fast-growing coalfield industrial areas especially in South Wales, the West Midlands, South Lancashire, West and South Yorkshire, Northumberland and Durham, and the ports of Humberside and Merseyside (Fig. 6.10). All these areas combined the advantages of rapidly growing and varied employment, improved living conditions (especially after the Public Health Act of 1875) and greater opportunities for educational and social advancement. The vast majority of the rural migrants were young and this rapid urban population growth was the result of both in-migration and high birth rates. The urban population increased from just under 9 million in 1851, when it accounted for 54.2% of the population, to just under 28 million in 1911, by which time 80% of the population were classified as urban. London, Birmingham, Liverpool and Manchester were the cities in which the greatest absolute population growth took place, followed by Leeds, Newcastle and Sheffield. Among other rapidly growing urban areas were seaside resorts such as Blackpool, Bournemouth and Brighton, inland resorts such as

Bath, Cheltenham and Harrogate, 'new towns' such as the industrial creations of Middlesbrough, Scunthorpe and St Helens, and the railway towns of Crewe and Swindon.

Migration trends between 1911 and 1951

The 40 years between 1911 and 1951 saw the continuation of a number of trends from the nineteenth century, and the reversal of a number of others. Figure 6.11a, showing population losses by migration between 1921 and 1947, indicates clearly the continued depopulation of the remotest and most purely agricultural of the rural areas. Exmoor, Central Wales, northern East Anglia, the Fens, large parts of rural Lincolnshire, the Vale of Pickering, the North York Moors and the northern Pennines all recorded overall net migrational losses during this period. Increased mechanisation, low earnings and isolation continued to be important push factors.

In addition to the rural areas, out-migration became a feature of a number of areas which in the preceding 60 years had been areas of massive and almost continuous population increase. These were the conurbations and the coalfield industrial towns. The migration from the conurbations, which tended to slow down the overall increase of population rather than cause absolute decline, was in large part due to the relocation of population in adjacent rural districts and small towns outside the conurbation boundaries. This took the form of voluntary movement by those seeking rural residential locations while continuing to work in the conurbations, and planned rehousing of populations from inner-city slums. This was a marked feature around London, the West Midlands conurbation and Merseyside, especially after 1945. The out-migration from the coalfield towns, which was especially severe in South Wales, Lancashire and North-east England, resulted from the stagnation or decline of the staple industries of these regions, namely cotton spinning and weaving, textile machinery, shipbuilding, coal mining and heavy engineering. Not only did employment fail to expand in the staple industries, but many towns in these regions were dependent upon a narrow range of occupations,

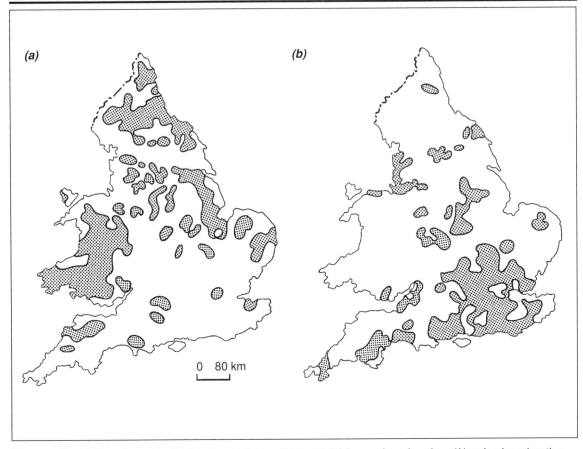

Fig. 6.11 Population change in England and Wales, 1921–47: (a) losses by migration, (b) gains by migration. *Source:* simplified from Willatts and Newsom, 1953.

often all declining. The contraction of employment opportunities, coupled with continued high levels of natural increase, inevitably led to widespread unemployment and heavy out-migration. The designation in 1934 of three Special Areas (the North-East, West Cumberland and South Wales) in which government assistance was available for industrial development, wartime measures to direct industry to new locations, and the reconstitution of the Special Areas as Development Areas in 1945 (with the addition of Wrexham, South Lancashire and North-east Lancashire between 1947 and 1953), all reduced outward migration from the declining areas to some degree although it continued to be important both relatively and absolutely throughout the period.

The most notable features of the map showing areas of net gain through migration in the period 1921–47 (Fig. 6.11b) are the concentrations of such areas in the Midlands and particularly in South-east England. This was the result of the so-called 'drift to the South' from the declining industrial regions. The industrial structure of the towns and cities of the Midlands and South-east England was strikingly different from that of the towns of South Wales and Northern England in two respects. Since the end of the First World War, growth industries such as electrical engineering, the manufacture of electronic and radio apparatus, motor vehicle assembly and component manufacturing, aircraft manufacturing, paper making and printing and food products had greatly increased and one-industry towns were far less common. Additionally, service industries such as banking, finance and insurance were overwhelmingly concentrated in the South East.

Two other features of migration between 1911 and 1951 are worth noting. First, there were significant net gains in rural coalfield areas where deep, concealed coal measures were being exploited for the first time. This was particularly marked in the eastern parts of the Yorkshire, Derbyshire and Nottinghamshire coalfield. Secondly, there were important rural and urban gains, including many retired people, in the coastal areas of Kent, Sussex, Hampshire, Devon, Cornwall, North Wales and Lancashire.

Migration between 1951 and 1971

Between 1951 and 1971 the most remote Welsh counties and the most northerly English rural counties continued to suffer migrational losses. Northumberland had the greatest population loss among English counties between 1961 and 1971, and Montgomery and Radnor (now Powys) in Central Wales, which had suffered from severe and continuous out-migration for well over a century, were by 1971 the most thinly populated counties in England and Wales.

There were also continued losses from the old industrial regions of Northern England and South Wales and from the conurbations and largest cities. Successive British governments since the mid-1940s had been pursuing planning policies designed to slow down and eventually eradicate the large-scale migration from the old industrial regions (Assisted Areas policy) and to relocate population and industries outside the largest conurbations (Green Belt and New Town policies).

By the early 1970s the whole of Wales, almost the whole of Northern England north of Nottingham, and much of South-west England were included within the assisted areas. These varied from Intermediate Areas, which were growing only slowly economically and were considered to be potential problem areas, to Development Areas, which had bad economic and social problems, and Special Development Areas in which the economic and social problems were particularly severe. In all these areas government subsidies were available, varying in size according to the type of area and including grants for new industrial buildings, new plant and machinery, capital loans on favourable terms for expansion schemes,

and grants towards the costs incurred when a business moved to a new area. In addition there were government-built factories for sale or rent at specially reduced rates. These measures were successful in promoting industrial development and in slowing down out-migration, but unemployment, substandard housing, derelict land and levels of out-migration were all above the national average in assisted areas in the 1950s and 1960s.

The New Towns Act of 1946 was also an important means of regulating population movement and distribution. The towns built during the first phase (1946–50) were overwhelmingly concentrated in the South East and, with one exception, Corby, they were concerned either with the planned decentralisation of population and employment from Greater London or with the creation of growth points in the assisted areas. The new towns of the second phase (1961–7) were fewer in number, more widely distributed and more diverse in function. Skelmersdale and Redditch were designed as overspill towns, Runcorn as a comprehensive redevelopment scheme and Washington and Newtown as regional growth centres. The third-phase new towns (1967–79) were all expansions of existing medium-sized or large towns and their projected sizes were much greater than those of the towns of the first two phases. Milton Keynes, Peterborough and Northampton were designed to act as counter-magnets to conurbation development in the South East, and Warrington, Telford and the Central Lancashire New Town as urban renewal schemes with overspill and counter-magnet functions.

The planned relocation of urban populations and voluntary out-migration resulted in a marked decentralisation of population from the conurbations and large cities, particularly in the period 1961–71. In the 1960s, Greater London lost more than 500,000 people and losses were also recorded in the Tyneside conurbation (from 0.86 million to 0.80 million), West Midlands (2.38 million to 2.37 million), South-east Lancashire (2.43 million to 2.39 million) and Merseyside (1.38 million to 1.26 million). Only the West Yorkshire conurbation (1.70 million to 1.73 million) recorded a population increase in the 1960s and significantly this has no related new towns.

In spite of regional and urban planning on a large scale, population and employment continued to increase most rapidly in the Midlands and the South East. Between 1951 and 1961 and between 1961 and 1971 the greatest growth of population was recorded in the area south and south-east of a line from the Wash to the mouth of the Severn. One significant difference between the 1950s and 1960s in this area of marked growth was that the rates of growth of those counties nearest to London which grew very rapidly in the 1950s were lower in the 1960s than those of the outer parts of the region in the East Midlands, East Anglia and the South West. This change in growth rate suggests that the planned and voluntary population and industrial decentralisation from the inner parts of the Midlands and the South East was gradually diffusing outwards.

Migration since 1971

Between 1971 and 1981 the conurbations continued to lose population at an accelerating rate.

Inner London's population declined by 17.7% and several individual boroughs by over 20%. Not far behind were some of the largest provincial metropolises. Manchester and Liverpool declined by 17% and 16% respectively, each losing between 90,000 and 100,000 people during the decade. In London, decline was not restricted to the inner areas. Outer London as a whole lost 221,000 people, a decrease of 5%, and some boroughs declined by as much as 10%.

Nor was population decline restricted to the largest urban areas, as Fig. 6.12 clearly shows. Those districts in the metropolitan counties not dominated by the principal city also declined by 2%, large cities outside the metropolitan counties declined as a whole by 5.1%, and even the smaller cities and towns beyond the metropolitan counties declined by 3.2%. The decade, then, was marked by a further contraction of the high and middle levels of the urban system and this contraction was overwhelmingly the result of out-migration. The detailed results of the 1991 census

Category of district	1971–81 population change	
	Thousands	**%**
England and Wales	262	0.5
Greater London Boroughs	−756	−10.1
1 Inner London	−535	−17.7
2 Outer London	−221	−5.0
Metropolitan Districts	−546	−4.6
3 The principal cities	−386	−10.0
4 Others	−160	−2.0
Non-Metropolitan Districts	1,564	5.3
5 Large cities (over 175,000)	−149	−5.1
6 Smaller cities	−55	−3.2
7 Industrial districts		
a) Wales and the three northern regions of England	42	1.3
b) Rest of England	158	5.0
8 Districts that include new towns	283	15.1
9 Resorts and seaside retirement districts	156	4.9
10 Other urban, mixed urban-rural and more accessible rural districts		
a) Outside the South East	307	8.8
b) In South East	468	6.7
11 Remoter, largely rural districts	354	10.3

Fig. 6.12 Population change for different categories of districts, 1971–81.

are not available at the time of writing but estimates made since 1981 suggest that these *counter-urbanisation* trends are continuing. An important exception to this conclusion is London which in recent years has been undergoing a population recovery. Between 1961 and 1971 its population fell by 538,000 and between 1971 and 1981 by 756,000. In contrast, between 1981 and 1987 the capital's population fell by only 45,000 and in each year between 1983 and 1985 there was a slight population increase.

Despite London's recovery, the highest relative increases in population in the 1970s and 1980s were beyond the conurbations and the largest free-standing towns and cities, particularly in an area in the East and South East from the Wash to the Solent. Other accessible districts showing noticeable increases of population in the same period occur around Birmingham and Manchester. Large population increases also took place in those districts containing new towns and overspill settlements. These trends are considered further in Exercise 6.3. Resort and seaside retirement districts, most notably on the South coast and in the South West, and remote districts in Central Wales and the Northern region (which for over a century had been areas of decline) have also seen significant population increases since 1971 (Fig. 6.12).

What appears to have taken place since 1971 is an accelerated out-migration from the major urban areas accompanied by what has been termed the 'rush Southwards'. This selective migration has been particularly marked among the younger age groups and the more skilled, leaving behind relatively large proportions of the old, the unskilled and the unemployed. As in the United States (see Case Study 3B) this changing distribution of the population has been, in large part, a response to changes in the structure of the economy, principally a move from an economy dominated by manufacturing to one dominated by service industries. Those manufacturing industries still holding their own or expanding are mainly technologically based industries which tend to be *footloose* in terms of locational preferences. At the same time service industries such as banking, insurance and corporate headquarters are less tied to the largest urban centres because of high rates, inadequate accommodation, congestion and employee dissatisfaction with house prices and long and difficult journeys to work. For example, East Anglia, for much of the nineteenth and first half of the twentieth century a region of population decline or very slow growth, has been a major recipient of people and decentralised employment since 1951, particularly since 1971. Its population grew by 11.7% between 1971 and 1981, and that rate of growth was almost equalled in the 1980s. Between 1983 and 1987 alone, manufacturing employment in the region grew by 21% and service industry employment by 25%. Both of these rates were the highest in the United Kingdom as a whole in that period.

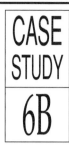

CASE STUDY 6B

Transmigration in Indonesia

The term 'transmigration' is used in Indonesia to describe the resettlement of people from densely populated parts of the country in the islands of Java, Bali, Madura and Lombok to some of the less densely populated 'outer islands' such as Sumatra, Sulawesi, Kalimantan, and Irian Jaya (Fig. 6.13). This process began during the Dutch colonial period in the early years of the twentieth century – at first mainly to provide labour for plantations. Later, the government saw transmigration as a means of solving problems of population pressure in the intensive rice-growing areas of Java, of similar areas in other islands and in some overcrowded urban areas. The first large-scale migrations in the 1930s, which were predominantly conservative migrations, to use Petersen's terminology (see Chapter 8), involved the move-

ment to newly irrigated areas in Lampung province, southern Sumatra, of rice farmers from parts of Java where land fragmentation resulting from subdivision for inheritance purposes was creating a situation where holdings were too small to support a family.

Altogether over 200,000 transmigrants were re-settled under government programmes before the Japanese invasion in 1941, over 85% of them in Sumatra with smaller numbers in what are now Sulawesi and Kalimantan. After the Japanese occupation and the fight for independence from the Dutch that led to full independence in 1949, transmigration resumed with a further 424,000 transmigrants resettled in the next 20 years, the vast majority still moving to Sumatra. The nature of this migration was similar to that of earlier years, being designed to relieve pressure on the main zone of origin, the densely populated rice-producing areas of Java, with the new settlers aiming to become self-sufficient in food crops at their destinations though some were also involved in growing cash crops.

Since 1970 ideas about transmigration have altered markedly and there have been various changes in transmigration policies. The increasing awareness that there were major problems of land shortage and landlessness as a result of popula-

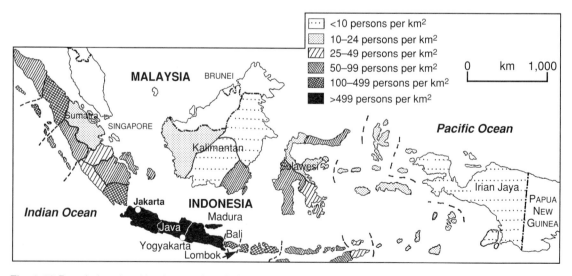

Fig. 6.13 Population densities by province in Indonesia, 1985.
Source: based on data from Department of Information, Republic of Indonesia, 1990.

tion increase in areas outside Java, such as Bali and Lombok, and that the land:population equation in Java was not going to be solved solely by transmigration, had a strong influence on attitudes and approaches. Massive rural–urban migration, especially from the pressurised rural areas of Java, also influenced the government to seek new solutions in both rural and urban areas. In rural areas, intensification of rice production was encouraged and, partly because of this, double-cropping is widespread in Java today, and triple-cropping in Bali. This has been helped to some extent by the use of improved grain varieties with shorter growing seasons but, in general, rice production still follows a much more traditional pattern in these areas than in much of the rest of Asia with only limited mechanisation and therefore probably fewer employment problems than might have been the case if the methods of the Green Revolution had been more fully adopted. In Lombok, most farmers are still restricted to one crop per year by water supply problems, and poverty is often more overt than in Bali or Java despite lower population densities. By the late 1980s, Indonesia had achieved a rather precarious state of self-sufficiency in rice production while rural poverty, though still widespread, had been somewhat reduced. Investment in the urban economy, housing and social services had also brought about some improvement but many cities still had major problems of overcrowding, with Jakarta and Yogyakarta officially designated as sources of transmigrants. In addition, between 1970 and 1990 official family planning policies helped to reduce the birth rates from 47 to below 30 per thousand, thus reducing the scale of potential future pressures.

Despite the changes outlined above, numbers registering for transmigration after 1970 continued to exceed the places available. Migration was selective, with transmigrants usually aged below 30. Most typically such migrants were from farming families. Faced with the prospect of becoming landless or inheriting an area of land inadequate to support a family in their home area, many young men found the government's offer of two hectares of land and a house in another island attractive enough to overcome any positive factors in the zone of origin. Many urban residents with employment problems and low living standards found such an offer equally attractive.

Between 1950 and 1970 over 900,000 people (185,000 families) were resettled under the transmigration scheme. During the 1970s transmigration continued as a major policy with over 480,000 settlers moving to the outer island areas. From 1979 to 1986 the process accelerated markedly with over half a million more families moving under the scheme, a peak of 80,000 families being reached in 1986. By then, over 700,000 families, more than 3 million people, had moved as official transmigrants from Java, Madura, Bali and Lombok to other islands. A further 200,000 families are estimated to have moved without government help (Madeley, 1988b), forming part of a process of chain migration as they responded to positive feedback from earlier transmigrants. In 1987, however, the transmigration programme slowed dramatically, with only some 10,000 families migrating in that year under the official scheme. Reasons for this included government financial shortages, largely resulting from falling oil revenues and growing foreign indebtedness (it costs about US$10,000 to resettle a family); increased concern about the social and environmental impacts of transmigration; and a growing acceptance that transmigration has had only a limited effect on the situations it was designed to resolve in the densely populated zones of origin. The numbers migrating annually under the general transmigration scheme had shown an increase over the 1987 figure to about 25–30,000 by the end of the decade but were outnumbered by a ratio of more than 4 to 1 by what the government calls spontaneous transmigrants (*Indonesia Official Handbook, 1990*), i.e. those moving outside the official scheme.

Figure 6.13 indicates that great contrasts in population density still existed within the country in the mid-1980s despite the markedly increased densities in some transmigration destination areas. By 1990, about 110 million of Indonesia's estimated 182 million people lived in Java at a mean density of over 800 per square kilometre while Sumatra, the main early destination for transmigrants and the second most populous island, supported some 35 million people at a mean density only one-tenth that of Java. Bali had fewer than 4 million inhabitants but a density approaching 500 per square kilometre while the large area of Irian Jaya, an important destination for recent transmigrants, had a density of only 6 per square kilometre. Although such contrasts imply that there is still much scope for further transmigration to even out population densities between islands, Hardjono (1983) and others have pointed out that it is naive to view the outer islands as grossly underpopulated when, in fact, there is a shortage of suitable sites for development.

Much of the early migration was to drained coastal swamps in southern Sumatra with rich soils, satisfactory water supplies for wet rice cultivation, and few indigenous people. Migrants to this area have generally been very successful, though some problems have arisen more recently as we shall discuss later. In other areas, much of the resettlement has been in forested areas, previously occupied by shifting cultivators or by people who lived by hunting and gathering. In such areas, the indigenous peoples have often suffered as a result of transmigrant settlement and there has been some criticism that such settlement has been politically motivated in 'planting' pro-government populations in areas where indigenous groups may be more hostile to the government, notably in Irian Jaya. Moreover, such areas are usually unsuitable for wet rice cultivation and attempts to grow various other annual crops on forest soils have sometimes proved unsuccessful as fertility has declined after a few years, causing major ecological damage and creating problems for settlers, considerable numbers of whom have found themselves in severe financial difficulties as crop yields have declined. This has resulted in counter-streams of disgruntled migrants returning home from some areas. Attempts to clear both primary and secondary forest for re-settlement purposes have been widely criticised by environmental groups. Indonesia has some 120 million hectares of forest land and has recently designated 60 million hectares of this as protected forest, 30 million hectares as forest available for selected cutting and the final 30 million hectares, mainly secondary forest, as land to be available for non-forest uses. It is in this last category that

future resettlement sites will be made.

Whatever the longer-term results of this policy it is clear that transmigration has had a range of impacts on the areas to which people have moved. A slightly more detailed examination of the situation in Lampung province, Sumatra, the destination of over 100,000 transmigrant families, emphasises the complexity of such impacts and some of the problems encountered in planning migration. Sasdi (1990) has described how transmigrants have transformed formerly forested resettlement areas into fertile irrigated farming areas in South and Central Lampung. These contrast strongly with adjacent land occupied by indigenous peoples. Many settlers are now relatively affluent and have planted cash crops such as coffee, cloves and pepper to supplement their incomes, often turning protected forest land and unauthorised zones along river banks into plantations to increase their earnings. Local officials have estimated that migrants have been responsible for the destruction of 70% of the protected forest in the province and settlers are being evicted from unauthorised areas in South and Central Lampung and moved into the less densely populated district of North Lampung which occupies 54% of the province's 35,000 square kilometres but holds under 30% of its 7.5 million people. New plantations are being developed in this area growing oil palm, coconuts, sugar cane, rubber and cassava. With an overall population density of over 200 per square kilometre, Lampung is relatively densely populated – largely because of transmigration – and official transmigration to this area has now ceased. Contacts maintained by earlier migrants with their rural areas of origin have resulted in much positive feedback, however, and there is a continuing pattern of chain migration involving what Mabogunje would classify as passive migrants. These individuals, despite the absence of the government help provided under the official transmigration scheme, are maintaining the flow of migrants to Lampung. Many of them are relatively affluent by the standards of the areas from which they come and so are able to afford to pay their own travel expenses, and establish themselves in their new home. Their presence is, however, likely to increase ecological pressures in

Lampung as they add to the existing problems of a population growth rate that was over 5.5% in the mid-1980s.

Clearly transmigration has had a major impact on Lampung and this is true of most other destination areas for transmigrants, though the nature of such impacts has varied from place to place. The impact on areas of origin has been less obvious and has only marginally reduced population pressures in such areas. Family planning policies may ultimately prove to be much more significant in this respect. Government-aided transmigration in future seems likely to be less important than spontaneous migration but represents a significant attempt to use migration as a primary means of development policy. Its impact, both on settlers and on the areas settled, has been varied – but in a country as vast and complex as Indonesia this is perhaps not surprising.

7
Circulation

The concept of circulation was briefly discussed in Chapter 5 but the significance of such temporary, often short and repetitive movements in different societies demands more detailed treatment. Not only is a study of circulation important because of its economic and social significance, but also because of the planning problems that it gives rise to at local, regional and national levels in many countries. There are great variations in type, nature and intensity of circulation, and it is beyond the scope of this chapter to deal in depth with every aspect. What we shall try to provide is a review of the changing form and function of circulation as the modernisation of societies takes place. Particular emphasis will be placed on the journey to work, one of the most important types of circulation in developed countries and a feature of growing importance to developing countries.

Circulation in developing countries

In many sedentary peasant societies, both in the historic past in what are now developed countries, and at the present time in parts of the developing world, ideas and behaviour, including patterns of movement, have traditionally been rigidly circumscribed. Inherited class, occupation and gender were, and still are in many societies, formidable barriers to personal mobility. In such societies *fields of information* are usually small and ideas and attitudes change only slowly. (An information field is the area from which a sedentary individual receives information. Such fields normally show the effects of distance-decay. In addition they tend to vary in size in relation to the degree of modernisation of the society to which the individual belongs.) In such circumstances, circulation is often restricted to movements concerned with tilling the land, pasturing animals, trips to local markets and visits related to religious observance. Local communities, especially in broken country, may in such conditions have relatively little contact with their neighbours except in times of inter-community disputes and at marriages. Such relatively immobile societies are still quite common in isolated regions of Latin America, Africa and Asia.

The decline of traditional forms of circulation

In many other forms of traditional society some type of circulatory movement has been important though today this is often in decline. Food gatherers such as the Semang in the Malay peninsula, the Inuit seal and caribou hunters of Arctic North America, shifting cultivators such as the Boro of the Amazon Basin, camel and goat herders of North Africa and the Middle East, horse and sheep herders in Central Asia and cattle herders in East Africa have all relied upon some form of circulation to provide themselves with food. Traditional lifestyles amongst such groups have involved rhythms of movement evolved over long periods of time. In the case of shifting cultivators, movement from one area to another has occurred at fairly regular intervals (though the number of years between moves has varied in relation to soil fertility and other factors) and usually within fairly well-defined territories. Even when land may have appeared to outsiders to have been abandoned, it often formed part of a long-fallow system (see Chapter 4). Recent population growth and commercial pressures to develop areas formerly under shifting cultivation for other purposes (e.g. cattle ranching or timber production) have often led to the intensification of cultivation and a deterioration in the quality of land still being cultivated. In some cases shifting cultivators have become sedentary farmers as in parts of East and West Africa; in others they have participated in government settlement schemes, as in Malaysia; in yet others they continue to follow their traditional lifestyle in conditions of increasing difficulty, as in parts of northern Thailand.

The movements of nomadic livestock herders are usually marked by a seasonal rhythm determined in relation to water supply and pastures, with particular areas regarded as the exclusive property of certain groups. Annual movements have frequently involved crossing international boundaries as with the Somali herders who moved between Somalia, Ethiopia and Kenya in some cases. Because of the frequent movement of such groups, homes have traditionally been relatively impermanent – a tent or a hut made from branches covered with mud and/or dung being typical (see Fig. 7.1). Only in a very few cases do societies of this kind continue to live in isolation from the outside world – the rise to power of new political regimes and a greater emphasis on the significance of political boundaries, agricultural expansion, mineral exploitation, road and railway construction, and military considerations have all brought such groups into contact with modern society. In extreme cases, groups have been forced to settle permanently, either through environmental deterioration as in parts of the Saharan margins or by government direction as in parts of the former USSR.

Even where traditional ways of life persist, they are much infiltrated by outside influences, and circulatory movements have often been severely curtailed. Thus the Maasai in Kenya and Tanzania have during the twentieth century lost parts of their former pastures to provide land for cultivators, for urban and industrial developments and for national parks and game reserves. Their movements have thus been restricted and most Maasai groups have altered their lifestyle as a result of modern influences. Some still follow their traditional way of life with only minor modifications, others have become less nomadic and changed their lifestyle dramatically, with a few even becoming largely dependent on cultivation (usually carried out by wives from a different tribal background) and some involved in tourism through allowing tourists to visit their homes and selling them trinkets of various kinds. Additionally, the spread of modern education has led to some Maasai becoming teachers, government workers and the like, abandoning their traditional way of life completely in some cases. Case Study 7A illustrates how dramatic economic and political changes have affected nomads in the western Sahara.

Fig. 7.1 A traditional dwelling of the Maasai. Many of the younger Maasai no longer live in the traditional wattle and dung dwellings of the type shown here but build houses of concrete blocks with corrugated metal roofs. This is indicative of the changing lifestyles and reduced degree of nomadism of the Maasai in recent times.

Commuting to urban areas in developing countries

The significance of migrants in the urbanisation process in developing countries has already been mentioned in earlier chapters but in many cases so-called migrants are involved in a process perhaps more accurately described as 'long-term commuting'. This term describes a situation in which an individual retains a rural home but moves to live and work in the city for much of the year. This is generally a response of the poor to improve their situation by keeping their rural home – and often an associated small plot of land from which other members of the family will strive to produce as much food as possible – while earning as much as possible and living as cheaply as possible in the urban area. The development of cheap, informal housing areas in many cities is partly related to this process and forms part of a pattern sometimes described as 'earning in the city, spending in the village' which has a wide range of impacts on both rural and urban areas. Early movement of this kind mainly involved young men with the women staying in the village and this still tends to be common in areas where women take responsibility for much or most farming activity, as with the Kikuyu people of Kenya, for example.

In a detailed examination of villages in West Java, Hugo (1979) found circulation to be the dominant form of rural–urban mobility in more than two-thirds of the villages surveyed. Most of those involved were young men and the mean length of time that non-daily commuters were absent from their village varied between a week and six months, the frequency of links being largely related to transport costs and the commuter's ability to meet these out of his urban income. Although many of these long-term commuters received very low incomes in the city in which they worked (usually Jakarta or Bandung), remittances sent to the village ranged between 21% and 44% of their income and formed a significant factor in providing the basic necessities of life for their families, accounting on average for nearly half the family income. Many of these Javanese commuters worked in informal sector occupations in the city and this enabled most of them to work also in their home village for part of the year – usually timed to coincide with periods of maximum labour requirement in agriculture. One adverse impact of the absence of young men for much of the year noted by Hugo was a decline in the amount of communal work making general improvements to the village in off-season agricultural periods. He also recorded various possible social effects of the system including high divorce rates, increased pressures on wives and mothers caused by the absence of fathers for much of the year, some problems of village leadership, and the introduction of new ideas and attitudes (about which villagers had mixed feelings).

Government attempts to provide universal education and the recent expansion of employment opportunities for women in some areas have helped to increase the amount of both migration and commuting of women to urban areas in many developing countries. Drakakis-Smith (1987) suggests that much female labour of this kind is of short duration and targeted at obtaining a dowry prior to marriage; it is non-unionised, docile, cheap and more dextrous than male labour. Thus it is in much demand for intricate assembly work in industry. While these factors do not always apply, they have been significant in creating a situation in some industrialising countries such as South Korea and the Philippines in which the number of young women involved in migration and long-term commuting now exceeds that of men of a similar age.

Daily commuting has also increased in many developing countries in recent years. It is particularly evident in association with the larger urban centres. Naipaul's (1981) description of commuters as 'lemminglike crowds stampeding in and out' of the Victoria rail terminus in Bombay is indicative of similar scenes in other large Indian cities and the sight of trains, seemingly carrying almost as many commuters clinging to their exteriors as in their carriages, is a familiar one in and near many cities in the developing world. Journey-to-work times by rail may be in excess of two hours in some of the largest cities and, while commuting by private car is generally much less common than in many developed countries because of the cost, a mass of cheap, informal public transport services has developed, principally to serve the needs of the less affluent commuters. In Kenya, *matatus* (minibuses named after the 30-cent flat fee they used to charge) now dominate commuter transport services in much of the country, despite a notable disregard for passenger safety. The cacophony of varied horn-blasts of these vehicles at the crack of dawn in Kakamega, Western Kenya, warning commuters to Kisumu and other towns that they are about to leave, is a sound one of the authors will never forget. Cheap transport of this kind is likely to facilitate the growth of commuting in developing countries in future. Case Study 7B illustrates something of the nature of commuting to a small Indian town where industrial growth has provided a recent stimulus to commuting.

Circulation in developed countries

Circulation in economically advanced nations has reached unprecedented levels in recent years. Much of this is economically motivated, with trips to and from work and during the course of work accounting for a large proportion of adult circulation. In addition, the number of trips made to shops, to hotels and restaurants, to sports stadia, to friends and relatives and to holiday resorts (Fig. 7.2) is also significant. For example, according to a recent *National Travel Survey*, 27% of all journeys made in Great Britain in 1985–86 were to or from work or in the course of work. These accounted for 32% of the mileage travelled. Journeys for social or entertainment purposes, holidays and day trips accounted for 33% of all journeys and 42% of the mileage travelled. Although shopping accounted for about 20% of all journeys, it accounted for only 12% of the mileage travelled, reflecting the predominance of short shopping trips. The survey also showed the significance of gender and age in circulatory habits. Figure 7.3, which summarises the survey findings concern-

Fig. 7.2 Holiday traffic on the M5 motorway near Bristol, one of the main routeways to the tourist resorts of the South West. In the United Kingdom and other developed countries, shorter working hours, longer holidays and widespread car ownership allow a much wider range and greater volume of recreation-oriented circulation than ever before. Despite massive extension of road networks to cater for this, traffic congestion related to holiday traffic is still a common problem in many areas.

ing the number of journeys made and the distance travelled per week, reveals some marked differences between men and women in the economically active age range, and between these two groups and the young and old. The same survey also showed some interesting changes over time. In 1965, people on average were making 11 journeys per week compared with 13 in 1985–86, and the average journey length increased from 6.5 to 7.5 miles in the same period. In 1972–73, 54% of all journeys to and from work were by car, van or lorry, compared

				Journey purpose						
				Escorting						
	To or from work	In course of work	Educ- ation	Work	Educ- ation	Shopping	Other personal business	Social or entertain- ment	Holidays/ day trips/ other	All purposes
Number of journeys										
0–15 years	0.1	–	2.6	0.2	0.2	1.8	1.0	3.0	0.7	9.8
16–59 years										
Males	6.5	1.2	0.3	0.5	0.1	2.3	2.0	4.3	0.8	18.0
Females	3.7	0.3	0.3	0.3	0.5	3.1	1.8	3.8	0.7	14.5
60 years and over	0.8	0.1	–	0.1	–	2.9	1.4	2.5	0.8	8.6
All ages	3.1	0.4	0.7	0.3	0.2	2.6	1.6	3.5	0.8	13.2
Distance travelled (miles)										
0–15 years	0.5	0.1	8.1	1.1	0.6	8.5	4.5	21.9	11.4	56.6
16–59 years										
Males	54.8	28.2	1.9	2.0	0.6	11.3	12.1	37.6	14.8	163.2
Females	19.8	3.7	1.8	1.7	1.5	14.8	9.8	32.0	15.2	100.2
60 years and over	4.5	2.2	–	0.6	0.1	11.5	7.5	19.2	12.5	58.2
All ages	22.2	9.5	2.8	1.4	0.7	11.8	8.8	28.7	13.1	99.5

Fig. 7.3 Number of journeys and distance travelled per person per week in Great Britain by purpose and age, 1985–86.
Source: National Travel Survey, and given in *Social Trends* 19 (HMSO, 1989).

with 67% in 1985–86. By contrast, there was a downward trend in the use of buses in the same period from 23% to 11%.

One thing that the table does not show is the relative importance of internal and international circulation, the latter being an increasingly important element of the total circulatory pattern in advanced countries. Entertainers, skilled workers, business managers and other 'specialists', from politicians to athletes, spend hundreds of hours each year journeying around the world, and at certain times of year these regular international travellers are joined by holiday-makers. By the late 1980s, for instance, over 20 million British tourists annually were visiting foreign destinations, more than twice as many as a decade earlier. Although many factors are involved in the rapid growth of international tourism since the 1960s, a major element is the removal or easing of many of the previously existing 'intervening obstacles' to travel,

brought about by such factors as the development of jet aircraft capable of carrying large numbers of people rapidly over long distances, and the growth in 'package holidays' that ease the physical, psychological and financial barriers to travel for many people. Exercise 7.1 examines some aspects of circulation relating to international tourism.

The significance of the journey to work

Despite the growth of international travel, internal circulation is a far more general feature of modern life than circulation at an international level. Multi-lane road networks, widespread car ownership, high-speed railways (see Fig. 7.4), 'shuttle' air services and increased levels of affluence coupled with shorter working days and weeks and longer annual holidays have all contributed to the high levels of internal circulation in economically advanced countries. In the last 40 years, car ownership has been a potent

Exercise 7.1

International tourist circulation: Singapore visitors

Consider the table below and then answer the questions that follow.

Tourist visitors to Singapore by place of residence and purpose of visit, 1987

Residence	Holiday & pleasure		Business		Business		In transit		Other		Total
	Nos	(%)	Nos	(%)	Nos	(%)	Nos	(%)	Nos	(%)	Nos
Americas (total)	158,743	60.9	38,199	14.7	20,205	7.7	29,378	11.3	14,055	5.4	260,580
Canada	26,538	72.5	2,963	8.1	2,139	5.8	3,239	8.8	1,742	4.8	36,621
USA	122,820	58.1	34,588	16.4	17,475	8.3	25,404	12.0	11,082	5.2	211,369
Asia (total)	1,522,167	66.2	305,468	13.0	109,033	4.7	149,399	6.4	228,291	9.7	2,344,358
ASEAN*	638,577	59.5	144,086	13.4	59,938	5.6	87,104	8.1	144,281	13.4	1,073,986
India	159,265	65.4	30,697	12.6	14,038	5.8	10,903	4.5	28,611	11.7	243,514
Japan	447,337	82.6	56,418	10.4	9,438	1.8	16,074	3.0	12,132	2.2	541,399
Europe (total)	417,076	67.4	75,023	12.1	28,687	4.6	65,270	10.5	33,212	5.4	619,268
UK	133,138	68.2	24,535	12.6	10,439	5.3	18,752	9.6	8,374	4.3	195,238
West Germany	63,651	68.2	11,786	12.6	4,186	4.5	10,078	10.8	3,618	3.9	93,319
Oceania (total)	293,391	69.7	34,822	8.3	12,854	3.0	57,472	13.6	22,665	5.4	421,204
Australia	229,939	69.6	29,363	8.9	9,854	3.0	44,097	13.4	16,925	5.1	330,178
New Zealand	54,021	70.6	4,515	5.9	2,545	3.3	10,848	14.2	4,578	6.0	76,507
Others	22,087	66.1	2,845	8.5	1,474	4.4	4,293	12.9	2,700	8.1	33,399
Total	2,443,464	66.4	456,357	12.4	172,253	4.7	305,812	8.3	300,923	8.2	3,678,809

* ASEAN = Brunei, Indonesia, Malaysia, Philippines, Thailand

Source: Singapore Tourist Promotion Board, 1987

1 a) Outline the main features of the pattern of visitors to Singapore at the continental scale in terms of place of origin and purpose of visit.

b) The number of visitors from Africa is so low that it is not even mentioned separately in the table. Suggest why there are so few visitors from this continent to Singapore.

2 To what extent does the table suggest that distance-decay is of significance in the patterns of holiday tourism to Singapore?

3 Select *four* of the following countries or areas. Suggest why they are the source of large tourism flows to Singapore, highlighting any differences between the flows from the countries/areas you select:
USA, Japan, the ASEAN countries, UK, Australia, India.

Fig. 7.4 Tokyo: an underground train in the rush hour. Although private cars play an increasingly significant role in commuting to small and medium-sized towns, rapid public transport systems, either underground as in this case, or at or above ground level, are the most important means of travelling to work in many of the largest metropolitan areas. The white-gloved 'pushers' who help to pack people tightly into the Tokyo trains emphasise the intensity of use of this means of transport.

force (except in the largest urban areas where rapid rail transport is very important) in allowing a wider separation of place of residence from place of work. This has resulted in the decline of population in many large metropolitan areas and a corresponding population growth in small towns and villages. During this period of *decentralisation of population* there has been a marked increase in the number of commuters, who live in one community but travel regularly, often daily, to work in another. In terms of circulation this has increased the significance of the journey to work and in settlement terms has resulted in the growth of large num-

bers of commuter towns and villages at varying distances from the major metropolitan areas. Commuter villages are also called dormitory villages, suburbanised villages, metropolitan villages, incipient suburbs and discontinuous suburbs. Case Study 7C illustrates some typical characteristics of a commuter village. Other aspects of such settlements are considered in *An Introduction to Settlement Geography*, the companion volume to this book.

The distinction between self-contained communities on the one hand and predominantly dormitory settlements on the other is sometimes quite clear, but in many cases communities fall neither into one group nor the other. One method of identifying dormitory settlements and gauging the degree of decentralisation of population is to calculate *job ratios* using the following formula:

$$\frac{\text{People } working \text{ in the area (both residents and commuters)}}{\text{Total number of employed people } living \text{ in the area}}$$

For example, a mining settlement in which 1,000 people were employed, 900 of whom lived in the settlement, and from which only 150 people made journeys to work elsewhere, would yield a job ratio of 95.2. (People working in area = 1,000. Employed people living in the area = 900 + 150 = 1,050. Job ratio therefore

$$\frac{1,000}{1,050} \times 100 = 95.2.)$$

In contrast, a commuter village containing 550 economically active people but with only 55 jobs within its boundaries would have a job ratio of only 10. (People working in area = 55. Employed people living in area = 550. Job ratio therefore

$$\frac{55}{550} \times 100 = 10.)$$

Journey-to-work patterns are, however, not confined to movements into towns and cities from outside. Complex intra-urban (within cities) patterns of circulation are also characteristic of large urban areas. These patterns are in part the result of intra-urban migrations by individuals and families who when they change their place of residence often retain their previous employment and shopping and leisure patterns (see pages 153 et seq.). Such migration is predominantly outward to the periphery of the city – although there may also be significant inward movements especially among older intra-urban migrants – and is usually connected with the life-cycle as individuals and families adjust to changing circumstances (e.g. income) and demands (e.g. family size). As intra-urban migration takes place, houses tend to 'filter down' and people tend to 'filter up'. When first built, a new neighbourhood contains housing units of basically similar style and quality and is usually located near the edge of the built-up area (exceptions to this are, for instance, re-development schemes and some fashionable apartment developments). As time passes the houses and the neighbourhood become older and usually less fashionable than newer developments. At the same time, the incomes of many of the original inhabitants increase and family sizes change. Many families therefore move to newer, often larger houses in more fashionable neighbourhoods further out, even though this may result in increased circulation in order to reach work, schools, shops and certain leisure facilities. Families of relatively lower income move into the housing in the initial neighbourhood and for most of these families this area represents an improvement on the housing and neighbourhood from which they have moved.

So far, attention has been focused on the nature of population decentralisation and on the emergence of commuting on a large scale from the outer suburbs and accessible rural areas to centres of employment in the metropolitan areas. We must now consider the question of *why* people commute. Although some people may enjoy a long journey to work, many commuters resent the loss of time involved, and investigations suggest that substantial numbers of residents of commuter settlements – particularly wives not in formal employment – dislike many aspects of their lives. Why then do people commute? Surveys in various parts of the United Kingdom suggest the existence of at least four groups of commuters as follows:

1 Commuters who are prepared to travel long distances from what they believe are better environments. Journey time may be a limiting factor to them but cost (of travelling and house purchase) is not. Such people may travel, for example, from Kent and Sussex to Central London, or from the Peak District to Sheffield, Nottingham, Derby or Manchester.
2 Young commuters, usually young married couples, who commute because housing is cheaper in certain outlying towns and villages than in the cities where they work.
3 Commuters nearing retirement who buy a house in the country or at the seaside and commute until they retire.
4 Commuters who – unlike those in the first three groups – are not migrants but commute from their life-long place of residence, because of lack of opportunities in their local area. Some of these may plan to do this indefinitely, and others, particularly young single people living with their parents, only until they marry.

The term *voluntary commuters* is often used to describe those in the first three groups and the term *inertia commuters* applied to those in the final group (Fig. 7.5). In those areas where employment as well as population has been decentralised a further group of commuters may be identified who are called *reverse commuters*. These workers, who live in the inner parts of large cities, may need to make a long journey to work every day from the centre to the periphery of the urban area. Indeed in a large number of metropolitan regions in the United States where the decentralisation of both population and employment has reached an advanced stage, many middle-class people who have decentralised make shorter journeys to work than those in lower socio-economic groups who still live in inner urban areas.

Plane (1981) has summarised the spatial complexity of commuting patterns within, into and out of metropolitan areas in the United States (Fig. 7.6). The term *metropolitan area* in the USA is used to denote a large city (called a *central city*) and its surrounding hinterland, which may include smaller cities and many towns and vil-

Fig. 7.5 The morning rush hour at Waterloo Station, London. Voluntary and inertia commuters leave the train after travelling to Central London from towns to the south and west: Alton, Basingstoke, Farnham, Guildford, Winchester and Woking.

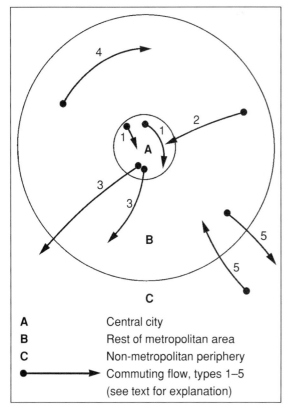

A	Central city
B	Rest of metropolitan area
C	Non-metropolitan periphery
●——▶	Commuting flow, types 1–5
	(see text for explanation)

Fig. 7.6 Typology of commuting flows within, into and out of metropolitan areas in the United States.
Source: after Plane, 1981.

lages. The smaller cities, towns and villages are popularly referred to as suburbs. A metropolitan area is, therefore, akin to a conurbation in which there are many distinct local governments, on average about 100. The significance of this latter fact will be returned to later in the chapter.

Plane has identified five types of commuting flows typical of such areas.

1 *Flows (inward, outward and lateral) restricted entirely to the central city.* These are relatively short-distance movements and predominantly from peripheral residential areas to more centrally located industrial districts and the central business district (CBD).

2 *Movement from the suburbs to the central city.* This is the type of commuting that grew rapidly in the first half of this century, but which is now of decreasing importance as employment decentralises and regroups on less congested, highway-oriented 'greenfield' sites in the suburbs.

3 *Reverse commuting.* Workers residing in the central city travel each day to the decentralised places of employment in the suburbs and beyond.

4 *Lateral commuting.* This is a rapidly increasing form of commuting in which workers who live in one suburban community travel to work in another. Such commuting typically takes place by car along multi-lane highways that have encouraged suburban residential expansion and given rise, especially at intersections, to much sought-after sites for manufacturing industry, office development and shopping centres. In the Boston metropolitan area, for example, one of these highways, Route 128, has acquired the nickname 'Technology Road' and another, the Interstate 495, has been labelled the 'Platinum Perimeter' because of its attractiveness to electronics industries.

5 *Cross-commuting.* This involves the movement out of the metropolitan area to non-metropolitan workplaces and vice versa.

Exercise 7.2 provides an opportunity to consider Plane's ideas in greater detail.

Exercise 7.2

Commuting flows within, into and out of US metropolitan areas

Study carefully the table and map provided. The table shows commuting flows within, into and out of five metropolitan areas in the New England region of the United States in 1970 as calculated by Plane (1981). Re-read the relevant section of Chapter 7 and then:

a) Define the following clearly in your own words: central city; suburbs; metropolitan area; the five types of commuting flow as defined by Plane (1981).

b) i) Calculate how many commuters in the Boston metropolitan area regularly undertook type 2 and type 4 commuting journeys in 1970.

   ii) Explain why type 2 commuting flows had become relatively unimportant by 1970 whereas type 4 commuting flows had become predominant.

c) Suggest reasons why Manchester, Portland and Providence/Pawtucket generate such large type 5 flows.

Metropolitan areas in the New England region.

Importance (%) of Plane's (1981) five types of commuting flow in selected metropolitan areas in the New England region of the United States in 1970.

Metropolitan area	Types of commuting flow as defined by Plane (1981) %					Total flow (thousands)
	Type 1	Type 2	Type 3	Type 4	Type 5	
Boston, Mass.	11.0	13.6	3.2	68.2	3.9	1,616
Hartford, Conn.	3.6	7.5	1.7	75.7	11.4	947
Manchester, NH	9.8	3.3	1.4	49.1	36.3	291
Portland, Me.	7.3	6.8	1.7	52.0	32.3	259
Providence– Pawtucket, RI/Mass.	4.4	4.7	1.5	64.3	25.1	1,519

Source: Plane, 1981.

Commuting hinterlands and megalopolis

One outcome of the mixing of urban and rural life is that there is now often no clear break between town and country. Indeed in many 'rural' areas only the landscape remains truly rural. Because of this it is no longer realistic in many regions to speak of urban or industrial areas as opposed to rural or agricultural areas. An alternative approach is to view areas in terms of cities and their *commuting hinterlands*. Commuting hinterlands are also called urban fields, although the latter are not based solely on commuting patterns. The term *daily urban system* has been used in the USA to describe a city and its commuting hinterland. In England and Wales some of these hinterlands, as in South-west England, South Wales, East Anglia, Humberside and northern England are, in the main, separated from one another and from other commuting regions by rural areas. But the main body of hinterlands stretching from South-east England across the Midlands to industrial Lancashire and West Yorkshire forms one mass and this has been called the English *megalopolis* (Fig. 7.7). The term megalopolis is usually associated with the vast interlocking region of cities and their hinterlands on the north-eastern seaboard of the USA, but it is increasingly used as a general term to describe large urban and urban-oriented regions. It was originally popularised by Lewis Mumford to describe any large shapeless urban area. It was then used by Jean Gottman in his book *Megalopolis: the urbanised north-eastern seaboard of the United States* (1961) to describe a specific urbanised region. Such regions do not constitute vast zones of houses and factories; indeed, in most megalopolises only a small part of the land is truly urban – about 18% in the case of the English megalopolis. They are, however, urban in a functional sense, i.e. those parts which appear at first sight to be rural are urban in that they act as dormitories for urban employees, they are supply areas for commodities such as dairy produce and water consumed in the urban areas and they are recreation areas for urban people. Such is the degree of decentralisation of both employment and population

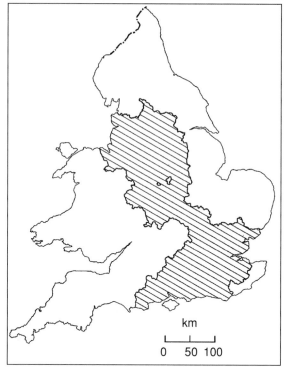

Fig. 7.7 'Megalopolis England' as defined by Peter Hall (1973). In 1961 this area contained 56% of the population of England and Wales at a density of 2,446 people per square kilometre.

in the United States, and such is the inter-relatedness and overlap between daily urban systems that it was postulated in the 1970s that by the year 2000 more than half the United States population would live in three giant megalopolises, rather unhappily named Boswash (from Boston to Washington D.C.), Chipitts (Chicago to Pittsburgh) and Sansan (San Francisco in Central California to San Diego on the Mexican border).

Commuting patterns and local government boundaries

At the beginning of this chapter it was hinted that problems often arise as circulation becomes more complex. Brief discussions of planning issues in England and the United States will illustrate clearly the need to respond in planning terms to increased levels of commuting and continuing population decentralisation. It became increasingly obvious in England after the Second World War that the pattern of local government areas did not fit the pattern of work and life in the country. The division of England into 79 county boroughs and 45 counties, exercising independent authority and dividing urban areas from rural areas (and hence the places of work and places of residence of millions of people) made physical, social and economic planning very difficult. As a result of this a Royal Commission was set up in 1966 to make recommendations on local government reform, and the report (popularly known as the Redcliffe-Maud Report) was published in 1969. The main conclusions of the report were that the county boroughs and counties (excluding London which was outside the terms of reference of the inquiry) should be replaced by 61 new local government areas, each covering town and country. Three of the largest areas – centred on Birmingham, Manchester and Liverpool – would be called metropolitan areas and would be further subdivided into metropolitan districts. A major criticism of the recommendations was that population size rather than the extent of commuting and service hinterlands had formed the basis of the new administrative structure. Indeed, one member of the Commission wrote a minority report suggesting a two-tier system of 35 new local government areas (to be called provinces) based much more closely on present and possible future hinterlands, and subdivided into 148 districts.

In the end the government of the day opted for a compromise solution of 47 counties and 333 districts, plus 6 metropolitan counties that were subdivided into metropolitan districts. The system came into operation in April 1974 and, apart from the abolition of the 6 metropolitan counties in 1984, remains virtually intact at the time of writing though there is increasing pressure for further reform. The new local government map has, however, disappointed most

applied geographers because of the failure, for the most part, to match county boundaries with existing and possible future commuting and service hinterlands, thus restricting the effectiveness of planning. Figure 7.8 shows a small-scale example of this.

In the United States the problems associated with high levels of circulation are further aggravated by racial issues. Since 1960 most American central cities have lost population and much of this loss has been the result of the out-migration of families who are, in the main, White and in the middle and upper income brackets. Rapid-transit railways, widespread car ownership, complex motorway systems and decentralisation of employment and retailing have all combined to encourage such residential dispersal. At the same time the large cities have attracted substantial numbers of Black and Hispanic Americans and their arrival has tended to accelerate the out-migration of Whites. Thus the old cities that grew up in the nineteenth and early twentieth centuries house large numbers of Black Americans, while the politically independent suburban communities are predominantly White and middle class. For example, 63% of the population of Detroit in 1980 were Black Americans. In Newark the proportion was 58% and in Baltimore 55%. New York's Black population was only 25% of the total but a further 20% were of Hispanic origin.

This residential segregation has given rise to a number of severe problems. The affluent middle classes who live in the suburbs but use the central city's highways, museums, art galleries, golf courses and other institutions and amenities do not pay city rates. This is a particularly crippling problem to the cities because their relatively poor and often ageing populations demand a high level of health and welfare services. Similarly the cities have been deprived of rates and rents from industry as a result of factory re-location in the suburban communities. If the remaining industry is more heavily taxed to make up this deficit, then accelerated industrial decentralisation is likely to ensue. On the other hand, lowering of taxes to induce industry to stay inevitably leads to reduced city health and

Fig. 7.8 Part of the greatly expanded residential community of Gosforth Valley in Dronfield, north-east Derbyshire. Writing in the *Sheffield Morning Telegraph* in 1970 under the headline 'Epitaph for Dronfield, the vanishing village', a locally born resident commented that the population of Dronfield had grown from 6,000 to 20,000 since 1950 and that there seemed no end to its growth as an extension of the South Yorkshire city of Sheffield, the centre of which lies less than 10 kilometres to the north. Many of Dronfield's new residents originated in Sheffield, which is the major destination of the thousands of commuters who leave the settlement every weekday to work in the surrounding region. Recent surveys also show that Sheffield is the most visited major centre for shopping, easily outstripping the town of Chesterfield a few kilometres to the south. Yet despite recommendations in the past by Boundary Commissions and academic observers that logically it should be part of Sheffield, and proposals by Sheffield City Council for its incorporation, Dronfield remains part of Derbyshire.

welfare services. Another problem arises from the stringent land-use regulations that operate in the suburban communities. By zoning potential residential areas into one-acre and half-acre plots, the lower-income groups are effectively excluded through their inability to secure enough capital.

The prospect of any metropolitan area-wide re-organisation of local government in the USA looks bleak. So far it has happened in only a tiny minority of places, usually in the South where suburbanisation came late and fragmentation is less advanced. The federal government is prevented by the constitution from intervening in local affairs and the suburban communities seem unlikely to cede any of the political, economic and environmental advantages they have gained over the years. Meanwhile, more and more middle-class White Americans live, work, shop and spend their leisure time in suburbia, increasingly distanced from and apparently indifferent to the problems of the old urban cores.

It is apparent from these brief summaries of trends in England and the United States that sensible physical, social and economic planning can only take place when local government responsibilities are rationalised and the areas that these bodies serve correspond more closely with current or predicted patterns of work and leisure. It is also clear that local government boundaries and responsibilities need to be kept under continuous review.

CASE STUDY 7A

Politics and pastoral nomadism in the western Sahara

Like many other nomadic peoples, the Sahrawi camel and goat herders of the western Sahara have undergone significant changes in lifestyle in recent years. A major factor in this has been the political changes that have occurred in this area, these in turn being motivated to some extent by economic factors, most notably the discovery and development of vast deposits of phosphates in the region.

The formal establishment of colonial boundaries interfered only slightly with the nomadic circulation patterns of the various Sahrawi tribes in the first half of the present century. Seasonal patterns of circulation established over several hundred years, involving a variety of cross-border movements, continued largely unhindered in areas of Spanish (later to become Western) Sahara, Mauritania, Morocco and Algeria (see Fig. 7.9). The discovery of phosphates in Spanish Sahara and the beginnings of industrial development based on this, led to rapid urbanisation from the 1960s onwards. Many Sahrawis were attracted by waged employment in growing urban centres such as Layune (El Ayoun) and Smara, and abandoned completely their traditional way of life. Others adopted a sedentary way of life but retained an interest in their herds through trading and similar activities. According to a Spanish census in 1974, over half the Sahrawis in Spanish Sahara had become urban residents by this time.

The tendency to abandon a nomadic existence was reinforced by droughts in the 1970s that dramatically reduced the size of Sahrawi herds and by the political upheaval that followed Spain's relinquishment of control in Spanish Sahara in 1975. Initially the new state of Western Sahara was partitioned between Morocco and Mauritania though Morocco has since taken over control of the whole area. Throughout the period since 1975 the Polisario Front, which claims to represent the majority of Sahrawi people in the whole region of the western Sahara (as well as in the new state), has been in conflict with Morocco in an attempt to establish the independence of the state of Western Sahara. By 1976 an estimated 40,000 Sahrawi refugees had undergone a forced migration from Western Sahara to Algeria as a result of the conflict. Here they were joined by many thousands of other Sahrawis forced by the effects of drought in the Algerian and Mauritanian sections of the

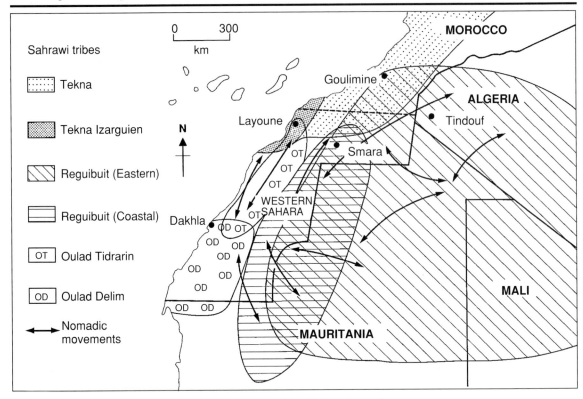

Fig. 7.9 Location and traditional circulation patterns of the Sahrawi people.
Source: after Arkell, 1991.

Sahara to settle in camps provided by the Algerian government, who have supported the Polisario Front in their battle for independence. By the beginning of the 1990s, Polisario claimed that over 165,000 Sahrawi refugees were living in the Tindouf region of Algeria though this may be an overestimate (Moroccan sources estimate the figure at under 50,000!). During the period of conflict between Morocco and the Polisario Front, circulation involving the crossing of borders has decreased dramatically, especially since the construction of a pattern of defensive walls and minefields along the border between Western Sahara and Mauritania closed that border almost completely to nomadic peoples.

Arkell (1991) suggests that these political developments, together with the effects of drought, have led to the establishment of two very

different groups of Sahrawis, one based in Western Sahara, the other in the Algerian camps. Both these groups show considerable differences in lifestyle from the Sahrawi pastoral nomads who were typical of the region before the 1960s. The first group of Sahrawis resident in Western Sahara are outnumbered two to one by Moroccan settlers, encouraged to migrate to Western Sahara by the Moroccan government. Massive investment by Morocco has created an abundance of new jobs, especially in the urban areas, and many Sahrawis are now employed in urban industry and trade – though usually not in the most highly paid forms of employment. Other Sahrawis in the country are still pastoralists but few are now truly nomadic. Most manage to combine a semi-nomadic lifestyle with residence in an urban area. Helped by government subsidies and the increased market for their pastoral products brought about by the growth of the urban population, they are also generally more affluent than was the case when they followed a more traditional lifestyle.

The second Sahrawi group comprises those based in the Algerian camps, run by the Polisario Front's 'government-in-exile', the Sahrawi Arab Democratic Republic (SADR). With the help of foreign aid from countries such as Algeria and Libya the SADR leaders have developed a society that is well organised and takes full advantage of the economic potential of the area in which the camps are based. In a political situation where the operation of traditional pastoral nomadism was more difficult and at a time when many former nomads had lost many of their animals because of drought, the SADR established a new economic base. This includes irrigated vegetable gardens, some small industrial establishments and some animal husbandry. The latter has been adapted to the new situation, however, rather than being a simple continuance of traditional practices. Although some camel herds graze in parts of the Saharan region that are outside Moroccan control, the majority now use grazing areas close to the camps and their owners are either sedentary or, at most, semi-nomadic. Though not fully self-sufficient, the Sahrawi population in this area has moved well away from a reliance on their traditional means of livelihood and even the remnants of this form only a part of the total economic pattern. With an exten-

sive education system also having been established, the people are being educated in new economic and political attitudes. This suggests that a return to the old way of life is highly unlikely even if the political situation should change dramatically as a result of current UN peace initiatives or for other reasons.

This is equally true of the Sahrawis in Western Sahara and it seems that the traditional pattern of pastoral nomadism as the dominant lifestyle in this part of the Saharan region has disappeared for ever – though that is not to say that small numbers of nomadic pastoralists may not continue to follow the old ways for a long time to come. Elsewhere in the Sahara similar changes have been taking place, with a general decline in nomadism albeit usually with less dramatic political overtones. Thus, for example, many of the Tuareg herders of the Ahaggar region in south-east Algeria have, since the 1960s, also adopted a more sedentary way of life with some now working in areas of irrigated cultivation and others modifying the pattern of their pastoral activities in the light of changing economic and political influences and the problems brought about by drought. Although the political background against which the decline in pastoral nomadism of the Sahrawis has been set may be unique, many of the changes they have made in their lifestyle are mirrored elsewhere in the Sahara and even further afield.

CASE STUDY 7B

Commuting to a small town in India

Although daily commuting to large cities is now a well-established feature of many developing countries alongside circulation based on more lengthy periods of residence, it is considerably less significant in relation to smaller urban settlements. A study of Hosur in the state of Tamil Nadu by Heins and Meijer (1990) provides some interesting insights into the process in a small Indian town. Hosur is near the north-west border of Tamil Nadu in Dharmapuri, one of the most backward districts in the state. The nearest large town is Bangalore, 45 kilometres away in the neighbouring state of Karnataka (see Fig. 7.10). Rapid development of industry in Hosur since the 1970s, when Hosur became established as a growth pole, has been largely dependent on government planning and assistance through the State Industries Promotion Corporation and the Small Industries Development Corporation of Tamil Nadu (SIPCOT and SIDCO) with more than 100 factories being established in a decade. The population of Hosur more than doubled to over 35,000 between 1971 and 1985. Migration, much of it from larger urban centres outside the local district, was a major factor in this with young, skilled migrants attracted by the many, often well-paid job opportunities. A sample survey in 1985 suggested that almost half of Hosur's population were in-migrants.

By contrast the significance of commuting is fairly limited with only about 10% of those employed in the industrial areas and town centre being commuters although the commuting hinterland extends as far as Bangalore. Heins and Meijer carried out a sample survey of commuters working in Hosur based on roughly equivalent

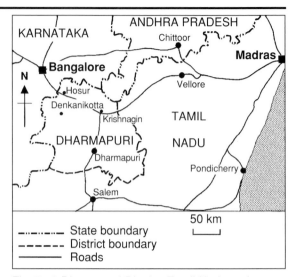

Fig. 7.10 Dharmapuri District, Tamil Nadu and adjacent areas.
Source: after Heins and Meijer, 1990.

numbers from the SIPCOT/SIDCO industrial area and the town centre, the latter including those employed in retailing, workshops, street vending, etc. Of the commuters surveyed only 14% were from villages (here classified as settlements of fewer than 3,000 people), 59% from small towns (over 3,000 people) and the remainder from the one metropolitan centre involved, Bangalore. Just over one-quarter of all the commuters lived within 10 kilometres of Hosur, including more than half of those commuting from villages. Almost one-third of the commuters from small towns to Hosur lived between 5 and 10 kilometres away but 28% lived within the 20–25 kilometre distance band with smaller numbers commuting from the intervening 10–15 and 15–20 kilometre bands. This principally reflects the geographical distribution of settlements of this kind. Somewhat surprisingly at first glance, nearly 40% of all Hosur's commuters came from more than 25 kilometres away, but this is largely explained by the fact that two-thirds of this group were from Bangalore and most travelled by company buses that overcome the problems of cost and distance involved in such a long journey to work for many employees on the SIPCOT/SIDCO sites while ensuring a supply of skilled labour for the companies concerned. Thus, for a variety of reasons, a pattern of commuter residence in conformity with distance-decay theory does *not* occur in this area.

Heins and Meijer recognise six categories of workers in Hosur:

1 Permanent wage workers earning a 'high' income (over 1,000 rupees (Rs) per month).
2 Permanent wage workers earning a 'low' income (below Rs1,000 per month).
3 Short-term wage workers (casual and temporary workers in registered factories and workshops plus 'permanent' employees in unregistered workshops whose jobs are not secured by legislation).
4 Casual wage workers (those employed outside manufacturing or service establishments, e.g. construction workers, porters).
5 Dependent and self-employed workers (more or less independent traders and producers earning less than Rs1,000 per month).
6 'Petit-bourgeois' (as in category (5) but earning more than Rs1,000 per month).

Figure 7.11 shows the distances travelled to work by the different categories of workers together with some information concerning their incomes. Most of the high-income permanent wage workers travelled more than 25 kilometres to work, mainly by company bus from Bangalore, and they formed the largest group of long-distance commuters. The fact that average incomes

of those commuting more than 25 kilometres were more than twice as high as those of commuters in any other distance band emphasises the way in which material benefits can help to overcome the friction of distance, especially if the costs and inconvenience of travel can also be kept to a minimum – a function served by the company buses. Lower-income permanent wage workers showed a more varied pattern of distance travelled with considerable numbers of both short- and long-distance commuters whereas short-term wage workers tended to live nearer to Hosur. Many of the latter lived in villages where their income, even if relatively low, was likely to provide an important supplement to the limited household incomes from agriculture and other rural activities. Over 30% of the Hosur commuters (mostly members of the lower wage-earning groups who still lived with their parents) provided less than 40% of the income of the household in which they lived but this amount could contribute to a significant improvement in living standards for a poor rural family as well as marking, for some, the crucial first stage in a move away from traditional forms of employment.

Relatively few commuters to Hosur were in the self-employed or petit bourgeois categories but over half of each of these groups travelled more than 15 kilometres to their place of work. When questioned, however, about 40% of those in each of these categories said they had plans to move to live in Hosur compared with fewer than 20% in any

	Distance from Hosur					Total workers surveyed (by wage category)
	5–10	**10–15**	**15–20**	**20–25**	**>25**	
Permanent high wage	14.0	3.5	1.8	5.3	75.4	(57)
Permanent low wage	33.3	4.9	12.3	19.8	29.6	(81)
Short-term wage	44.9	11.6	17.4	8.7	17.4	(69)
Casual wage	42.9	14.3	–	42.9	–	(7)
Dependent and self-employed	32.1	10.7	21.4	25.0	10.7	(28)
Petit bourgeois	42.9	–	28.6	–	28.6	(7)
Total	32.5	7.2	12.4	14.1	33.7	(249)
Average income in Rs	545	546	705	618	1,614	932

Fig. 7.11 Distance from Hosur to place of residence of different categories of commuters (by percentage within each wage category), and income of commuters in relation to distance travelled to work.
Source: Heins and Meijer, 1990.

of the other commuting categories. A housing shortage in Hosur and the high rents of available houses were obstacles to potential migrants while a variety of family commitments and other personal factors may also, of course, have influenced the potential for migration. Many of the commuters were still relatively young (55% under the age of 30) and unmarried and their attitudes to movement may well change as they grow older and their marital status changes. Here, as in other parts of the world, decisions about whether to commute or migrate to a place of work may involve a balancing of many different factors, some of which will change significantly as individuals move through their family life-cycle.

The development of Hosur as a growth pole with considerable new employment opportunities has obviously altered the structure of the labour force by encouraging migration but commuting is, as yet, of considerably less significance than migration in Hosur. Commuters tend to be relatively young, with only 13% of commuters over the age of 40 at the time of the survey, but commuting may well increase if employment opportunities continue to expand and contact with those already commuting opens up the field of information for other potential commuters, especially in the more traditional rural areas.

The commuters who travel more than 25 kilometres to earn high wages in the SIPCOT/SIDCO industrial area form an interesting minority group. They do little to fulfil the normal growth pole aim of spreading wealth to the rural area adjacent to the growth pole but serve an important function, together with some of the recent migrants to Hosur, of providing skilled labour in an area where it was formerly in relatively short supply. This has been facilitated by the provision of private transport by the companies in the industrial area, a development that largely resolves the problems associated with the limited and relatively expensive transport provision that serves as one of the main limitations on commuting to smaller settlements in the developing world. Heins and Meijer indicate that only small numbers of commuters use the public bus services to Hosur. This perhaps suggests that any expansion in commuting might be linked to the development of more flexible, possibly informal, transport systems that provide an inexpensive but efficient means of travelling to work for less affluent commuters in many other parts of the developing world. Commuting is still at an early stage in this area and it will be interesting to see to what extent both commuting itself and transport systems to better serve commuter needs develop in the next few years.

Detling, Kent: profile of a metropolitan village

Detling is a small settlement at the foot of the chalk scarp of the North Downs in Kent in South-east England. It lies 4 kilometres north-east of the county town, Maidstone, 10 kilometres to the south of Chatham and Gillingham, and about 55 kilometres from central London (Fig. 7.12). It is linked by road to the capital by the M20 and M25, and there is also a nearby rail link. The core of the settlement consists of attractive timber-framed houses, the village pub and a neat parish church. Surrounding the historic core of the village are twentieth-century extensions to the settlement in the form of small groups of houses and larger, estate-like adjuncts. Altogether by the beginning of the 1980s there were 338 houses in the village, 286 of them (85%) owner-occupied; 146 of the houses (43%) had been built since 1945. The total population in 1981 was 800, an increase of more than 175% since 1901 and 34% since 1951.

In the Kent County Structure Plan Review published in 1980 the parish of Detling was identified as one of 25 rural parishes in the county with predominantly non-rural functions. These parishes were characterised by largely owner-occupied housing, mostly built since 1920, with household heads in managerial and professional occupations, and with low levels of unemployment. What were being identified in fact were parishes containing once-rural villages that had been transformed by commuting into metropolitan villages, a term coined by Masser and Stroud in 1965. They

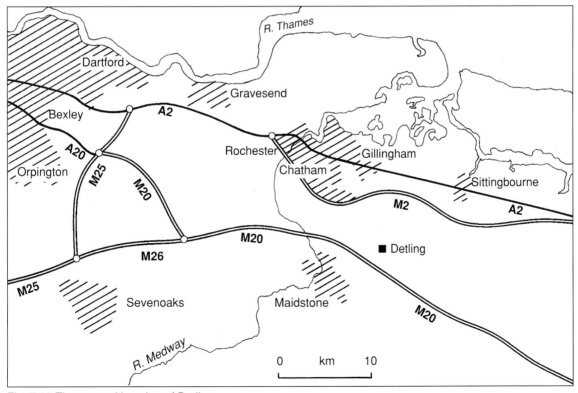

Fig. 7.12 The general location of Detling.

have proliferated in those parts of the countryside within commuting distance of towns and cities. Some came into being immediately after the opening of the railways in the mid-nineteenth century but their period of greatest growth has been in the last 40 years.

In such villages the old social and occupational structures have been largely obliterated (Connell, 1974). Before the suburbanisation of the countryside took place, villagers usually worked in their home village or in the surrounding countryside. A social hierarchy was usually easily identifiable in such communities extending from the village squire, vicar, doctor and farm owners at the top, through the village craftsmen and tradespeople, down to the farm labourers and house servants. Although socially divided, and with very different qualities of life, the inhabitants of such villages shared a close-knit, localised lifestyle (Newby, 1979). In metropolitan villages these characteristics have disappeared. Populations have expanded rapidly, fewer and fewer of the inhabitants are locally born and only a minority of the working population works on the land or in the immediate locality. Moreover, the old social hierarchy has been replaced by two co-existing populations – long-established residents, who may form only a minority of the total population, and newcomers who may have been born in another part of the country and may only reside in the village for a relatively short period of time. When metropolitan villages first came into being there were often marked contrasts between the long-established residents and the newcomers in terms of where they worked, how they travelled to work and where they shopped, but these differences are becoming less obvious.

To summarise, the main characteristics of the population geography of a metropolitan village are as follows:

a) Long-established residents usually live in a village core, in council properties outside the core or in farmhouses in and around the village. There is a sizeable community of newcomers in the village, mostly living outside the old village core, usually in the newest housing; in large villages this housing is in the form of estates. Some newcomers live in the core in renovated properties and buildings converted from non-residential uses. The newcomers have often migrated from nearby towns or cities, but a substantial proportion may be from other parts of the country. The average age of the newcomer households is usually lower than that of the village as a whole and such households tend to be simple nuclear families of two, three or four persons.

b) Few of the newcomers work in the village. They usually work in nearby towns and cities, but some may travel considerable distances to neighbouring counties. They usually travel to work by car or train. These are the so-called voluntary commuters. Additionally, increasing numbers of the long-established residents also commute to work in nearby urban areas (inertia commuters). In some parts of the country there may be substantial numbers of retired newcomers in the community. In many metropolitan villages it is the long-established residents who are dominant in this category.

c) Because of the rapidly rising numbers of people, including large numbers of newcomers, in such villages, there is a much greater degree of anonymity than in the past and there may be a much weaker sense of 'community'. Additionally, because more and more adults work outside the village, have social contacts elsewhere, and have access to cars, a large proportion of the village population may choose not to make the village the focus of all their social activities. Some researchers have also found a sense of hostility between the long-established residents and the newcomers (e.g. Newby, 1979, Pacione, 1980). This may be due, for example, to the newcomers feeling that the long-established residents are being slow to accept change and resent the presence of the newcomers, or because the long-established residents feel that the newcomers do not understand country ways or are taking over and changing the nature of village institutions.

A small-scale study completed in the early

1980s (Day, 1982), using a questionnaire survey, investigated the extent to which some of the above characteristics, namely the influx of newcomers, their origins in nearby urban areas, the decline of the village as a place of work, high levels of car ownership, and heavy use of the car as the means of travelling to work, were true of Detling. The author questioned 83 heads of household in the village which was roughly the equivalent of a 25% sample. He used a stratified sample survey in which his households were selected in strict proportion to the numbers of the various types and tenures of housing in the village in order to ensure that he was sampling a representative cross-section of the village community.

The survey showed that 45.6% of his 83 respondents lived in detached houses, 24.1% in bungalows, 15.7% in semi-detached properties and only 10.8% in cottages; 54% of the properties visited had been built since 1946 and 79.3% since 1919; 85.3% were owner-occupied, 12.1% council rented and 3.4% privately rented or tied cottages. The picture that emerges is of an expanded village containing a predominantly middle-class population living in comfortable surroundings.

In terms of length of residence in the village, Day found that 34 (40.9%) of the 83 heads of household had lived in the village for 10 years or less. Of the rest, 38 (45.8%) had lived there for more than 16 years, but only 8 (9.6%) of these had been born in the village. When asked where they had lived immediately prior to moving to Detling he found that of the 75 'migrant' households, 40 (53.5%) had moved 8 kilometres or less, mainly from Maidstone, a further 15 (20.0%) had moved from other parts of Kent, 13 (17.3%) from other parts of the South East and 7 (9.3%) from elsewhere in the United Kingdom. When asked what the main reason was for moving to Detling, the most common answers were the appeal of a particular house (22 respondents), the location within commuting distance of work (20 respondents) and the countryside setting (13 respondents).

The answers to the questions concerning the journeys to work of heads of household confirm Detling's status as a well-developed metropolitan village. Thirty-three (39.8%) heads of household said they were retired. A further 10 (12.0%) worked in the village or from home. Of the 40 (48.2%) heads of household who worked outside the village, 17 worked in Maidstone, 7 in London, and all but one (who worked abroad) of the rest elsewhere in Kent, in places as far apart as Tonbridge, 23 kilometres to the south-west, Gravesend, 22 kilometres to the north-west, and Canterbury, 36 kilometres to the east. Car ownership in Detling was found to be high with 69 (83.1%) of the respondents stating that their household owned at least one car, and 33.7% of the respondents saying that their household had more than one car. Not surprisingly the car was the chief means of travelling to work, with more than 80% of the economically active heads of household (41 out of 50) travelling to work by that means or, in the case of those working in the village or from home, using it in the course of their work.

It is clear that Detling in the early 1980s shared many of the characteristics of metropolitan villages described on page 148. The size and appearance of the village, the geographical origins and socio-economic characteristics of its residents, and the volume and spatial extent of their regular journeys were a far cry from those of Detling and its inhabitants of a century earlier when the population was only 275. Its setting may still be rural but the village is a component part of the English megalopolis.

8

Typologies of migration

General considerations

Advances in the understanding of the processes and patterns of migration have often been marked by attempts to summarise findings in large-scale classificatory models. Such classifications of migrations into types are called *migration typologies*. As research has progressed and data have increased in volume, detail and reliability, old typologies have been modified or discarded and others have been proposed.

Most, but not all, typologies take the form of a 'multi-dimensional matrix with some cells empty and some occupied by distinguishable types' (Kosinski and Prothero, 1975). In Fig. 8.1, for instance, two criteria are used: on one axis boundaries crossed are employed and on the other the voluntary or involuntary nature of migration is used. This provides six cells; whether or not all six would be filled by distinctive types would depend upon the region or country under investigation.

A critical decision in classifying migrations is the choice of classificatory criteria. The list and commentary below indicate the most important variables traditionally employed in classifying migrations and highlight some of the problems surrounding their use.

	Voluntary	Forced
Intra-regional		
Inter-regional		
International		

Fig. 8.1 A simple typology of migration.

1 *Distance travelled*
This apparently straightforward and reasonable way of classifying migrations is fraught with difficulties. Physical distance, for example, may be of less significance than cost distance or time distance. Of even more importance, but often unmeasurable, may be cultural or social distance, i.e. the large cultural or social gap that may occur between an origin and a potential destination even though the physical distance may be small. This may be the case when a Flemish-speaking family moves into a French-speaking village in Belgium or a Catholic family moves into a Protestant-dominated community in Ulster.

2 *Internal as opposed to international migration*
This distinction may not always be as significant as it first appears to be. For example, in countries like China and India, long-distance internal migrations involve the crossing of many economic, cultural and linguistic boundaries. Such migrations would involve much greater re-adjustments on the part of migrants than international migrations from, say, the southern Netherlands to northern Belgium or from northern Italy to the Italian-speaking cantons of neighbouring Switzerland.

3 *The temporary or permanent nature of migration*
As has already been pointed out in Chapter 5, it is notoriously difficult to distinguish between 'temporary' and 'permanent' migration when time scales of many years or even several decades are involved. Even when data are collected personally from migrants there is no certainty about whether individuals will do what they say they intend to do. Migration counter-streams always contain a substantial number of migrants who intended to be permanent migrants.

4 *The causes of migration*
In this case categories such as economic, retirement, education and political are employed. A weakness of this approach is that migration is often triggered not by one but by a combination of factors, a possibility

acknowledged in both Lee's theory of migration and Wolpert's place utility concept (see Chapter 6).

5 *The selectivity of migration*

Here the emphasis is on the characteristics of the migrant: gender, age, stage in family life-cycle, ethnicity, educational background, occupational status. A problem here is that many migrants move in family groups, sometimes as extended families. Should every member of the group be classified according to the above criteria? Or only adults? Or only the migration decision-makers? How can the migration decision-makers be identified?

The question naturally arises: why construct typologies? This may be answered from two viewpoints. For the individual scholar they may constitute summaries of the findings of his own investigations, and for planners and politicians they provide the raw materials and guidelines for the drafting of regional and national plans. Detailed proposals in such plans may capitalise on known migratory or circulatory trends; they may attempt to contain, slow down or stop them or they may encourage such movements.

Examples of typologies

Perhaps the best-known typology is Petersen's 'General typology of migration', which dates from 1958. (It originally appeared in the *American Sociological Review* but is reprinted in Jansen, 1970.) It is summarised in Fig. 8.2. This typology hinges on the identification of five broad classes of migration: primitive, forced, impelled, free and mass (column 3 in Fig. 8.2). Each class of migration is seen to be related to general and specific activating forces (columns 1 and 2 respectively) and each class of migration is subdivided into two types: *conservative*, when migrants move in order to retain their previous way of life, and *innovating*, when migrants move to achieve a new way or standard of life (columns 4 and 5).

Petersen sees *primitive migration* as the outcome of people's relationships with their natural environment, in particular their inability to cope with natural forces because of their limited technology. This leads to two types of migration: on the one hand, the conservative wanderings of cultivators and the conservative ranging of gatherers and nomads, and on the other, innovating flight from the land. Petersen cites the Irish migration to the United States following the 1840s famine as an example of flight from the land of a 'primitive' people. He points out that they steadfastly avoided the extremely cheap methods of purchasing for farming purposes the publicly owned land in the United States; instead they overwhelmingly went to the great cities and became urban Americans. They

Relation	Migratory force	Class of migration	Type of migration	
			Conservative	Innovating
Nature and man	Ecological push	Primitive	Wandering Ranging	Flight from the land
State (or equivalent) and man	Migration policy	Forced Impelled	Displacement Flight	Slave trade Coolie trade
Man and his norms	Higher aspirations	Free	Group	Pioneer
Collective behaviour	Social momentum	Mass	Settlement	Urbanisation

Fig. 8.2 Petersen's 'general typology of migration'.

stand in contrast to the many rural folk who took part in the migrations from Sweden to the United States in the last four decades of the nineteenth century. Many of these went to the northern Midwest, to the states of Minnesota and Wisconsin, and theirs was a conservative migration in that they farmed or became small-town craftsmen and merchants.

Petersen analyses politically motivated migration in the same way. In this case he recognised two classes: *impelled migration* when the migrants, although under great pressure to migrate, have the power to decide whether or not to leave, and *forced migration*, when the migrants no longer have that power. Petersen illustrates the difference between the two by the example of Jewish migration in and from Germany between 1933 and 1945 (and after 1938 in other German-occupied lands). Between 1933 and 1938 the Nazis impelled Jews to migrate from Germany by means of anti-Semitic legislation; between 1938 and 1945 Jews were system-atically rounded up and forced to migrate to work camps and concentration camps. Both of these migrations, using Petersen's criteria, were conservative; the 1933–38 migrations would come under the heading of flight and the later forced migrations are examples of what he calls displacement. Two examples of more recent forced migration are illustrated in Figs. 8.3 and 8.4.

Petersen's innovating types of politically motivated migrations are interesting in that the innovating agent is not the migrant but the individuals or agencies that, with the backing of prevailing laws and attitudes concerning labour recruitment, organise the migrations. Thus the plantation owners, the colonial powers and their officials were, among others, the innovators in, for example, the forced migrations of slave labour from West Africa to the West Indies and the impelled migrations of 'coolies' (contract labourers) from India to work on the Mombasa–Nairobi railway in the 1890s. Petersen des-

Fig. 8.3 Ugandan exiles arriving in Britain in 1972, following a decision by the then President Amin to expel all Asians from Uganda. Most of the 30,000 or so Ugandan Asians involved in this forced migration were British passport holders, and many settled in the United Kingdom. By Petersen's definition this was a conservative migration, as most of the migrants had been involved in commercial activities in Uganda and, after arriving in Britain, continued to function economically as traders and shopkeepers and in small businesses, much as they had in Uganda.

ignated these types of movement as innovating because they resulted in changes in work patterns and social patterns among the migrants at their destination.

The vast majority of modern migrations are included in Petersen's last two classes of migration, free and mass. In his definition, *free migration* consists of individuals and small groups moving of their own free will. There is an element of risk involved in the early stages of such migrations (risk of starvation, non-assimilation, death, and so on) and so such migrants set examples for others, who may eventually transform these small-scale migrations into *mass migrations*. Mabogunje (see Chapter 6) made the same distinction when he differentiated between active and passive migrants. During periods of mass migration the propensity to migrate appears to be almost inborn in particular groups. Again Petersen differentiates between conservative and innovating migrations. In the case of mass migrations he gives the name *settlement* to those conservative movements that result in modes of life similar to those at the areas of origin, and he designates as *urbanisation* those migrations that result in an urban lifestyle taking the place of a former rural

one. Case Study 6B, of transmigration in Indonesia, considers an example of a mass migration that is essentially conservative in character, with the vast majority of the migrants being from farming areas in Java, Madura, Bali and Lombok, and having a similar lifestyle at their destination to that in their zone of origin. The movements of people from the Caribbean and parts of the Indian subcontinent to the United Kingdom between the end of the Second World War and the first of the Commonwealth Immigrant Acts in 1962 are examples of what began as an innovatory free migration but was beginning to assume the characteristics of mass migration until legislation was introduced to reduce the flow of migrants. Exercise 8.1 provides an opportunity to consider Petersen's typology in more detail.

A rather different approach to migratory classification is that of Roseman (1971), who places all human movements into just two broad classes (Fig. 8.5, page 156). The first he calls *reciprocal movements* (Fig. 8.5a). These are circulatory movements such as the journey to work, shopping trips, leisure trips and so on. The second class of movements consists of *migratory movements*, in which Roseman recognises two

Fig. 8.4 A group of Kurdish refugees arriving at a temporary camp on the Turkish border in 1991, having been driven out of their homes in Iraq following a Kurdish uprising in the aftermath of the Gulf War. This is one of a number of forced migrations in recent years in areas as diverse as the former Yugoslavia, Afghanistan, Mozambique, Cambodia, Albania and the Middle East resulting from political upheavals and/or persecution of minority groups.

Exercise 8.1

Petersen's general typology of migration

a) Suggest the appropriate class of migration in Petersen's typology into which each of the migratory movements listed below fits. In each case indicate whether the migration is of the conservative or innovating type.

You may find it useful to produce an enlarged outline of Petersen's typology (Fig. 8.2). Columns 1and 2 ('Relation' and 'Migratory force') can be written up exactly as shown in Fig. 8.2. In column 3, underneath the appropriate heading, the listed migratory movements can be

entered. A tick can be entered in either column 4 or column 5 to indicate whether it is, in your opinion, conservative or innovating. The migration of the Irish to the United States in the 1840s is used below to show the suggested arrangement.

b) In a separate set of notes, for each of the migratory movements listed below, justify why you have allocated it to a particular *class* and *type* of migration, commenting on any difficulties encountered in doing so.

Relation	Migratory force	Class of migration	Type of migration	
			Conservative	Innovating
Nature and man	Ecological push	Primitive – Migration of the Irish to US in 1840s		✓
State and man	Migration policy	Forced		

List of migratory movements

1 The 20,000 Hungarian refugees who settled in the United Kingdom after fleeing Hungary in 1956 following the invasion by Soviet armed forces to put down a national uprising against the Communist government of the country.

2 The 20,000 Dutch farmers who migrated to Canada after the end of the Second World War. Many worked as farm labourers before buying or renting their own farms.

3 The Pebble family who moved from Warwick, England in 1976 to Nova Scotia, Canada. George Pebble moved from a middle-management position in an engineering firm to start his own firm of consulting engineers in Halifax, Nova Scotia.

4 The 1.5 million Turks (Turkish immigrant workers and their families) living in Germany. Turkish male workers moved to the former West Germany mainly in the 1950s and 1960s to escape poverty. Many

came from rural areas. They undertook unskilled and dirty jobs in Germany's major cities and industrial regions.

5   John O'Grady, a university graduate from Dublin in the Republic of Ireland, who has moved to work as an accountant in the City of London.

6   John Branston who was transferred by his British firm of food manufacturers to be director of their New York office in 1985.

7   A bank clerk from Harare, Zimbabwe, who has moved to England to become a professional cricketer. He is currently playing as a full-time professional with a leading county side.

8   Jose Sanchez, an illegal immigrant to the United States from Mexico. He has moved from a small town in northern Mexico where unemployment is high to a resort town on the Texas Coast where he works as a gardener.

9   The 60,000 Sri Lankan women who were living in Kuwait on the eve of the invasion by the Iraqis in August 1990. They were working as maids for rich Kuwaiti and Western families.

10 The 20,000 Vietnamese political refugees (including boat people) who have been resettled in the United Kingdom since 1979. These migrants were among the first wave of refugees from the defeated South Vietnam. They left because of persecution by the Communist government. They have had to adapt to a new culture and language.

subtypes: partial displacement migration (Fig. 8.5b) and total displacement migration (Fig. 8.5c). In a *partial displacement migration* the location of the home changes but other areas of activity (e.g. place of work, shopping centres visited) remain largely as before. This is true of much intra-urban migration. In *total displacement migration* a move is made to a new location that results in the creation of a completely new set of reciprocal movements. The emphasis in this classification is on the impact of different types of migration on other spatial processes and patterns.

So far the typologies described have been of general application. There are others that have been devised to relate to specific continents, countries or regions – although they too may, in some cases, have wider applicability. An attempt to clarify the complexities of human mobility in a particular region has been made for tropical Africa by Gould and Prothero (in Kosinski and Prothero, 1975). In their typology they use the two variables of space and time (Fig. 8.6). Space is seen in terms of 'urban' and 'rural', and movements within and between each of these spheres are considered. Time is considered in terms of periodicity, ranging from circulatory movements of a few hours' duration to those resulting in a permanent change of residence. In all, the authors recognise four types of spatial movement and six types of temporal movement, thus giving 24 separate categories within the typology. Exercise 8.2 involves using and evaluating this typology by reference to specific examples.

Perhaps the most provocative typology is Zelinsky's hypothesis of the *mobility transition* (Zelinsky, 1971) shown in Fig. 8.7 (page 159). Zelinsky summarises his hypothesis: 'There are definite patterned regularities in the growth of personal mobility through space-time during recent history, and these regularities comprise an essential component of the modernisation process'. Basically he considers that changes in personal mobility through time consist of a number of stages, and that these stages (the mobility transition) closely parallel the stages of the demographic transition, or as Zelinsky terms it, the vital transition. As a

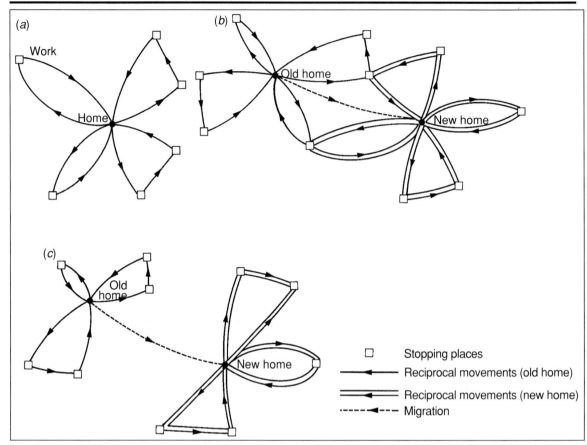

Fig. 8.5 Roseman's reciprocal movement, partial and total displacement migrations.

	Time					
	Circulation				Migration	
Space	Daily	Periodic	Seasonal	Long-term	Irregular	Permanent
Rural–rural						
Rural–urban						
Urban–rural						
Urban–urban						

Fig. 8.6 Gould and Prothero's typology of African population mobility.
Source: Kosinski and Prothero, 1975.

Exercise 8.2

Gould and Prothero's typology

Gould and Prothero's typology of African population mobility (Fig. 8.6), though originally devised with reference to situations in tropical Africa, might be expected to have a wider application to similar areas in other parts of the world. The list that follows includes examples of population movements in and from Africa, Asia and Latin America.

1 Suggest the appropriate space/time category into which each of the following circulatory/migratory movements might fit in Gould and Prothero's typology. (You may find it helpful to produce an enlarged copy of Fig. 8.6 and enter your answers into it in the appropriate spaces.)

a) A Tuareg camel herder to provide water and grazing for his stock throughout the year.

b) A Peruvian peasant farmer who leaves his land and goes to live in a squatter settlement in Lima.

c) A Hausa worker who travels from his rural home in northern Nigeria to work as a seasonal labourer in the cocoa belt.

d) A refugee family from their village in Mozambique to a 'safe' rural area in neighbouring Malawi.

e) A woman from her 'shanty' home in Belém, Brazil, to her daily work in a brazil-nut factory in another part of the same city.

f) A Muslim pilgrim who travels by air from Jakarta, Indonesia, on pilgrimage to Mecca.

g) A Malaysian rubber-tapper to his work on a plantation near his home in a nearby village.

h) A young man from the slums of Rio de Janeiro to work as a 'garimpeiro' (gold miner) for a year or two in the Amazon Basin.

i) An Indian woman from her home village to live in her husband's village after their marriage.

j) A Tanzanian student from his home in Dodoma to attend university in Dar es Salaam.

k) A young woman from Manila in the Philippines to be an 'au pair' girl in New York.

l) A man who has just retired after working for 30 years in Accra back to his home village in Ghana.

m) A woman from a village near Kisumu, Kenya, taking some of her crop of bananas for sale in the nearest periodic rural market.

n) A building worker from Cairo to work on construction sites in Saudi Arabia as a temporary labourer.

o) A Moroccan woman collecting drinking water from the nearest well some two miles from her isolated farmstead.

p) A Singaporean businessman employed by a Japanese company visiting prospective clients in North American cities.

2 Comment on any difficulties you encountered in allocating particular movements in the above list to specific categories within the Gould and Prothero typology and explain how you resolved these.

3 Discuss how effective this particular typology is and suggest how wide an application it might have. (Is it appropriate to other developing countries as well as those in Africa, for example? Could it also be used effectively in the context of Europe or North America? Can you suggest any appropriate amendments to it?)

(a)

The vital transition	The mobility transition
Phase A: *The pre-modern traditional society* (1) A moderately high to quite high fertility pattern that tends to fluctuate only slightly (2) Mortality at nearly the same level as fertility on the average, but fluctuating much more from year to year (3) Little, if any, long-range natural increase or decrease	**Phase I:** *The pre-modern traditional society* (1) Little genuine residential migration and only such limited circulation as is sanctioned by customary practice in land utilisation, social visits, commerce, warfare or religious observances
Phase B: *The early transitional society* (1) Slight, but significant, rise in fertility, which then remains fairly constant at a high level (2) Rapid decline in mortality (3) A relatively rapid rate of natural increase, and thus a major growth in size of population	**Phase II:** *The early transitional society* (1) Massive movement from countryside to cities, old and new (2) Significant movement of rural folk to colonisation frontiers, if land suitable for pioneering is available within country (3) Major outflows of emigrants to available and attractive foreign destinations (4) Under certain circumstances, a small, but significant, immigration of skilled workers, technicians, and professionals from more advanced parts of the world (5) Significant growth in various kinds of circulation
Phase C: *The late transitional society* (1) A major decline in fertility, initially rather slight and slow, later quite rapid, until another slow-down occurs as fertility approaches mortality level (2) A continuing, but slackening, decline in mortality (3) A significant, but decelerating, natural increase, at rates well below those observed during Phase B	**Phase III:** *The late transitional society* (1) Slackening, but still major, movement from countryside to city (2) Lessening flow of migrants to colonisation frontiers (3) Emigration on the decline or may have ceased altogether (4) Further increases in circulation, with growth in structural complexity
Phase D: *The advanced society* (1) The decline in fertility has terminated, and a socially controlled fertility oscillates rather unpredictably at low to moderate levels (2) Mortality is stabilised at levels near or slightly below fertility with little year-to-year variability (3) There is either a light to moderate rate of natural increase or none at all	**Phase IV:** *The advanced society* (1) Residential mobility has levelled off and oscillates at a high level (2) Movement from countryside to city continues but is further reduced in absolute and relative terms (3) Vigorous movement of migrants from city to city and within individual urban agglomerations (4) If a settlement frontier has persisted, it is now stagnant or actually retreating (5) Significant net immigration of unskilled and semi-skilled workers from relatively underdeveloped lands (6) There may be a significant international migration or circulation of skilled and professional persons, but direction and volume of flow depend on specific conditions (7) Vigorous accelerating circulation, particularly the economic and pleasure-oriented, but other varieties as well
Phase E: *A future super-advanced society* (1) No plausible predictions of fertility behaviour are available, but it is likely that births will be more carefully controlled by individuals – and perhaps by new socio-political means (2) A stable mortality pattern slightly below present levels seems likely, unless organic diseases are controlled and lifespan is greatly extended	**Phase V:** *A future super-advanced society* (1) There may be a decline in level of residential migration and a deceleration in some forms of circulation as better communication and delivery systems are instituted (2) Nearly all residential migration may be of the inter-urban and intra-urban variety (3) Some further immigration of relatively unskilled labour from less developed areas is possible (4) Further acceleration in some current forms of circulation and perhaps the inception of new forms (5) Strict political control of internal as well as international movements may be imposed

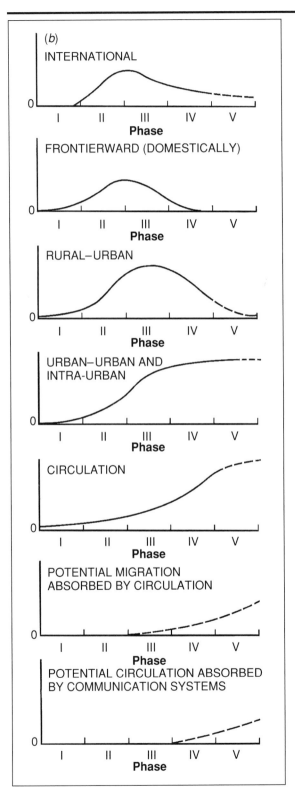

nation or region progresses through the various stages of the demographic/mobility transitions, Zelinsky argues that there are orderly changes in the type as well as the amount of spatial mobility, including changes in function, frequency, duration, periodicity, distance and types of migrants. As these changes take place they are accompanied by changes in the flow of information and technology so that in the later stages of the transition, potential circulation is cancelled out by improved inter-personal communications such as the telephone, and potential migration by improved commuting opportunities. Zelinsky further suggests that when a country begins to move through the mobility transition at a late date, then (as in the demographic transition) the progression tends to be more rapid than in countries where this happened in the relatively distant past. He cites Japan as an example of a nation that was still in the late stages of phase I of the mobility transition in 1920. Evidence suggests that Taiwan was still in phase I in 1930 and Sri Lanka as recently as the late 1940s. These countries contrast markedly with England and Wales where the onset of Phase II of the mobility transition began in the second half of the eighteenth century. Although Zelinsky's hypothesis remains largely untested it provides a valuable attempt to reduce to some semblance of order the apparently chaotic nature of human spatial mobility and to relate that mobility to other developments. The hypothesis is applied to England and Wales in Case Study 8A.

Fig. 8.7 Zelinsky's Hypothesis of the Mobility Transition: (a) the phases of the mobility transition and their relationship to the phases of the vital transition, and (b) changes in the volume of different kinds of mobility during the five phases of the mobility transition.
Source: Zelinsky, 1971.

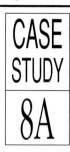

Application of Zelinsky's Hypothesis of the Mobility Transition to England and Wales

Figure 8.8 summarises an attempt to apply Zelinsky's 'Hypothesis of the Mobility Transition' to England and Wales. On the left-hand side of the tabulation is a summary of trends in birth rates, death rates and total population for each of the first four phases of the model. This contains no surprises as Zelinsky based his mobility phases on the established phases of the model of the demographic transition and, as we have already pointed out in Case Study 2A, vital trends in England and Wales over the last 250 years show a close similarity with the basic model. On the right-hand side of the tabulation an outline commentary is given on the major features of migration and circulation in England and Wales in each of the four phases, emphasising the extent to which these conform with or diverge from those suggested by Zelinsky. The text that follows expands on that outline commentary.

Phase 1: the pre-modern traditional society, ending in the 1740s

It is difficult to argue with Zelinsky's assertion that circulation was severely limited in the pre-modern period, which in England and Wales ended in the mid-eighteenth century. Even towards the end of the period, roads were poor or non-existent, there were no canals or railways, tourism was extremely limited, and workplace and place of residence were still overwhelmingly the same place. As Zelinsky points out, the main types of movement engaged in by the ordinary population would be time-honoured ones such as moving animals between upland and lowland pastures, driving livestock to market, carting goods over relatively short distances between producers, manufacturers and customers (e.g. hides to tanneries, corn to manorial grinding mills, timber from woods to building projects), and visits to distant parish churches on the occasion of baptisms, marriages and burials. All these trips would have been slow and time-consuming.

Zelinsky may have underestimated the volume, complexity and spatial extent of some of these circulatory movements, but in the absence of reliable data and the paucity of research on the subject these must remain a matter of conjecture. However, when attention is turned from circulation to migration, there is a large and growing volume of research to suggest that, as far as England and Wales are concerned, Zelinsky's view that in the pre-modern period there was 'little genuine residential migration' must be rejected.

Recent research suggests, for example, that in the late medieval and early modern periods (1500–1750), there were high levels of migration in England and Wales, though most of the migration was short-distance. Such migration was encouraged by the fact that many adolescents left their parents' houses to work in service or as apprentices in the households of others, production of goods was mainly for exchange rather than for direct consumption thus widening knowledge of other places and opportunities, and there was a large measure of personal choice in the selection of marriage partners which stimulated much inter-parish migration, especially of brides, and cemented inter-community links.

A few specific examples of research findings will illustrate the levels of migration that are being discovered. In a study of the Nottinghamshire village of Clayworth and the Northamptonshire village of Cogenhoe in the seventeenth century it was found that over periods of about a decade population turnover in the two villages was between 50 and 60%, with only about one-third of this being accounted for by deaths (Laslett, 1977). Using parish registers, Levine (1977) has calculated that in the Leicestershire village of Bottesford between 1600 and 1679 only 6.3% of marriages were between couples both of whom were born in

(b)

The vital transition	The mobility transition
Phase A: *The pre-modern traditional society (high stationary), ending in the 1740s* (1) High and fluctuating birth rates (2) High and fluctuating death rates (3) Alternating periods of population stability, slow growth and decline; total population small	**Phase 1:** *The pre-modern traditional society* (1) Available evidence suggests levels of circulation were very low by modern standards as Zelinsky suggests (2) Zelinsky overlooked or ignored known major movements of peoples into and within England and Wales in prehistoric and early historic period, and early emigrations to Ireland and North America. His conclusions about residential migration are challenged by recent research suggesting high levels of short-distance migration in England and Wales in late medieval period and Tudor and Stuart times
Phase B: *The early transitional society (early expanding), 1740s–c.1880* (1) Birth rates remain at high level, peaking in second and third decades of nineteenth century (2) Death rates steadily decline (3) Total population rises steeply from 5.6 million to 25 million	**Phase 2:** *The early transitional society* (1) The following trends conform with Zelinsky's suggested characteristics: – high levels of rural–urban migration – major emigration flows – significant increases in levels of circulation (2) The following characteristics are not found in England and Wales in this phase: – movement to colonisation frontiers – immigration from more advanced parts of the world
Phase C: *The late transitional society (late expanding), c.1880–1920* (1) Birth rates decline sharply (2) Death rates fall steeply (3) By 1900 this has caused rate of population increase to slow	**Phase 3:** *The late transitional society* (1) Continual but slackening depopulation of many rural areas is a noticeable feature as Zelinsky suggests, though accessible rural areas become suburbanised (2) The sharply rising levels of circulation also accord with Zelinsky's prognostications, the result of an expanded railway system and the introduction of trams, cars and buses (3) Emigration continues at a high level contrary to Zelinsky's suggestion (4) As in the previous phase, movement to colonisation frontiers is not found in England and Wales
Phase D: *The advanced society (low stationary), since 1920* (1) Birth rates at a low level with marked fluctuations (2) Death rates at low level (3) Population growth rate has slowed down and is now growing more slowly than at any time since the early eighteenth century	**Phase 4:** *The advanced society* (1) The following trends accord with Zelinsky's predictions: – high levels of residential mobility – vigorous inter-urban migration – influx of unskilled and semi-skilled workers from undeveloped parts of the world – significant international migration/circulation of skilled workers – high and accelerating levels of internal circulation (2) His suggestion that rural out-migration would continue to be important is not borne out by trends in England and Wales. Throughout the period suburbanisation of the accessible countryside has been a marked feature and since 1971 many remote rural areas have seen population growth (3) His comments about settlement frontiers are again not relevant to England and Wales

Fig. 8.8 The application of Zelinsky's Hypothesis of the Mobility Transition to England and Wales. This table should be compared with Fig. 8.7.

the village, and only 26.4% of marriages in the same period involved one partner who was native to the village. Even more surprising are the results of an analysis of marriages in the parish of Hartland in Devon which is relatively isolated and surrounded by sea on two sides. There it was found that between 1600 and 1850, 60% of brides had been baptised (and, therefore, presumably, born) outside the parish (Smith, 1978). Many other studies testify to the high levels of migration into and out of small communities, usually over short distances as in the case of the 126 serfs leaving the manor of Forncett in Norfolk between 1400 and 1575, over 70% of whom settled within 12 miles of it (Phythian-Adams, 1987).

When migration to towns is considered, Zelinsky's conclusion is found equally wanting. For example, London's population grew from approximately 400,000 to about 575,000 between 1650 and 1700. Wrigley (1978) has estimated that during that period an average of about 8,000 more people each year moved to London than left it, with migrants being recruited from considerable distances. The population changes in some provincial towns in the seventeenth century also indicate high levels of rural–urban migration. In a study of population change in Norfolk and Suffolk, Patten (1975) estimated that the towns in the two counties had grown by 50% between 1603 and 1670, while the rural areas grew by only 11%, even though there was a constant population growth rate over the region as a whole. The population of Norwich, the region's largest town, almost doubled in the same period from 11,000 to 20,000 in spite of high levels of urban mortality at that time. The only reasonable explanation is that in-migration was an important factor in this growth.

Neither does Zelinsky's contention seem to fit the known facts of emigration from and immigration to England and Wales in the period before 1740. There were, for example, important movements from England and Wales to Ireland between the late twelfth century and the late seventeenth century. For instance, contemporaries estimated that 80,000 people moved from Scotland, England and Wales to Ulster in the second quarter of the seventeenth century with a further 50,000–80,000 moving there in the 1690s. It has been estimated

that in 1670 the population of the whole of Ireland was 1.3 million of whom 0.5 million were immigrants or the descendants of immigrants from Great Britain. Emigration also took place over longer distances from the beginning of the seventeenth century to the colonies on the eastern seaboard of North America.

Much earlier, a number of major immigrations into England and Wales had taken place, namely the Scandinavian colonisations of the ninth and tenth centuries, the Anglo-Saxon migrations of the fifth and sixth centuries, and the successive waves of Neolithic, Bronze Age and Iron Age peoples from continental Europe and the Mediterranean basin in the prehistoric period. Phase 1 of Zelinsky's mobility transition seems to take no account of major movements such as these.

Phase 2: The early transitional society, 1740s – c.1880

Three of the five generalisations put forward by Zelinsky for this phase of the mobility transition unquestionably apply to England and Wales – massive rural–urban migration, major emigration flows, and significant increases in the levels of circulation. His remaining two points are of little significance: there was little or no movement of migrants to colonisation frontiers because such frontiers were virtually non-existent in England and Wales by 1740, and there was little flow of migrants from more advanced parts of the world because England and Wales were at or near the leading edge of world economic development throughout the period in question.

Between 1740 and 1790 short-distance migration from surrounding rural areas fed the population growth of the major provincial towns and cities and the new industrial areas. There were also important long-distance movements of skilled craftsmen into the wide range of growing manufacturing industries. Migration, often from considerable distances, was also a key factor in the massive growth of London from about 600,000 at the beginning of the eighteenth century to about 750,000 by 1780, despite very high levels of mortality. Altogether the urban population grew from about a quarter of the total in 1750 to one-third by 1801.

Between 1780 and 1830 the population of England and Wales grew by 83%, and the period saw the continued rapid growth of the industrial regions to which net migration made a significant contribution. During the period London grew by more than 1.3 million with perhaps 0.75 million contributed by net migration. After 1830, and particularly after 1850 (see Case Study 6A), most rural areas of England and Wales suffered continued and heavy depopulation with London and the fast-growing coalfield industrial areas as the main destinations of out-migrants. This period also saw the establishment and rapid growth of new towns such as the industrial towns of Middlesbrough, Scunthorpe and St Helens, the railway towns of Crewe and Swindon, and the seaside resorts of Cleethorpes and Skegness.

The establishment of the railway system after 1825 aided long-distance migrants. It also encouraged the separation of place of residence and place of work, and the journey to work became an increasingly common feature among the middle classes. The railways also increased circulation in another important way at this time by creating the day excursion to inland and coastal resorts. In 1845, for example, it was estimated that 150,000 had left Manchester by train over the Whitsuntide holidays.

Finally, this period of rapid population growth and internal redistribution also witnessed a massive emigration to the colonies, principally Canada, Australia, New Zealand and South Africa, and to the United States. Between 1820 and 1880, 9.5 million immigrants entered the United States; about 1.5 million were from England, Scotland and Wales.

Phase 3: The late transitional society, *c.*1880 –1920

In the first characteristic that Zelinsky attributes to this phase, the slackening of the level of rural–urban migration, he hints that this period is marked by the drying up of the rural reservoir of population. In England and Wales many decades of out-movement of young people had left a dwindling and ageing population in some regions, but nevertheless, considerable rural out-migration continued to take place throughout the 40 years

from 1880, though it varied from region to region and from decade to decade.

As in the previous phase Zelinsky's suggestion that there would be movement to colonisation frontiers was not true of England and Wales; indeed this period was marked by the abandonment of settlements in some upland farming areas and worked-out mining districts.

Exception can also be taken to Zelinsky's view that emigration falls off in this phase. Migration to the colonies from England and Wales continued at a high level in the three decades before the First World War and emigration to the United States from Great Britain amounted to 2 million people between 1880 and 1919, half a million more than in the 60 years up to 1880.

However, there can be full agreement with Zelinsky's final point. This phase in England and Wales was not only a period of continued expansion of the passenger railway network, it also saw the establishment and rapid expansion of electric tramway systems and the early years of the motor car and bus era. Circulation reached new levels and a suburban explosion occurred extending well into the countryside around the major towns and cities.

Phase 4: The advanced society, since 1920

Zelinsky's first (high and oscillating levels of residential mobility), second (vigorous inter-urban migration), and seventh (high and accelerating levels of circulation) points are well documented features of the population geography of England and Wales during the last 70 years, with a marked growth of all three in the last 40 years. His fourth point about settlement frontiers is again not relevant to England and Wales.

His second point, concerning continued rural out-migration, was true up to a point in the 1920–71 period when remote areas continued to lose population. However, in the same period more accessible rural areas experienced rapid population increases. Since 1971 relatively remote areas in Central Wales, the Pennines, and parts of East Anglia and southern Lincolnshire have shared in this rural resurgence.

The second half of the phase since 1920 has, in

accordance with Zelinsky's fifth point, seen an influx of unskilled and semi-skilled workers from 'relatively underdeveloped' parts of the world. These immigrants have originated in the so-called New Commonwealth (India, Pakistan, Bangladesh, the West Indies and Guyana, and various parts of Africa). In 1951 there were 0.2 million people living in the United Kingdom who had been born in the New Commonwealth and by 1971 the figure had risen to 1.2 million. By the mid-1980s there were some 2.4 million people in Great Britain of New Commonwealth origin, though two-fifths were born in this country.

What Zelinsky calls in his sixth point the international circulation or migration of highly skilled and professional persons, is thought to be the predominant type of British emigration at the present time. These *skilled transients* are prepared to move from one country to another and back again for the purposes of employment. Findlay and Garrick (1990) have identified three main channels through which such skilled transients move (Fig. 8.9). The first of these channels is the labour market of multi-national companies. These companies send expatriate workers to branches around the world to fulfil certain key managerial tasks. Most of the skilled transients in this category tend to originate in those regions where multi-national companies have their headquarters, in the case of England and Wales, in London and the South East. By the same mechanism the UK attracts skilled multi-national company transients from other advanced countries, particularly the USA and Japan. The second channel includes British companies which have been invited to undertake specific development projects abroad and which then recruit staff on fixed-term contracts. The third channel includes those skilled transients who have been selected by international recruitment agencies on behalf of foreign governments, state organisations and private companies.

Fig. 8.9 The channels through which skilled international transients move.
Source: after Findlay and Garrick, 1990.

Concluding comment

This commentary shows that it is possible to see close parallels between most of Zelinsky's characteristics for phases 2, 3 and 4 of the mobility transition and trends in England and Wales in the last 250 years. However, his conclusions about the levels of migration in Phase 1 are at odds with history and the findings of recent research on internal migration in England and Wales in the medieval and early modern period.

Other researchers suggest that further modifications to the detailed framework are necessary when the hypothesis is subjected to detailed scrutiny in relation to other countries in both the developed and developing world (e.g. Skeldon, 1990).

Bibliography and further reading

This selective bibliography includes both sources specifically referred to in the text and some suggestions for further reading within the general field of study. A wide range of statistical sources related to themes introduced in this book is available in most large libraries. These include statistical reports produced by various government agencies, national yearbooks and international publications such as the *United Nations Statistical Yearbook*, the *United Nations Demographic Yearbook*, the *World Bank Atlas*, and the annual reports of the Food and Agricultural Organisation of the United Nations – *The State of Food and Agriculture* and the *FAO Yearbook (Production)*. *People*, the quarterly journal of the International Planned Parenthood Federation, also frequently contains statistical summaries as well as providing up-to-date articles on many topics relating to population growth and change. The annual *World Population Data Sheet* issued by the Population Reference Bureau Inc., Washington D.C. (and available in the UK via Population Concern) is an extremely useful source of up-to-date data.

Chapter 1

Clarke, J.I. (ed.) (1984) *Geography and Population: Approaches and Applications*, Pergamon, Oxford.

Haggett, P. (1975) *Geography: A Modern Synthesis*, 2nd edition, Harper and Row, New York.

McGirk, T. (1991) 'India Census shows 25% rise', *The Independent*, 26 March 1991.

Chapter 2

Caldwell, J. (1980) 'Mass education as a determinant of the timing of fertility decline', *Population and Development Review*, 6, 225–55.

Clarke, J.I. (1985) 'Islamic populations: limited demographic transition', *Geography*, 70, 118–28.

Cliff, A. and Haggett, P. (1989) 'Plotting disease', *Geographical Magazine*, 61 (6), 26–29.

Dwyer, D.J. (1987) 'New population policies in Malaysia and Singapore', *Geography*, 72 (3), 248–50.

Howe, G.M. (1972) *Man, Environment and Disease in Britain*, David and Charles, Newton Abbot.

— (1986a) 'Death in Britain', *Geographical Magazine*, 58 (10), 502–05.

— (1986b) 'Does it matter where I live?', *Transactions of the Institute of British Geographers*, 11, 387–414.

Jones, H. (1990) *Population Geography*, 2nd edition, Paul Chapman, London.

Krishnan, G. (1989) 'Fertility and mortality trends in Indian states', *Geography*, 74, 53–56.

People (1989) 'Eastern Europe', *People*, 16 (3) (full issue devoted to Eastern Europe).

Sutton, K. and Nacer, M'H. (1990) 'Population changes in Algeria, 1977–87', *Geography*, 75 (4), 335–47.

Turley, G. (1990) 'Malaria: world-wide search for solutions', *Geographical Magazine*, 52 (2), 22–27.

Wrigley, E.A. and Schofield, R.S. (1981) *The Population History of England 1541–1871: a reconstruction*, Arnold, London.

Chapter 3

Berry, B.J.L., Simmons, J.W., and Tennant, R.J. (1963) 'Urban population densities: structure and change', *Geographical Review*, 53, 389–405.

Bohland, J.R. (1988) 'Population geography of the US', pp. 11–48 in Knox, P.L. *et al.*, *The United States: a contemporary human geography*, Longman, Harlow.

Borchert, J.R. (1967) 'American metropolitan evolution', *Geographical Review*, 57, 301–22.

Brunn, S.D. and Williams, J.F. (1983) *Cities of the World*, Harper and Row, New York.

Castles, I. (1990) *Yearbook Australia 1990*, Australian Bureau of Statistics, Canberra.

Chalkley, B. and Winchester, H. (1991) 'Australia in transition', *Geography*, 76, 97–108.

Clark, C. (1967) *Population Growth and Land Use*, Macmillan, London.

Clark, D. (1985) *Post-industrial America: a geographical perspective*, Methuen, London.

Cloke, P. (1985) 'Counter-urbanisation: a rural perspective', *Geography*, **70**, 13–23.

Drakakis-Smith, D. (1987) *The Third World City*, Methuen, London.

Estall, R. (1972) *A Modern Geography of the United States*, Penguin, Harmondsworth.

Fielding, G.J. (1974) *Geography as Social Science*, Harper and Row, New York.

Gilbert, A. and Gugler, J. (1982) *Cities, Poverty and Development*, Oxford University Press, Oxford.

Gleave, M.B. (1988) 'Changing population distribution in Sierra Leone, 1974–85', *Geography*, **73**, 351–54.

Haggett, P. (1975) *Geography: a modern synthesis*, 2nd edition, Harper and Row, New York.

Hicks, D.A. (1982) *Urban America in the Eighties*, Transaction Books, New Brunswick/London.

Hornby, W.F. and Jones, M. (1991) *An Introduction to Settlement Geography*, Cambridge University Press, Cambridge.

Johnston, R.J. (1982) *The American Urban System*, Longman, London.

Kagambirwe, E.R. (1972) *Causes and Consequences of Land Shortage in Kigezi*, not known, Kampala.

Knox, P.L. *et al.* (1988) *The United States: a contemporary geography*, Longman, London.

Lockhart, D.G. and Mason, K.T. (1988) 'Malta: the 1985 census', *Geography*, **73**, 261–65.

Morgan, W.T.W. (1973) *East Africa*, Longman, London.

Short, J. (1988) 'Urbanisation in Australia', *Geography Review*, **2** (1), 7–11.

Taylor, J. (1991) 'Anchorage and Darwin – a tale of two (sister) cities', *Geography*, **76**, 151–54.

United Nations (1989) *World Population Prospects, 1988*, United Nations, New York.

United Nations Development Programme (1990) *Human Development Report 1990*, Oxford University Press for UN Development Programme, New York/Oxford.

Watson, J.W. (1982) *The United States: habitation of hope*, Longman, London.

Chapter 4

Agnew, C. (1990) 'Green belt around the Sahara', *Geographical Magazine*, **62** (4), 26–30.

Bass, T. (1988) 'Feeding a continent', *Geographical Magazine*, **60** (5), 32–37.

Boserup, E. (1965) *The Conditions of Agricultural Growth*, Allen and Unwin, London.

— (1987) 'Population and technology in pre-industrial Europe', *Population and Development Review*, **13**, 691–701.

de Freitas, C.R. (1991) 'The greenhouse crisis: myths and misconceptions', *Area*, **23**, 11–18.

Evans, R. (1989) 'A debt trap with no way out', *Geographical Magazine*, **61** (10), 10–16.

— (1990) 'Women in Asia and sub-Saharan Africa', *Geographical Magazine*, **62** (4), 32–35.

FAO (1989) *The State of Food and Agriculture 1989*, FAO, Rome.

— (1990) *FAO Yearbook (Production)*, FAO, Rome.

Farmer, B.H. (1986) 'Perspectives on the "Green Revolution" in South Asia', *Modern Asian Studies*, **20**, 175–99.

Findlay, A.M. and Findlay, A.M. (1987) *Population and Development in the Third World*, Methuen, London.

Frankel, F.R. (1971) *India's Green Revolution: Economic Gains and Political Costs*, Princeton University Press, Princeton.

Funnell, D.C. (1988) 'Crisis in Africa: the Agrarian Dimension', *Geography*, **73**, 54–59.

Griffiths, I.L. and Binns, J.A. (1988) 'Hunger, help and hypocrisy: crisis and response to crisis in Africa', *Geography*, **73**, 54–59.

Haggett, P. (1975) *Geography: a modern synthesis*, 2nd edition, Harper and Row, New York.

Harrison, P. (1987) *The Greening of Africa*, Paladin/Grafton, London.

Jenkins, A. and Cannon, T. (1987) 'The Chinese socialist experience: from utopia to myopia', *Geography*, **72**, 335–40.

Jowett, A.J. (1986) 'China: population change and population control', *Geo Journal*, **12**, 349–63.

— (1989a) 'Mao's man-made famine', *Geographical Magazine*, **61** (4), 16–19.

— (1989b) 'Demographic Development', *Geography*, **74**, 346–48.

Kebbede, G. and Jacob, M.J. (1988) 'Drought, famine and the political economy of environmental degradation in Ethiopia', *Geography*, **73**, 65–70.

Kopp, D. and Wallace, I. (1990) 'The wheat imports of non-traditionally wheat-producing countries', *Geography*, **75**, 148–52.

Leeming, F. (1985) *Rural China Today*, Longman, London.

— (1989) 'Rural change and agricultural development', *Geography*, **74**, 348–50.

Luling, V. (1989) 'Wiping out a way of life', *Geographical Magazine*, **61** (7), 34–37.

Meadows, D.H. et al. (1972) *The Limits to Growth*, Earth Island, London.

Nowikorski, F. (1987) 'A child killer revealed', *Geographical Magazine*, **59**, 487–89.

People (1989) 'China 40 years on', *People*, **16** (1) (full issue devoted to China).

Petersen, W. (1975) *Population*, 3rd edition, Collier Macmillan, New York.

Redclift, M. (1991) 'The multiple dimensions of sustainable development', *Geography*, **76**, 36–42.

Rigg, J. (1989) 'The green revolution and equity: who adopts the new rice varieties and why?', *Geography*, **74**, 144–50.

Robinson, C. (1989) *Hungry Farmers: world food needs and Europe's response*, Christian Aid, London.

Taylor, G.R. (1972) 'The concept of optimum population', in **Stanford, Q.H.** (ed) *The World's Population*, Oxford University Press, Toronto.

Third World Planning Review (1989) 'Green for Danger', editorial in Third World Planning Review, **11** (4), iii–vi.

United Nations Development Programme (1990) *Human Development Report, 1990*, Oxford University Press for UN Development Programme, New York/Oxford.

Wrigley, E.A. (1967) 'Demographic models in Geography', in **Chorley, R.J. and Haggett, P.** (eds), *Socio-economic Models in Geography*, Methuen, London.

— (1969) *Population and History*, Weidenfeld and Nicolson, London.

Zhu Ling (1990) 'The transformation of the operating mechanisms in Chinese agriculture', *Journal of Development Studies*, **26**, 229–42.

Chapter 5

Bulusu, L. (1989) 'Migration in 1988', *Population Trends*, **58** (4), 33–39.

Kosinski, L.A. and Prothero, R.M. (eds) (1975) *People on the Move: Studies in Internal Migration*, Methuen, London.

United Nations (1958) *Multilingual Demographic Dictionary*, United Nations, New York.

Zelinsky, W. (1971) 'The hypothesis of the mobility transition', *Geographical Review*, **61**, 219–49.

Chapter 6

Barker, D. and Ferguson, A.F. (1983) 'A goldmine in the sky faraway: rural-urban images in Kenya', *Area*, **15** (3), 185–91.

Brown, L. and Moore, E. (1970) 'The intra-urban migration process: a perspective', *Geografiska Annaler*, **52B**, 1–13.

Champion, A.G. (1973) 'Population trends in England and Wales', *Town and Country Planning*, **56**, 80–82.

— (1987) 'The changing pace of population deconcentration in Great Britain since 1971', *Geoforum*, **18**, 379–401.

— (1988) 'Momentous revival in London's population', *Town and Country Planning*, **56**, 80–82.

Clarke, J.I. (1984) *Geography and Population: Approaches and Applications*, Pergamon, Oxford.

Craig, J. (1981) 'Migration patterns in Surrey, Devon and South Yorkshire, *Population Trends*, **23** (1), 16–21.

Department of Information, Republic of Indonesia (1990) *Indonesia 1990: an official handbook*, DOI, Jakarta.

Desai, R. (1963) *Indian Immigrants in Britain*, Oxford University Press, Oxford.

Gould, W. (1982) 'Emigrants from fear', *Geographical Magazine*, **54**, 494–98.

Hardjono, J. (1983) 'Rural development in Indonesia: the top-down approach', in **Lea, D.A.M. and Chaudhri, D.P.** (eds) *Rural Development and the State*, Methuen, London.

Hocking, J.A. and Thomson, N.R. (1981) *Migration and Urbanisation in West Africa*, Moray House, Edinburgh.

Jansen, C.J. (ed) (1970) *Readings in the Sociology of Migration*, Pergamon, Oxford.

Johnson, J.H. (1990) 'The context of migration: the example of Ireland in the nineteenth century', *Transactions of the Institute of British Geographers*, **15**, 259–76.

Jones, H. (1990) *Population Geography*, 2nd edn, Paul Chapman, London.

Jones, P.N. (1990) 'Recent ethnic German migration from Eastern Europe to the Federal Republic', *Geography*, **75**, 249–52.

Keown, P.A. (1971) 'The career cycle and the stepwise migration process', *New Zealand Geographer*, **27**, 175–84.

Lawton, R. (1967) 'Rural depopulation in nineteenth century England', in **Steel, R.W. and Lawton, R.** (eds), *Liverpool Essays in Geography*, Liverpool University Press, Liverpool.

Lee, E.S. (1961) 'A theory of migration', *Demography*, **3**, 47–57.

Mabogunje, A.K. (1970) 'Systems approach to a theory of rural–urban migration', *Geographical Analysis*, **2**, 1–18.

Madeley, J. (1988a) 'Indonesia slows migration', *Earthwatch*, **30**, 1–4.

— (1988b) 'People transplanted, forests uprooted', *Geographical Magazine*, **60** (7), 22–25.

Monbiot, G. (1989) 'The transmigration fiasco', *Geographical Magazine*, **61** (5), 26–30.

Ravenstein, E.G. (1885) 'The Laws of Migration', *Journal of Royal Statistical Society*, **48**, 167–235.

Sasdi, A. (1990) 'Lampung: new home to migrants from Java and Bali', *The Jakarta Post*, 13 July 1990.

Stouffer, S.A. (1960) 'Intervening opportunities and competing migrants', *Journal of Regional Science*, **2**, 1–26.

Warnes, A. and Law, C. (1984) 'The elderly population of Great Britain: locational trends and policy implications', *Transactions of the Institute of British Geographers*, **9**, 37–59.

White, P. and Woods, R. (1980) *The Geographical Impact of Migration*, Longman, London.

Wolpert, J. (1965) 'Behavioural aspects of the decision to migrate', *Papers of the Regional Science Association*, **15**, 159–69.

— (1966) 'Migration as an adjustment to environmental stress', *Journal of Social Issues*, **22**, 92–102.

Woods, R. (1982) *Theoretical Population Geography*, Longman, London.

Chapter 7

Arkell, T. (1991) 'The decline of pastoral nomadism in the Western Sahara', *Geography*, **76**, 162–66.

Asher, M. (1991) 'How the mighty are fallen', *Geographical Magazine*, **64** (3), 24–26.

Berry, B.J.L. (ed) (1976) *Urbanisation and Counter-urbanisation*, Sage Publications, Beverley Hills/London.

Connell, J. (1974) 'The Metropolitan Village: spatial and social processes in discontinuous suburbs', in **Johnson, J.H.** (ed) *Suburban Growth*, Wiley, London.

Day, C. (1982) *Contrasting impacts of the suburbanisation process upon selected villages in Kent*, unpublished undergraduate dissertation, Sheffield City Polytechnic.

Dicken, P. and Lloyd, P.E. (1981) *Modern Western Society*, Harper and Row, London.

Drakakis-Smith, D. (1987) *The Third World City*, Methuen, London.

Evans, R. (1991) 'Born to roam free', *Geographical Magazine*, **64** (3), 22–23.

Findlay, A.M. and Findlay, A.M. (1987) *Population and Development in the Third World*, Methuen, London.

Gottman, J. (1961) *Megalopolis: The Urbanised North-eastern Seaboard of the United States*, MIT Press, Cambridge (Mass.).

Hall, P. (1973) *The Containment of Urban England*, Allen and Unwin, London.

Heins, J.J.F. and Meijer, E.N. (1990) 'Population movements to a growth pole: the case of Hosur, Tamil Nadu', *Third World Planning Review*, **12**, 231–47.

Herington, J. (1984) *The Outer City*, Harper and Row, London.

HMSO (1969) *Local Government Reform (Redcliffe-Maud Report: short version)*, Cmnd 4039, HMSO, London.

Hornby, W.F. and Fyfe, E.M. (1990) 'Tourism for tomorrow: Singapore looks to the future', *Geography*, **75**, 58–62.

Hornby, W.F. and Jones, M. (1991) *An Introduction to Settlement Geography*, Cambridge University Press, Cambridge.

Hugo, G.J. (1979) 'The impact of migration on villages in Java', in **Pryor, R.J.** (ed) *Migration and Development in South-East Asia*, Oxford University Press, Kuala Lumpur/Oxford.

Masser, F.I. and Stroud, D.C. (1965) 'The metropolitan village', *Town Planning Review*, **36**, 111–24.

Naipaul, S. (1981) 'Bombay; refuge to all, home to none', *Geo*, **3** (9), 58–79.

Newby, H. (1979) *Green and Pleasant Land*, Penguin, Harmondsworth.

Pacione, M. (1980) 'Differential quality of life in a metropolitan village', *Transactions of the Institute of British Geographers*, **5**, 182–206.

— (1984) *Rural Geography*, Harper and Row, London.

Plane, D. (1981) 'The geography of urban commuting fields', *Professional Geographer*, **33**, 182–88.

Singapore Tourist Promotion Board (1987) *Annual Statistical Report on Visitor Arrivals to Singapore, 1987*, STPB, Singapore.

Thomas, C. (1988) 'Moscow's mobile millions', *Geography*, **73**, 216–25.

United Nations Development Programme (1990) *Human Development Report, 1990*, Oxford University Press for UN Development Programme, New York/Oxford.

Wheeler, J.O. (1974) *The Urban Circulation Noose*, Duxbury Press, North Scituate.

Chapter 8

Findlay, A.M. and Garrick, L. (1990) 'Scottish emigration in the 1980s: a migration channels approach to the study of skilled international migration', *Transactions of the Institute of British Geographers*, **15**, 177–92.

Gould, W.T.S. and Prothero, R.M. (1975) 'Space and time in African population mobility', in Kosinski, L.A. and Prothero, R.M. (eds) *People on the Move: Studies in Internal Migration*, Methuen, London.

Laslett, P. (1977) *Family Life and Illicit Love in Earlier Generations*, Cambridge University Press, Cambridge.

Lawton, R. (1978) 'Population and Society 1730–1900' in Dodgshon, R.A. and Butlin, R.A. (eds), *An Historical Geography of England and Wales*, Academic Press, London.

Levine, D. (1977) *Family Formation in an Age of Nascent Capitalism*, Academic Press, London.

Patten, J. (1975) 'Population distribution in Norfolk and Suffolk during the sixteenth and seventeenth centuries', *Transactions of the Institute of British Geographers*, **65**, 45–65.

Petersen, W. (1970) 'A general typology of migration', in Jansen, C.J. (ed), *Readings in the Sociology of Migration*, Pergamon, Oxford.

Phythian-Adams, C. (1987) *Re-thinking English Local History*, Leicester University Press, Leicester.

Roseman, C.C. (1971) 'Migration as a spatial and temporal process', *Annals of the Association of American Geographers*, **61**, 589–98.

Skeldon, R. (1990) *Population Mobility in Developing Countries: a re-interpretation*, Bellhaven Press, London.

Smith, R.M. (1978) 'Population and its geography in England 1500–1730', in Dodgshon, R.A. and Butlin, R.A. (eds), *An Historical Geography of England and Wales*, Academic Press, London.

Wrigley, E.A. (1978) 'A simple model of London's importance in changing England's society and economy 1650–1750', in Abrams, P. and Wrigley, E.A. (eds), *Towns in Societies* Cambridge University Press, Cambridge.

Zelinsky, W. (1971) 'The hypothesis of the mobility transition' *Geographical Review*, **61**, 219–49.

Index